D1471731

GENETIC ENTROPY

Dr. J.C. Sanford

GENETIC ENTROPY

Fourth Edition

ISBN 978-0-9816316-0-8
Copyright © 2005, 2006, 2008, 2014
Dr. John C. Sanford

Published by
FMS Publications
A Division of FMS Foundation

About the Author

Dr. John Sanford has been a Cornell University Professor for more than 30 years. He received his PhD from the University of Wisconsin in the area of plant breeding and plant genetics. While a professor at Cornell, John trained graduate students and conducted genetic research at the New York State Agricultural Experiment Station in Geneva, NY. At Cornell, John bred new crop varieties using conventional breeding and then became heavily involved in the newly-emerging field of plant genetic engineering. John has published over 100 scientific publications and has been granted several dozen patents. His most significant scientific contributions during the first half of his career involved three inventions: the biolistic ("gene gun") process, pathogen-derived resistance, and genetic immunization. A large fraction of the transgenic crops (in terms of numbers and acreage) grown in the world today were genetically engineered using the gene gun technology developed by John and his collaborators. John also started two biotech enterprises derived from his research, Biolistics, Inc., and Sanford Scientific, Inc. John still holds a position at Cornell (Courtesy Associate Professor), but has largely retired from Cornell and has started a small non-profit organization, Feed My Sheep Foundation (FMS).

Through FMS, John has conducted research in the areas of theoretical genetics and bioinformatics for the last 14 years. This book was the "first fruits" of those efforts.

Dedication and Acknowledgements

I feel I could only write this book by God's grace, and acknowledge and thank Him as the Giver of every good thing. This book is dedicated to the memory of Dr. Bob Hanneman, my graduate thesis advisor, who encouraged me in my science and provided an example for me regarding faith and godliness. I would like to thank my wife, Helen, for her unswerving support. I thank the many scientists who went before me, who courageously questioned the "Primary Axiom". Special thanks to my scientific colleagues who have collaborated with me during the last decade, doing research that strongly validates all of the themes of this book. These colleagues include Walter ReMine, John Baumgardner, Wes Brewer, Paul Gibson, Rob Carter, Franzine Smith, Chase Nelson, Chris Rupe, and others. I thank Lloyd Hight and Chris Rupe for this book's artwork.

J.C. Sanford

Genetic Entropy

Foreword

By Dr. John Baumgardner

During the past half century, the scientific enterprise has opened a door into an almost surrealistic, Lilliputian realm of self-replicating robotic manufacturing plants, with components whirring at tens of thousands of RPM, automated parcel addressing, transport and distribution systems, and complex monitoring and feedback control systems. Of course, this is the realm of cell and molecular biology. It is a realm in which tens of thousands of different kinds of sophisticated nanomachines perform incredible chemical feats inside the living cell. Above and beyond this cellular complexity is the equally complex realm of the organism, with trillions of cells working in astonishing coordination, and above that is the realm of the brain, with its multiplied trillions of neural connections. Confronted with such staggering complexity, the reflective person naturally asks, "How did all this come to exist?" The standard answer given to this question is what the author of this book calls "the Primary Axiom" (random mutations filtered by natural selection).

Genetic Entropy represents a probing analysis of the fundamental underpinnings of the Primary Axiom. In particular, it focuses on the genetic software that specifies life's astounding complexity. The author points out that, for higher organisms, and certainly for humans, the extent of these genetic specifications, called the genome, is vast. Not only is the genome huge, it is also exceedingly complex. It is filled with loops and branches, with genes that regulate other genes that regulate still other genes. In many cases, the same string of genetic letters can code for entirely different messages, depending on context. How such an astonishing information structure has come into existence is clearly an important question. But the author introduces a further question, namely, how can the human genome even be *maintained* against the degrading effects of the billions of new deleterious mutations that enter the human population each generation?

Concerning the Primary Axiom, the author acknowledges that, as a professional geneticist, he discerned no serious problems with its theoretical underpinnings for many years. He confides that during his training in graduate school he accepted this primarily by trust in the authorities, rather than by genuine personal understanding. At that point he felt he had no choice – he thought this abstract and highly mathematical field was beyond his own ability to assess critically. It was not until much later in his professional career that he became aware of how unrealistic and how vulnerable to critical analysis were the crucial assumptions on which the Axiom rests. The author concludes that most professional biologists today are just like he was earlier in his career. Most simply are not aware of the fundamental problems with the Axiom. This is because the Axiom's foundational assumptions are not critiqued in any serious way, either in graduate classes, or in graduate level textbooks, or even in the professional literature.

The conceptual models that population genetics has offered to the rest of the professional biology community, presented in the guise of mathematical elegance, have at their foundations a number of unjustifiable assumptions. The Primary Axiom, it turns out, depends on these assumptions for its support. Most professional biologists are simply not aware of this state of affairs.

The field of population genetics deals largely with complex mathematical models that attempt to describe how mutations are passed from one generation to the next after they arise, and how they affect the survival of individual members of a population in each generation. The reality of these conceptual models depends critically, of course, upon the realism of the assumptions on which they are built. In this book the author exposes the obvious lack of realism of many of the most crucial assumptions that have been applied for the past 75 years. Most professional biologists, like the author during the earlier part of his professional career, base much of their confidence in the Primary Axiom on claims derived from these conceptual models that have employed observationally unjustifiable assumptions. Most biologists today are unaware that the claims of population genetics to which they were exposed in graduate school can no longer be defended from a scientific standpoint. Most, therefore, can hardly imagine that when realistic assumptions are applied, population genetics actually repudiates the Axiom.

Genetic Entropy is a brilliant exposé on the un-reality of the Primary Axiom. It is written in a challenging but accessible style, understandable by non-specialists with a modest background in either genetics or biology. At the same time, this book has sufficient substance and documentation to cause the most highly trained biologist to seriously rethink what he or she probably has always believed about the Primary Axiom. In my opinion, this book deserves to be read by every professional biologist and biology teacher in the world. To me it has the potential of changing the outlook of the academic world in a profound way.

John Baumgardner has a PhD in geophysics from UCLA and worked as a research scientist in the Theoretical Division of Los Alamos National Laboratory for 20 years. He also received an MS degree in electrical engineering from Princeton University, where he first became aware of information theory and later its implications for biological systems. He is an expert in complex numerical simulations, and was instrumental in development of the computer program Mendel's Accountant *– currently the most realistic numerical simulation of the mutation/selection process.*

Prologue

In retrospect, I realize I have wasted much of my life arguing about things that don't really matter. It is my sincere hope that this book can actually address something that really does matter. The issues of *who we are, where we come from*, and *where we are going* seem to me to be of enormous importance. This is the real subject of this book.

Modern thinking centers around the premise that man is just the product of a pointless natural process (undirected evolution). This widely-taught doctrine, when taken to its logical conclusion, leads us to believe that we are just meaningless bags of molecules, and in the final analysis, nothing matters. If false, this doctrine has been the most insidious and destructive thought system ever devised by man. Yet, if true, it is at best meaningless, like everything else. The whole thought system which prevails within today's intelligentsia is built upon the ideological foundation of undirected and pointless Darwinian evolution.

Modern Darwinism is built upon what I will be calling "The Primary Axiom". The Primary Axiom is that man is merely the product of *random mutations* plus *natural selection*. Within our society's academia, the Primary Axiom is universally taught, and almost universally accepted. It is the constantly-mouthed mantra, repeated endlessly on every college campus. It is difficult to find professors on a typical college campus who would even consider (or dare) to question the Primary Axiom. It is for this reason that the overwhelming majority of youth who start out believing that there is more to life than mere chemistry – will lose that faith while at college. I believe this is also the cause of the widespread self-destructive and self-denigrating behaviors we see throughout our culture.

What if the Primary Axiom were wrong? If the Primary Axiom could be shown to be wrong, it would profoundly affect our culture and I believe it would profoundly affect millions of individual lives. It could profoundly change the way we think about ourselves.

Late in my career, I did something that would seem unthinkable for a Cornell professor. I began to question the Primary Axiom. I did this with great fear and trepidation. I knew I would be at odds with the most "sacred cow" within modern academia. Among other things, it might even result in my *expulsion* from the academic world. Although I had achieved considerable success and notoriety within my own particular specialty (applied genetics), it would mean stepping out of the security of my own safe niche. I would have to begin exploring some very big things, including aspects of theoretical genetics which I had always simply accepted by faith. I felt compelled to do all this, but I must confess that I fully expected to hit a brick wall. To my own amazement, I gradually realized that the seemingly "great and unassailable fortress" which has been built up around the Primary Axiom was really a house of cards. The Primary Axiom is actually an extremely vulnerable theory. In fact, it is essentially indefensible. Its apparent invincibility derives largely from bluster, smoke, and mirrors. A large part of what keeps the Axiom standing is an almost mystical faith – which the "true-believers" hold – regarding the omnipotence of natural selection. As I went deeper, I began to see that this unshakable faith in natural selection is typically coupled with a degree of ideological commitment which can only be described as religious. I started to realize (again with trepidation) that I might be offending the religion of a great number of people!

To question the Primary Axiom required me to re-examine virtually everything I thought I knew about genetics. This was the most difficult intellectual endeavor of my life. Deeply entrenched thought patterns only change very slowly (and, I must add, painfully). What I eventually experienced was a complete overthrow of my previous understanding. Several years of personal struggle resulted in a new and very strong conviction that the Primary Axiom was definitely wrong. More importantly, I became convinced that the Axiom could be *shown* to be wrong to any reasonable and open-minded individual. This realization was both exhilarating and frightening. I realized that I had an obligation to openly challenge this most sacred of cows. I also realized I would earn for myself the intense disdain of many of my colleagues within academia, not to mention very intense opposition and anger from other high places.

What should I do? It has become my conviction that the Primary Axiom is insidious on the highest level, having a catastrophic impact on countless human lives. Furthermore, every form of objective analysis I have performed has convinced me that the Axiom is clearly false. So now, regardless of the consequences, I have to say it out loud: *the Emperor has no clothes*.

I invite the reader to carefully consider this very important issue. Are you really just a meaningless bag of molecules, the product of nothing more than random molecular mutations and reproductive filtering? As you read this book, I am going to ask you to wrap your mind around something very challenging but also very exciting. I contend that, if you will invest a reasonable mental effort and follow just a handful of fairly simple arguments, I can persuade you that the Primary Axiom is false. Can you imagine anything more radical or more liberating? To the extent that the Primary Axiom can be shown to be false, it should have a major impact on your own life and on the world at large. For this reason, I have dared to write this book, which for some will be blasphemous treason and for others – revelation.

If the Primary Axiom is wrong, there is a surprising and very practical consequence. When subjected only to natural forces, the human genome must degenerate over time. Such a sober realization has more than just intellectual or historical significance. It should rightfully cause us to personally reconsider the basis of our hope for the future.

Update – Since the initial writing of this book, a series of dramatic new developments have been published, all of which powerfully reinforce the central themes of this book. These developments include the demonstration of the nonlinear nature of the genome, the poly-functional nature of many of the nucleotides which make up higher genomes, the fact that the genome encodes much more information than was even recently thought possible, and the collapse of the fallacy that most of the human genome is just "junk" or "silent" DNA. I have added in italics, very brief "Author's updates" on these various points at the end of most chapters. I have also added Chapter 11 which summarizes the major new scientific developments.

The Genome is the Book of Life. Where Did it Come From?

Newsflash – The genome is an instruction manual.

An organism's *genome* is the sum total of all its genetic parts, including all its chromosomes, genes, and nucleotides. A genome is an instruction manual that specifies a particular form of life. The human genome is a manual that instructs human cells how to be human cells and instructs the human body how to be the human body. There is no information system designed by man that can even begin to compare to the sophistication and complexity of the genome.

The complex nature of the genome can only be appreciated when we begin to grasp how much information it contains. When you assemble the little red wagon you bought for your child, there is a booklet that tells you how to put it together. The size of the booklet is deceptive. It does not contain all the information needed for fabricating the component parts, or for manufacturing the steel, rubber, and paint. The complete instruction manual would actually be a very large volume. If you compiled all the instruction manuals associated with creating a modern automobile, it would fill a library. That library would be very large if it included the information needed for making all the components for creating the robotic assembly lines. Likewise, the manuals required for creating a fighter jet and all its components, computers, and assembly lines would comprise an extremely large library. The manuals needed for building the entire space shuttle and all its components and all its support systems would be truly enormous. Yet the *specified complexity* of even the simplest form of life is arguably greater than that of the space shuttle. Try to absorb the fact that the jump in complexity from a bacterium to a human being is arguably greater than the jump from the little red wagon to the space shuttle. There is simply no human technology that serves as an adequate analogy for the complexity of a human being. The genome is the instruction manual encoding all the information needed for that human life!

We are only beginning to understand the first dimension of this book of life: a linear sequence of four types of extremely small molecules, called nucleotides. These small molecules make up the individual steps of the spiral-staircase structure of DNA. These molecules are the letters of the genetic code, and are shown symbolically as A, T, C, and G. These letters are strung together like a linear text. They are not just symbolically shown as letters, they are very literally the *letters* of our instruction manual. Small clusters or motifs of these four molecular letters make up the *words* of our manual, which combine to form genes (the *chapters* of our manual), which combine to form chromosomes (the *volumes* of our manual), which combine to form the whole genome (the entire *library*).

A complete human genome consists of two sets of 3 billion individual letters each. Only a small fraction of this genetic library is required to directly encode the hundreds of thousands of different types of human proteins and the uncounted number of functional RNA molecules found within our cells. Each of these protein and RNA molecular types are essentially miniature *machines*, each with hundreds of component parts, and with its own exquisite complexity, design, and function. But the genome's *linear* information, which is equivalent to many complete sets of a large encyclopedia, is not enough to explain the complexity of life.

As marvelous as all this linear information is, it must only be the first dimension of complexity within the genome. The genome is not just a simple string of letters spelling out a linear series of instructions. It actually embodies multiple linear codes that overlap and constitute an exceedingly sophisticated information system embodying what is called *data compression* (Chapter 9).

In addition to multiple, overlapping, linear, language-like forms of genetic information, the genome is full of countless loops and branches, like a computer program. It has genes that regulate genes that regulate genes. It has genes that sense changes in the environment and then instruct other genes to react by setting in motion complex cascades of events that can then respond to the environmental cue. Some genes actively rearrange themselves, or modify and methylate other gene sequences, basically *changing* portions of the instruction manual.

Lastly, there is good evidence that linear DNA can fold into two- and three-dimensional structures (as do proteins and RNAs), and that such folding probably encodes still higher levels of information. Within the typical non-dividing nucleus, there is reason to believe there are fabulously complex three-dimensional arrays of DNA, whose 3-D architecture controls higher biological functions.

The bottom line is this: the genome's set of instructions is not a simple, static, linear array of letters – but is dynamic, self-regulating, and multi-dimensional. There is no human information system that can even begin to compare to it. The genome's highest levels of complexity and interaction are probably beyond the reach of our understanding, yet we can at least acknowledge that these higher levels of information exist. While the linear information within the human genome is extremely impressive, the non-linear information must obviously be much greater. Given the unsurpassed complexity of life, this has to be true.

All this information is contained within a genomic package that is contained within a cell's nucleus – a space much smaller than a speck of dust. Each human body contains a galaxy of cells – more than 100 trillion – and every one of these cells has a complete set of instructions, directing the cell's own highly-prescribed duties. The human genome not only specifies the complexity of our cells and our bodies, but also the functioning of our brains. The structure and organization of our brains involves a level of organization entirely beyond our comprehension.

As we recognize the higher-order dimensions of the genome, I believe we can readily agree with Carl Sagan's oft-repeated statement that each cell contains more information than the Library of Congress. Indeed, human life is more complex than all human technologies combined. **Where did all this information come from, and how can it possibly be maintained? This is the mystery of the genome.**

The standard answer to the origin of biological information is that *mutation* and *selection* have created all biological information. This is the fundamental basis of the *Neo-Darwinian Theory*. It says that all genomes (instruction manuals) must have derived from a simple initial genome via a long series of mutations (typographical errors) and lots of natural selection (differential copying). This is the *Primary Axiom* of biological evolution: **Life is life because random mutations at the molecular level are filtered through a reproductive sieve acting on the level of the whole organism.**

What is an axiom? An axiom is a concept that is not testable but is accepted by faith because it seems obviously true to all reasonable parties. On this basis, it is accepted as an Absolute Truth. In this book, I am going to urge the reader to ask the question, "Should we accept today's Primary Axiom?" If the Primary Axiom could be shown to be wrong, it would mean that we would need to re-examine many other popular ideas, because the Primary Axiom has been so foundational to the establishment of modern thinking. This would justify a *paradigm shift* of the highest magnitude (a paradigm shift is a change in a fundamental idea that previously governed a group's collective thinking), and would allow us to completely reevaluate many of the deeply entrenched concepts which frame modern thinking.

It is important that we put the Primary Axiom into a framework that is honest and also realistic to our mind's eye. I would like to propose an honest analogy which very accurately characterizes today's Primary Axiom. My analogy involves the evolution of transportation technologies, as outlined below.

In our little red wagon analogy, the first primeval genome encoded the assembly instructions for the first wagon. That simple genomic instruction manual was copied by an invisible mechanical scribe, to make more instruction manuals. Each newly copied manual was used to make a new red wagon. However, the scribe, being imperfect, made errors. So each wagon came out differently. Each wagon had its own unique instruction manual taped to its bottom. When the first wagons were junked, their instruction manuals were lost with them. New copies of instruction manuals could only be imperfectly copied from the manuals of the immediately preceding generation of wagons, just before they were to be discarded. Since the copying of instructions was sequential (rather than using an original master copy), errors accumulated over time in every manual, and the resulting wagons started to change and vary. The accumulating errors are, of course, our analogy for mutations.

Are you uneasy with this picture? No doubt you realize we are looking at a deteriorating situation. Information is being lost, instructions are becoming degraded, and the wagons will doubtlessly deteriorate in quality. Eventually, the system will break down, the manual will become complete gibberish, and workable wagons will become extinct. We will examine this problematic aspect of mutation in more detail in Chapters 2 and 3.

At this point, we introduce our hero, natural selection. Natural selection is like a judge, or quality control agent, deciding which wagons are suitable models for further copying. Natural selection, as the judge, instructs the scribe not to copy manuals from inferior wagons. This represents differential reproduction (reproductive sieving), better known as *selection*. But it is important to understand there is never direct selection for good instructions, only for good wagons. As we will see, this is very important. Mutations are complex and happen at the molecular level, but selection can only be carried out on the level of the whole organism. The scribe and judge work entirely independently. Working on the level of molecules, the scribe is essentially blind; being extremely near-sighted, he can only see individual letters while he is copying. The judge is also nearly blind, but he is extremely far-sighted. He never sees the letters of the manual, or even the wagon's individual components; he can only see the relative performance of the whole wagon.

The scribe can be envisioned at the beginning of a robotic assembly line. He copies programs for the robots by blindly and imperfectly duplicating older programs, one binary bit at a time. The quality control agent looks at the performance of the finished wagons, and decides which wagons are better than others. The programs from the wagons he has chosen are then given to the scribe for the next round of copying and assembly.

In this way, many defective wagons can be eliminated, and so most errors in the instructions might presumably be eliminated. More exciting, some rare spelling errors might result in *better* wagons, and so the judge can instruct the scribe to preferentially copy these instructions. The process of evolution has begun!

Let us now examine the feasibility of the selection process as a mechanism for improving genomic information. The information within the instruction manual might not only be *improved* by this process, but it can also be *expanded*. If the imperfect scribe occasionally copies an extra (duplicate) page out of the manual, we might start adding information. Naturally, a duplicate page in an instruction manual is not really new information. In fact, it will invariably confuse and disrupt the reading of the manual. But again, the judge only allows copying of manuals from *good wagons*. So, bad duplications might presumably be eliminated and harmless duplications might be preserved. Now these harmless duplications will also begin to have copying errors within them, and some of these errors *might* create new and useful information, like instructions for new functional components in the wagon. With a little imagination, perhaps we can picture a variety of duplications eventually evolving, via misspellings, and specifying something entirely new, like an internal combustion engine, or wings, or an on-board computer navigational system. Hence we have a scenario whereby a little red wagon can, through a series of typographical errors, evolve into an automobile, a plane, or even the Space Shuttle.

But this analogy does not go far enough, because a human being is much more complex than a space shuttle. In fact, our *phenome* (the entire body including the brain), is immeasurably more complex than any known technology. Perhaps we can come closer to the mark if we imagine our little red wagon being transformed into the fanciful *Starship Phenome*, complete with warp-speed engines and a holodeck (Figures 1a-d, pp. 12-14). The Primary Axiom says that misspellings and some differential copying can simultaneously explain the library (the genome) and the starship (the phenome) illustrated in Figure 1d.

We must now ask, "Could misspellings and selective copying really do this?" A correct understanding of *selection* is essential for evaluating the merit of the Primary Axiom. No intelligence is involved in this scenario. The scribe is really just a complex array of senseless molecular machines that blindly replicate DNA. The judge is just the tendency for some individuals to reproduce more than others. Many people unconsciously attribute to natural selection a type of supernatural intelligence. But natural selection is just a term for a blind and purposeless process whereby some things reproduce more than others. It is crucial we understand that our scribe and our judge have neither foresight nor intelligence. Their combined IQ equals *zero*.

Isn't it remarkable that the Primary Axiom of biological evolution essentially claims that typographical errors and limited selective copying within an instruction manual can transform a wagon into a spaceship in the absence of any intelligence, purpose, or design? Do you find this concept credible? It becomes even more startling when we realize that the spaceship was in no way pre-specified under the Primary Axiom, not even in the mind of God. It truly "just happened" by accident. The spaceship is essentially just a *mutant wagon*. Yet this illustration is actually the best analogy for describing the Primary Axiom. The only weakness of this analogy is that there is no human technology that can compare to the actual complexity of life, and thus there is no human information system that can compare to the human genome.

This whole analogy stands in sharp contrast to the false picture portrayed by Dawkins (1986). The famous Dawkins argument, built around the phrase "methinks it is like a weasel", involved a *pre-specified language* and a *pre-specified message* being systematically uncovered through a simple-minded process equivalent to children's games such as "20 Questions" or "Hangman". In Dawkins' model, both the phrase and the carefully crafted and finely tuned method of uncovering it were intelligently designed and purposeful. Furthermore, his selection scheme allowed for direct selection of genotype (misspellings) rather than phenotype (wagon performance). Briefly, Dawkins set up a simple computer program which started with a simple random array of letters, having exactly the same number of characters as the phrase "methinks it is like a weasel". He designed his program to then begin to randomly mutate (change) the letters. When a new letter fell into place which matched the phrase "methinks it is like a weasel" the program would select the "improved" message. Obviously it would not take long for such a little program to create the desired phrase. However, even to make this simple program work, Dawkins had to carefully design the replication rate, the mutation rate, and other parameters to get the results he wanted. He also needed to impose perfect selection for each and every individual letter, each and every generation. This program supposedly proved that evolution via mutation/selection is inevitable (not requiring any intelligent design). Obviously, Dawkins used an intelligently designed computer, and then he used his own intelligence to design the program, to optimize it, and even to design the pre-selected phrase. For many reasons (see Chapter 9), Dawkins' argument cannot honestly be used to defend the Primary Axiom (which does not allow for the operation of any intelligence, purpose, or forethought, and does not allow for direct selection for any misspellings themselves).

In this book we are going to examine some basic aspects of genetics and determine if the known facts about the human genome are compatible with the Primary Axiom. As you read, if you come to the point where you feel that the Primary Axiom is no longer obviously true to all reasonable parties, then you should feel rationally obligated to reject it as an *axiom*. If the Primary Axiom cannot stand up as an axiom, it should be treated as an unproven hypothesis, subject to falsification.

*2014 Update – A milestone book was published in 2013 entitled "Biological Information – New Perspectives" (see **BINP.org**). This book was the compilation of research papers from a symposium held at Cornell University (Marks et al., 2013). These papers were authored by 29 well-credentialed scientists representing a very wide range of scientific disciplines. The 29 authors were in broad agreement regarding the true nature of biological information. **The nature of biological information systems is much more like an elaborate computer system than a book.** The DNA is like the cell's hard drive. The millions of RNA and protein molecules, and all their interactions, are like the active memory or RAM of the cell. Every individual gene functions as an executable computer program (indeed - there are multiple programs per gene). Each one of the protein and RNA molecules within a cell is itself a simple program (algorithm). The DNA, RNA, protein and countless other molecules are in constant communication with each other – constituting something like a vast internet system within every cell. Using data visualization techniques it has now been shown that higher genomes are remarkabley similar in structure to executable computer programs (Seaman, 2013).*

*For updated information on the topic of Genetic Entropy visit the website **GeneticEntropy.org**.*

Figure 1a. Some assembly required...

A little red wagon is not information, but it requires information to specify its assembly. A typical assembly booklet is not really all the information required to specify the production of a wagon. The truly complete production manual would be a very substantial book, specifying the production of all the components (wheels, etc.), and all raw materials (steel, paint, rubber).

Figure 1b. A library of information.

The complete instructions needed to specify a modern automobile would comprise a substantial library. If the assembly was to be done entirely by machines (no "intelligence" required), the information, including that required for making and programming the robots, would be massive, comprising a phenomenal collection of books.

Figure 1c. Many layers of information.

The complete instruction manual needed to specify a fighter jet, including its on-board computer systems and all the manufacturing and support systems inherent in creating and maintaining such a system, would be a massive library. Imagine the instructions if every component had to be made robotically!

Figure 1d. A galaxy of information...

The library shown above represents the human genome (all our genetic information). The spaceship represents the human phenome (our entire body, including our brain). We cannot really imagine how extensive the library would have to be were it to specify the fictional S.S. Phenome, complete with warp-speed engines and a holodeck. Wouldn't it have to be much larger than the Library of Congress? Yet it can be reasonably argued that a human is still more complex than a hypothetical S.S. Phenome. What type of starship could reproduce itself?

Are Random Mutations Good?

Newsflash – Random mutations consistently destroy information.

Mutations are typographical errors in the book of life. The subject of mutation in the human genome should be approached with sensitivity because people matter and people are hurt by mutation. The number of families affected by birth defects is tragically high, so this is not just a matter of "statistics". Genetic disease, in its broadest sense, is catastrophic. If we include all genetic predispositions to all pathologies, we must conclude that we are *all* highly mutant. Furthermore, nearly every family is impacted by the tragedy of cancer, which is fundamentally the result of accumulating mutations within our body cells. Indeed, growing evidence indicates that *aging itself* is primarily due to the accumulation of mutations within the cells of our body. Mutations are the source of immeasurable heartache. In fact, they are inexorably killing each one of us. So mutations are more than just an academic concern.

Can we say mutations are good? Nearly all health policies are aimed at reducing or minimizing mutation. Most personal health regimes are aimed at reducing mutations, to reduce risk of cancer and other degenerative diseases. How can anyone see mutation as good? Yet, according to the Primary Axiom, mutations are good because they create the variation and diversity which allow selection and evolution to occur, thus creating the information needed for life.

Before we go further, we need to realize that there are two types of variation: random variation and designed variation. Random variation is the type of variation I see in my car as time passes. It is the rust, the dings, the scratches, and broken parts. Such things create variation in cars, but do they ever lead to better cars? Can typographical errors realistically improve a student's term paper? Apart from accidents, there exists another type of variation, designed variation. When I bought my car I had many options: paint color, type of tire, size of engine, etc. These options were useful to me in making my selection. These designed variable components have also proven useful to me later on. I have added or taken away various options, replaced broken parts, etc. These designed forms of variation are beneficial, being useful for sustaining my car, and are even useful for *improving* my car, within limits. However, such variations, even when they are intelligently designed, will never transform my car into a spaceship.

Part of the Primary Axiom is that all genetic variation *must* come from random mutations, since no genetic variation by design is allowed. However, now that the era of genetic engineering has begun, this axiomatic assumption clearly is not true (because many living organisms now contain genetic variations designed and engineered by man). Perhaps this simple fact can open our minds to the possibility of designed genetic variation which preceded man! Apart from our ideological commitment to the Primary Axiom, it can very reasonably be argued that random mutations are almost universally bad. Speaking in terms of vehicles, they appear to be the *dings* and *scratches* of life, rather than the spare parts.

The overwhelmingly deleterious nature of mutations can be seen by the incredible scarcity of clear cases of information-creating mutations. It must be understood that scientists have a very sensitive and extensive network for detecting information-creating mutations, and most geneticists are diligently keeping their eyes open for them all the time. This has been true for about 100 years. The sensitivity of this observational network is such that even if only one mutation out of a million unambiguously creates new information (apart from "fine-tuning" which I will describe), the literature would be over-flowing with reports of this happening. Yet I am still not convinced there is a single, crystal-clear example of a known mutation which unambiguously *created* information. There are certainly many mutations which have been described as beneficial, but most of these beneficial mutations have not created information, but rather have destroyed it. For illustration, some of us (like me) would view a broken car alarm as "beneficial". However, such random changes, although they might be found to be "desirable", still represent a breakdown and not the creation of a new functional feature. Information consistently decreases. This is the actual case, for example, in chromosomal mutations that lead to antibiotic resistance in bacteria – cell functions are routinely lost. The resistant bacterium has not evolved. In fact it has digressed genetically and is *defective*. Such a mutant strain is rapidly replaced by the superior, natural bacteria as soon as the antibiotic is removed. Another example would be the hairless Chihuahua dog. In extreme heat, reduction of size and loss of hair may be useful adaptations, but these involve degeneration, not creation of new functions or new information. In such situations, although local adaptation is occurring, information is being lost, not added. Yet the Primary Axiom still insists mutations are good and are the building blocks with which evolution creates the galaxy of information currently existing within the genome. Let us continue to examine this concept more closely.

The nature of genetic deterioration via mutation can easily be seen using our analogy of an instruction manual. For example, a single line within a jet aircraft assembly manual might read as follows:

> *Step 6. When you have completed the last step, go back and repeat step 3, until part B is 10.004 mm thick – then wait no less than 3h before going to the next step.*

Limiting ourselves to just simple point mutations (misspellings), there are three possible levels of impact on the above instructions. Theoretically, some misspellings might have zero impact on the message (I don't see any obvious prospects in this instance). Most misspellings will have a very subtle effect on the clarity or coherence of the message (i.e., misspellings within all the portions not underlined). Lastly, a few changes (within the underlined areas), will have the potential for dramatic (essentially lethal) effects. What is *not* clear in the above example is which misspellings could actually improve the instructions to result in a better jet plane. While such changes are *conceivable*, they are unlikely, on a level that is difficult to fully describe. Any *possible* improvement in the instructions deriving from a misspelling would be expected to be very slight (i.e., changing the 4 to an 8, three places to the right of the decimal in the specified thickness). These types of changes do not actually *add* information, but really only *modulate,* or fine-tune, the system. It should be obvious to any reasonable person that we can't expect *any* misspellings that would result in a major advance in jet technology. For example, no misspelling in the above sentence is going to create a new patentable component or dramatically increase plane speed. Such major changes would obviously require intelligent design. For every hypothetical misspelling that might very subtly improve (or, more accurately, modulate) a jet plane's blueprint, there would be a multitude of misspellings which would be detrimental. The detrimental changes would range from a few lethal errors to a very large number of nearly-neutral changes in the text.

The above illustration can be extended to the genome (see Figure 2, p. 31). There are over 3 billion potential point mutation sites in the human genome. Only a small fraction of these, when mutated, will have a major effect. Yet none of the potential mutations can be conclusively shown to have zero effect. The vast bulk of the nucleotide positions are considered to be "nearly-neutral" sites, as will be seen more clearly below. Misspellings in life's instruction manual will sometimes be very deleterious, but in the overwhelming majority of cases they will be only slightly deleterious. No new information can be expected, although existing information can be modulated or fine-tuned to a limited extent. Biological modulation would involve adjusting the cell's "rheostats". For example, it is well known that mutations can adjust activity of a promoter or enzyme, either up or down. However, when we use a rheostat to dim a light, we are not creating a new circuit, nor are we in any way creating new information. We are just fine-tuning the system that is already there, which was, in fact, *designed to be fine-tuned.*

I have just stated that the overwhelming majority of mutations should be nearly-neutral. All population geneticists would agree, for many reasons. First, it can be seen by the nature of misspellings in any written language (as you can picture for yourself by changing any single letter in this book). Second, it can be seen by the total number of nucleotides. On average, each nucleotide position can only contain one 3-billionth of the total information. Third, it can be seen from innumerable studies on the mutation of specific coding sequences, promoters and enhancers. Experimentally, we can show that most nucleotide positions have very subtle effects on any given cell function, and only a few mutations are real "killers" of gene function (remember, any single gene function is just a miniscule part of the whole cell's system). Lastly, the near-neutral impact of most nucleotides can be seen from the very subtle role that single nucleotides play in *genome-wide patterns* (codon-preferences, nucleosome binding sites, isochores, "word" compositional differences between species, etc.). These patterns involve hundreds of millions of nucleotides which are dispersed throughout the genome. Individual nucleotide positions must play an immeasurably tiny role in maintaining all such genome-wide patterns. Yet as infinitesimal as these effects are, they are not zero. Such patterns exist because each nucleotide contributes to it. Each nucleotide still has an impact, and so carries information. No matter how we analyze it, we will see that most nucleotide positions must be nearly-neutral.

Are there *truly neutral* nucleotide positions? True neutrality can never actually be demonstrated experimentally (it would require infinite sensitivity). However, for reasons we will get into later, some geneticists have been eager to minimize the functional genome and have wanted to relegate the vast bulk of the genome to "junk DNA". Mutations in such DNA are assumed to be entirely neutral. However, actual research findings continually expand the size of the functional genome, while the presumed junk DNA keeps shrinking. In just a few years, many geneticists have shifted from believing that less than 3% of the total genome is functional to believing that much more than 30% is functional, and most recently evidence suggests 80% or more is functional (The ENCODE Project Consortium, 2012). As the functional genome expands, the likelihood of neutral mutations shrinks. Moreover, there are strong theoretical reasons for believing that there is no truly neutral nucleotide position. By its very existence, a nucleotide position takes up space, affects spacing between other sites, and affects such things as regional nucleotide composition, DNA folding, and nucleosome binding. If a nucleotide carries *absolutely no* information, it is, by definition, slightly deleterious, as it slows cell replication and wastes energy. Just as there are really no truly neutral letters in an encyclopedia, there are probably no truly neutral nucleotide sites in the genome. Therefore there is no way to change any given site without *some* biological effect, no matter how subtle. While most sites are probably nearly-neutral, very few, if any, should be absolutely neutral. This fallacy of absolutely neutral mutations is clearly refuted by Eyre-Walker and Keightley (2007). In their words:

> *"...it seems unlikely that any mutation is truly neutral in the sense that it has no effect on fitness. All mutations must have some effect, even if that effect is vanishingly small. However, there is a class of mutations that we can term effectively neutral... As such, the definition of neutrality is operational rather than functional; it depends on whether natural selection is effective on the mutation in the population or the genomic context in which it segregates, not solely on the effect of the mutation on fitness."*

So what does the real distribution of all mutations really look like? Figure 3a (p. 32) shows the naive, bell-shaped curve view of mutation, with half of the mutations being beneficial and half being deleterious. One of the founders of neo-Darwinian theory, R.A. Fisher, believed this was the actual distribution of mutational effects, and on this false premise he established what is called "Fisher's Fundamental Theorem of Natural Selection". His premise was clearly wrong, invalidating his entire mathematical analysis. It is easy to envision selective progress with such a distribution of mutations. Any level of selection, no matter how weak, would obviously favor at least some good mutations and eliminate at least some bad. In fact, if this distribution were correct, progressive evolution would be inevitable. But this view is clearly incorrect. **Beneficial mutations are so rare that they are typically not shown in such graphs**. Figure 3b (p. 33) shows a more realistic view of the distribution of mutations, ranging from lethal (-1) to neutral (0). However, this is still not quite right. Mutations are sharply skewed toward neutral values. In other words, most mutations are nearly-neutral, as we have just discussed. What does the real distribution of mutations look like? Figure 3c (p. 34) is modified and expanded from Kimura (1979). This curve very nearly represents the true distribution of mutations.

As can be seen from Kimura's curve, most mutations are negative, and pile up steeply near the zero mark. They are overwhelmingly deleterious and nearly-neutral. Kimura is famous for showing that there is a "zone of near-neutrality" (shown here as a box). Kimura calls near-neutral mutations "effectively neutral", meaning that they are so subtle that they are *not subject to selection*. We can see that Kimura does not show *any* mutations as being *absolutely* neutral. His curve approaches, but does not reach, the zero-impact point. Kimura's somewhat arbitrary cut-off point for "unselectable" (i.e., the size of his box) he calculates as a function of N_e (the number of reproducing individuals within a breeding population).

It is important to note that Kimura's box size, which he calculates based upon population size, is only a minimal estimate of the range of effectively neutral mutations. The actual box size should also be enlarged by any and all non-genetic factors that can affect reproductive probability. As we will see in Chapter 6, this fact very *significantly increases the size of the real box* (see Figure 9, p. 108). *Anything that decreases the "signal-to-noise ratio" will make proportionately more of a genome's nucleotides unselectable.* The importance of non-genetic factors in terms of making proportionately more nucleotides unselectable is clearly acknowledged by the famous geneticist Muller (Muller, 1964).

In Kimura's figure, he does not show any mutations to the right of zero – there are zero beneficial mutations shown. He obviously considered beneficial mutations very rare, and does not even discuss their fitness-effect distribution. Given this distribution of mutations, one would naturally ask, "How can theorists possibly explain evolutionary progress?" It is done as follows: everything in the "near-neutral box" is redefined as being *completely neutral,* and is thereby dismissed. It is then assumed that the mutations to the left of the near-neutral box can be entirely eliminated using natural selection. Having eliminated *all* deleterious mutations in these two ways, the theorists are then free to argue that no matter how rare selectable beneficial mutations may be (to the right of the box), there should now be enough time and enough selection power left over to rescue some of them and to use them as the building blocks of evolution. As we will soon see, they are wrong on all counts. The mutations in the box cannot be dismissed, the mutations to the left of the box cannot necessarily all be eliminated by selection, and there is neither time nor selection-power left for selecting the extremely rare mutations which might arise to the right of the near-neutral box.

Given the pivotal role beneficial mutations play in all evolutionary scenarios, I was puzzled as to why Kimura did not represent them in any way in his graphs. In fairness, I thought I should sketch them in. To the extent they occur, the distribution curve for beneficial mutations should be a reverse image of the deleterious mutations. Just like deleterious mutations, the overwhelming majority of the beneficial mutations should be nearly-neutral, being crowded toward the neutral mark. Crow (1997) clearly states this obvious fact. The overwhelming majority of beneficial mutations should have very slight effects (see Appendix 5 for more details). However, since beneficial mutations are so rare compared to deleterious mutations, their range and the area under their curve would also be proportionally smaller. I have seen estimates of the ratio of deleterious-to-beneficial mutations ranging from one thousand to one up to one million to one. I believe the best estimates are closer to one million to one (Gerrish and Lenski, 1998). The actual rate of beneficial mutations is so extremely low as to thwart any actual measurement (Bataillon, 2000; Elena et al., 1998). Therefore, I cannot draw a small enough curve to the right of zero to accurately represent how rare such beneficial mutations really are. Instead, I have shown the expected beneficial distribution, but very greatly exaggerated, so it can be seen (Figure 3d, p. 35). Figure 3d is an honest and true representation of the natural distribution of mutations, except that it is vastly too generous in terms of beneficial mutations. What is most interesting about this figure (and it came as a shock to me) is the realization that nearly all hypothetical beneficial mutations fall within Kimura's "effectively neutral" zone. That means that essentially all beneficial mutations (to the extent they actually happen), must be "unselectable". So selection could never favor any such beneficial mutations, and they would systematically drift out of the population. As we will see, there are some very rare beneficials that have a major effect, but they are anomalies – exceptions to the rule. These are shown in Figure 3d, as small arrows to the right of the 'no-selection zone'. Given the scale of the figure, these would be invisible apart from the arrows.

Figure 3d vividly illustrates why mutations cannot result in a net gain of information. As we will see more clearly in later chapters, selection cannot touch any of the mutations in the near-neutral box. Therefore, the very strong predominance of deleterious mutations in this box absolutely guarantees net loss of information. Furthermore, when mutations are recessive, or mutation rate is high and reproductive rate is moderate or low, selection cannot even eliminate all the deleterious mutations to the *left* of the box. We will see that constraints on selection even limit our ability to select for the extremely rare beneficial mutation that might lie to the right of the near-neutral box. **Everything about the true distribution of mutations argues against mutations leading to a net gain in information, as needed for forward evolution.**

Because beneficial mutations are so central to the viability of the Primary Axiom, I need to say a little more about them. During the last century, there was a great deal of effort invested in trying to use mutation to generate useful variation. This was especially true in my own area, plant breeding. When it was discovered that certain forms of radiation and certain chemicals were powerful mutagenic agents, millions and millions of plants were mutagenized and screened for possible improvements. Assuming the Primary Axiom, it would seem obvious that this would result in rapid "evolution" of our crops. For several decades this was the main thrust of crop improvement research. Vast numbers of mutants were produced and screened, collectively representing many billions of mutation events. A huge number of small, sterile, sick, deformed, aberrant plants were produced. However, from all this effort, almost no meaningful crop improvement resulted. The effort was for the most part an enormous failure, and was almost entirely abandoned. Why did this huge mutation/selection experiment fail – even with a host of PhD scientists trying to help it along? It was because even with all those billions of mutations, there were no significant new beneficial mutations arising. The exception proves the point. Low phytate corn is the most notable example of successful mutation breeding. Corn with low phytate has certain advantages in terms of animal feed. The low phytate corn was created by mutagenizing corn, and then selecting for strains wherein the genetic machinery which directs phytic acid production had been damaged. Although the resulting mutant may be desired for a specific agricultural purpose, it was accomplished through net loss of information (like the broken car alarm), and the loss of a biological function (a broken gene). Most of the other examples of successful mutation breeding are found within the area of ornamental plants, where dysfunctional anomalies are found to be novel and interesting to the eye. Examples of "useful" mutations within ornamental plants include sterility, dwarfing, mottled or variegated foliage, or misshaped floral organs.

If no truly positive mutations (resulting in a net gain of information) could be recovered from this vast science-guided process, why do we think the identical process, in the absence of any guiding intelligence, would be more fruitful in nature? However, the very same scientists who failed at mutation/selection were *extremely* successful in crop improvement when they abandoned mutation breeding and instead used the pre-existing natural variation within each plant species or genus. This would make sense if such pre-existing variation did not principally arise via mutation, but originally arose by *design*.

Bergman (2004) reviewed the topic of beneficial mutations. Among other things, he did a simple literature search via Biological Abstracts and Medline. He found 453,732 "mutation" hits, but among these only 186 mentioned the word "beneficial" (about 4 in 10,000). When those 186 references were reviewed, the presumed beneficial mutations were only beneficial in a very narrow sense and consistently involved *loss of function* (loss of information) changes. He was unable to find a single example of a mutation which unambiguously created new information. While it is almost universally accepted that beneficial, information-creating mutations *must* occur, this belief seems to be based upon uncritical acceptance of the Primary Axiom rather than upon actual evidence. I do not doubt there *are* beneficial mutations that create information, but it is clear they are exceedingly rare – much too rare for genome-building.

In conclusion, mutations appear to be overwhelmingly deleterious, and even when a mutation may be classified as beneficial in some specific sense, it is still usually part of an overall breakdown and erosion of information. As we will soon examine in greater detail, mutations, even when coupled with selection, cannot generally create new information. The types of variation created by mutation are more like the dings and scratches of life, and cannot be seen as life's spare parts (spare parts are designed). Mutations are the basis for the aging of individuals, and right now they are leading to our death, both yours and mine. Unless selection can somehow stop the erosion of information in the human genome, mutations will not only lead to our personal death, they will lead to the death of our species. We will soon see that in order to prevent continuous genomic degeneration, natural selection must be able to effectively select against extremely large numbers of nearly-neutral nucleotide mutations.

2014 Update – One of the things this book shows is that forward evolution requires a very high rate of beneficial mutations, and these must be sufficiently impactful so as to be selectable. Could such beneficial mutations be extremely common? Simple logic precludes this, as do most scientific observations over many decades. Logic tells us that genetic information represents specifications. Specifications are inherently specific, and random mutations destroy specificity – they systematically destroy any useful information. Yet there are a few isolated cases where it is claimed that certain laboratory experiments demonstrate remarkably high rates of beneficial mutation. My colleagues and I have very effectively refuted these claims in a recent scientific publication (see Montañez et al., 2013). The key to understanding these claims of super-abundant high-impact beneficial mutations, is that a large part (up to 50%) of any microbial genome consists of "just-in-case genes" which need to be precisely regulated.

These genes are crucial in the real world – conferring tolerance to a host of specific stress conditions. But in an artificial and unchanging laboratory environment, such genes are just dead weight. Breaking or deleting such non-essential genes will very often conserve energy and allow faster growth in the artificial environment. Likewise, disrupting their normal regulation can be advantageous in the artificial environment. Under these artificial conditions many diverse "beneficial" mutations can arise that involve loss of information, loss of function, and genetic degeneration (like stripping down a car for a race). Describing such mutations as "beneficial" is really a misnomer – they actually represent "adaptive degeneration". This is best seen in the famous long term Escherichia coli experiment by Lenski and colleagues (Barrick et al., 2009; Lenski, 2011). E. coli did indeed adapt to a certain artificial environment, and on specific artificial medium could grow slightly faster. But when the enabling "beneficial" mutations were analyzed – they all involved loss-of-function events (either broken genes or broken promoters). Genome size consistently shrank. This is clearly NOT how genomes are built, and speaks directly to the problem of genetic degeneration (manuscript in preparation).

Most recently a paper by Bataillon and Bailey (2014), examined the distribution of mutation effects. In their paper they specifically examine the distribution of beneficial mutations, and say; "direct experimental evidence confirms predictions on the DFE (distribution of fitness effects) of beneficial mutations favors distributions that are roughly exponential but bounded on the right." In other words their analysis agrees with mine – and supports Figure 3d. They go on to say; "...estimates consistently suggest shape parameters in the Weibull domain...." The Weibull-type distribution is the distribution my colleagues and I usually employ in our numerical simulations. Lastly, they address the rarity of beneficial mutations by saying; "The conventional assumption... is that populations are very close to their fitness optimum, and so beneficial mutations are exceedingly rare and can safely be ignored. Thus, in most cases, assumptions of the models used do not allow for beneficial fitness effects to be estimated at all... However, beneficial mutations are not so rare that they cannot be detected when looked for in evolution experiments, and depending on the particular selection environment, beneficial mutations can even be quite numerous... it could be argued that these data represent the DFE of extremely maladapted populations, important only in the artificial environment of the lab." These authors clearly understand that beneficial mutations are extremely rare anomalies. In the big picture, mutations systematically destroy biological information.

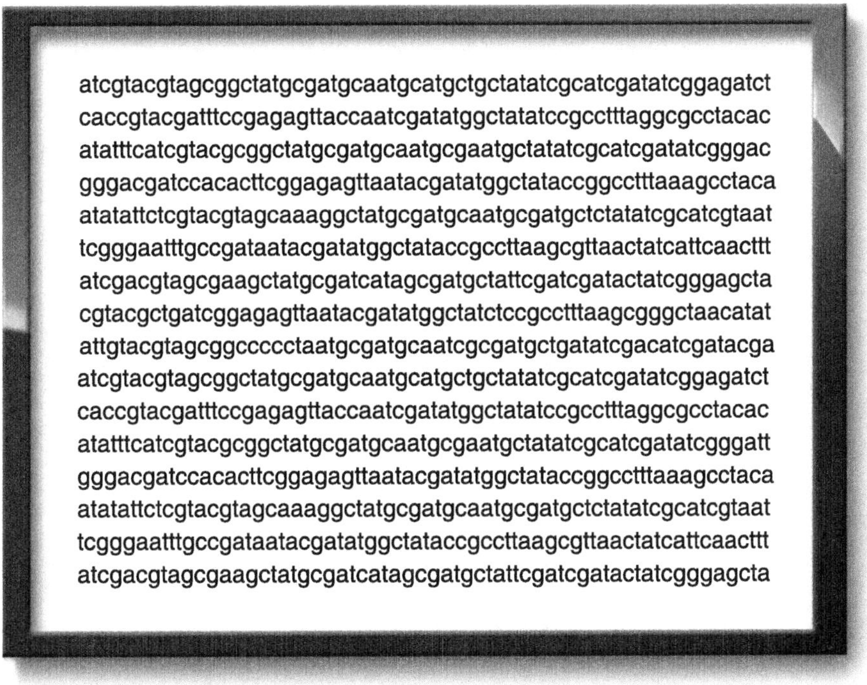

atcgtacgtagcggctatgcgatgcaatgcatgctgctatatcgcatcgatatcggagatct
caccgtacgatttccgagagttaccaatcgatatggctatatccgcctttaggcgcctacac
atatttcatcgtacgcggctatgcgatgcaatgcgaatgctatatcgcatcgatatcgggac
gggacgatccacacttcggagagttaatacgatatggctataccggcctttaaagcctaca
atatattctcgtacgtagcaaaggctatgcgatgcaatgcgatgctctatatcgcatcgtaat
tcgggaatttgccgataatacgatatggctataccgccttaagcgttaactatcattcaacttt
atcgacgtagcgaagctatgcgatcatagcgatgctattcgatcgatactatcgggagcta
cgtacgctgatcggagagttaatacgatatggctatctccgcctttaagcgggctaacatat
attgtacgtagcggcccccctaatgcgatgcaatcgcgatgctgatatcgacatcgatacga
atcgtacgtagcggctatgcgatgcaatgcatgctgctatatcgcatcgatatcggagatct
caccgtacgatttccgagagttaccaatcgatatggctatatccgcctttaggcgcctacac
atatttcatcgtacgcggctatgcgatgcaatgcgaatgctatatcgcatcgatatcgggatt
gggacgatccacacttcggagagttaatacgatatggctataccggcctttaaagcctaca
atatattctcgtacgtagcaaaggctatgcgatgcaatgcgatgctctatatcgcatcgtaat
tcgggaatttgccgataatacgatatggctataccgccttaagcgttaactatcattcaacttt
atcgacgtagcgaagctatgcgatcatagcgatgctattcgatcgatactatcgggagcta

Figure 2. The nature of genetic information...

The genome appears to us as a linear array of letters: A, T, C, G. The actual genome is 3 million fold greater than the sequence shown above. To view just half of your own genome, you would have to view 10 nucleotides every second, for 40 hours per week, for 40 years! The apparent simplicity of this language system is deceptive. A higher genome, almost certainly, must comprise a great deal of data compression (see Chapter 9), as well as a great deal of non-linear information. Except for certain short portions, we cannot view the genome as simply a linear text, like a book. Much of the information content is probably found in 3-dimensional structures, as is the case with folded proteins.

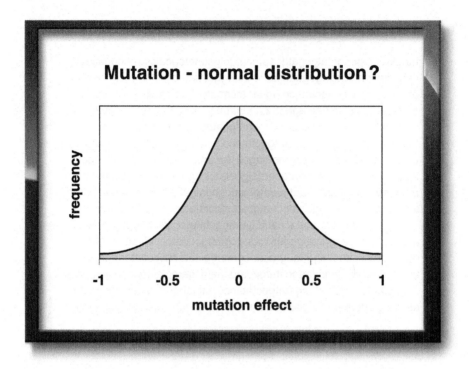

Figure 3a. Distribution of mutational effects on fitness – the naive view.

The naive view of mutations would be a bell-shaped distribution, with half of all mutations showing deleterious affects on fitness (left of center), and half showing positive effects on fitness (right of center). With such a distribution it would be easy to imagine selection removing some bad mutations and amplifying some good mutations, inevitably resulting in evolutionary progress. However, we know this is a false picture.

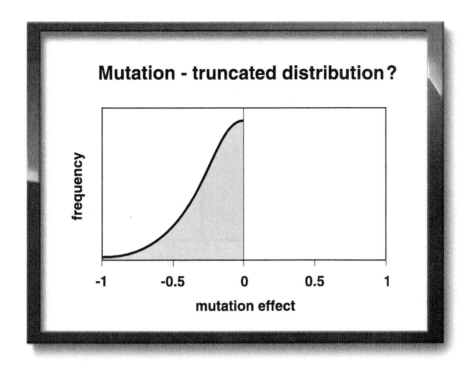

Figure 3b. Mutational effects on fitness – almost never beneficial.

Population geneticists know that nearly all non-neutral mutations are deleterious, and that mutations having positive effects on fitness are so rare as to be typically excluded from such distribution diagrams. This creates major problems for evolutionary theory. But this picture is still too optimistic.

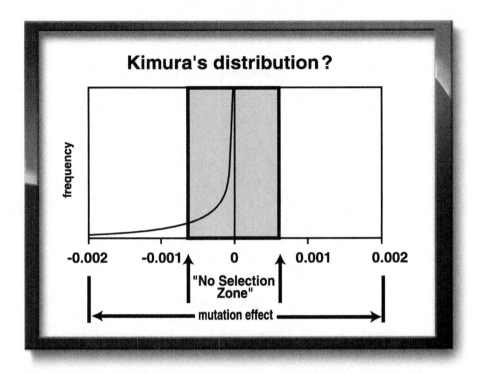

Figure 3c. Mutational effects – harmful effects usually very slight – invisible to natural selection.

Population geneticists know that mutations are strongly skewed toward neutral. Just like in an instruction manual, a few misspellings will be lethal but most will be *nearly harmless*. The nearly-neutral mutations create the biggest problems for evolutionary theory. This diagram is adapted from a figure by Kimura (1979). Note that the lower scale has changed – instead of ranging from -1 to +1, the scale ranges from -0.002 to +0.002. Kimura and his colleague, Ohta, are famous for showing that most mutations are nearly-neutral, and therefore are not subject to selection. Kimura's "no-selection zone" is shown by the grey box.

The general shape of this curve is important, but the precise mathematical nature of this curve is not. While Ohta feels the mutation distribution is exponential, Kimura feels it is a 'gamma' distribution (Kimura, 1979). However, regardless of which specific mathematical formulation best describes the natural distribution of mutation effects, they all approximate the picture shown above.

Geneticists agree that the frequency of highly deleterious mutations is almost zero (off the chart), while "minor" mutations are intermediate in frequency. Minor mutations are believed to outnumber major mutations by about 10-50 fold (Crow, 1997), but near-neutrals vastly outnumber them both.

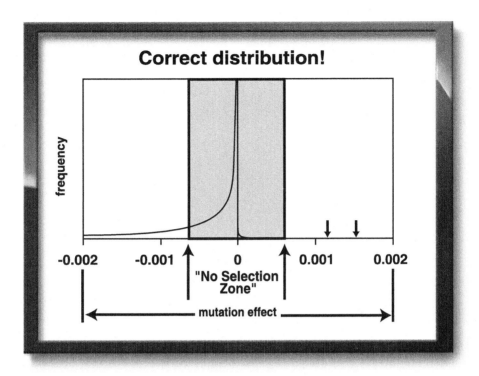

Figure 3d. Mutation effects – rare beneficial mutations do happen, but are generally un-selectable.

Kimura's Figure (3c) is still not complete. To complete the figure we really must show where the beneficial mutations would occur, as they are critical to evolutionary theory. Their distribution would be a reverse image of Kimura's curve, but reduced in range and scale, by a factor of somewhere between one thousand to one million. Because of the scale of this diagram, I cannot draw this part of the mutation distribution small enough, so a relatively large curve is shown instead. Even with beneficial mutations greatly exaggerated, it becomes obvious that essentially all beneficial mutations will fall within Kimura's "no-selection zone". This completed picture, which is correct, makes progressive evolution on the genomic level virtually impossible. Adaptation to a special circumstance can still happen, due to extremely rare high-impact beneficials – which are isolated anomalies (shown by arrows to the right of the "no-selection zone"). These rare beneficial mutations almost always involve loss of function and are therefore unproductive in terms of "forward evolution".

How Much Mutation is Too Much?

Newsflash – Human mutation rates are much too high.

For many decades geneticists have been worried about the impact of mutation on the human population (Muller, 1950; Crow, 1997). When these concerns first arose, they were based upon an estimated rate of deleterious mutation of *0.12 to 0.30 mutations per person per generation* (Morton, Crow and Muller, 1956). Since that time there have persisted serious concerns about deleterious mutation accumulation in man, leading to a high "genetic load" and a generally degenerating population. There has also been a long-standing belief that if the rate of deleterious mutations approached *one deleterious mutation per person per generation*, long-term genetic deterioration would be a certainty (Muller, 1950). This would be logical, since selection must eliminate mutations as fast as they are occurring. We need to prevent mutant individuals from reproducing, but we also need to leave enough remaining people to procreate and produce the next generation. By this thinking, deleterious mutations in man must actually be kept below one mutation for every three children – if selection is to eliminate all the mutations and still allow the population to reproduce. This is because global fertility rates are now less than 3 children for every 2 adults, so only one child in three could theoretically be selectively eliminated. For these reasons, geneticists have been naturally very eager to discover what the human mutation rate really is!

One of the most astounding recent findings in the world of genetics is that the human mutation rate (just within our reproductive cells) is in the range of 75-175 nucleotide substitutions (misspellings) per person per generation (Nachman and Crowell, 2000; Kondrashov, 2002; Xue et al., 2009; Lynch, 2010; Campbell and Eichler, 2013). These high numbers are now widely accepted within the genetics community. Furthermore, Dr. Kondrashov, the author of one of the publications, has indicated to me that 100 was only his *lower estimate*. He believed the actual rate of point mutations (misspellings) per person may be as high as 300 (personal communication). Even the lowest estimate, 75, is an amazing number, with profound implications. When an earlier study revealed that the human mutation rate might be as high as *30*, the highly distinguished author of that study concluded that such a number would have *profound* implications for evolutionary theory (Neel et al., 1986). Even if we assume that a very significant fraction of the genome is perfectly neutral junk, this would still mean that many new deleterious mutations are occurring per person per generation. So *every one* of us is a mutant, many times over. What type of selection scheme could possibly stop this type of loss of information? As we will see, given these numbers, there is no realistic method to halt genomic degeneration. Since the portion of the genome that is recognized as being truly functional is rapidly increasing, the number of mutations recognized as being actually deleterious must also be rapidly increasing. If the genome proves to be mostly functional, then most of these 75-175 mutations per person are actually deleterious. Because mutation-rate estimates have large margins of error, for the rest of this book I will just use 100 as a conservative estimate of the human mutation rate. However, this number is too conservative because it only considers point mutations (letter substitutions). This number does not include the many other types of common mutations, including tandem repeat mutations, deletions, insertions, duplications, translocations, inversions, conversions, and mitochondrial mutations.

To appreciate the extent of this underestimation of the mutation problem, we should first consider the types of mutation that fall outside the normal point mutation counts. Then we need to consider what portion of the whole genome is truly functional.

Within each cell are sub-structures called mitochondria, that have their own small internal genome (about 16,500 nucleotides), which is inherited only through the mother. However, because the mitochondrial genome is highly polyploid (hundreds of copies per cell), and because the mitochondrial mutation rate is extremely high, there are still a large number of mitochondrial mutations that must be eliminated each generation in order to halt degeneration. The human mitochondrial mutation rate may be as high as 2.5 mutations, per nucleotide site, per million years (Parsons et al., 1997). Assuming a generation time of 25 years and a mitochondrial genome size of 16,500, this approaches *a rate of 1.0 mitochondrial mutation per person per generation within the reproductive cell line*. Mitochondrial mutations, just by themselves, may put us over the theoretical limit of selective elimination. Even if the mutation rate is only 0.1 per person, we would have to select away a very substantial portion (10%) of the human population, every generation, just to halt mitochondrial genetic degeneration. Yet this would still allow the 100 or more nuclear mutations per person per generation to accumulate unabated. High rates of mitochondrial mutation are especially problematic in terms of selection (Chapters 4 and 5), because of a lack of recombination ("Muller's ratchet" – Muller, 1964), and a lower effective population size (only women pass on this DNA, so effective selection can only be applied to half the population).

The most rapidly mutating regions of the human genome are within the very dynamic micro-satellite DNA regions. These unique regions can mutate at rates nearly 1 million-fold above normal, and are not included in normal estimates of mutation rate. Yet these sequences are found to have biological impact, and their mutation results in many serious genetic diseases (Sutherland and Richards, 1995). It is estimated that for every "regular" point mutation, there is probably at least one micro-satellite mutation (Ellegren, 2000). This could conceivably double the mutation count per person per generation from 100 to 200.

In addition to nuclear point mutations, mitochondrial mutations, and micro-satellite mutations, there are a wide variety of more severe chromosomal mutations generally called "macro-mutations". These include deletions and insertions. According to Kondrashov (2002), such mutations, when combined, add another four macro-mutations for every 100 point mutations. This estimate appears to consider only the smallest of macro-mutations, and excludes the insertions/deletions affecting larger regions of DNA. Although there may be relatively few such macro-mutations (*minimally 4* per person per generation), these "major" mutations will unquestionably cause much more genomic damage, and so would demand higher priority if one were designing a selection scheme to stop genomic degeneration. Macro-mutations can affect any number of nucleotides – from one to one million – even as we might accidentally delete a letter, a word, or even an entire chapter from this book. These relatively few macro-mutations are believed to cause 3-10 fold more sequence divergence than all the point mutations combined (Britten, 2002; Anzai, 2003). This raises our actual mutation count to over 208 mutations per person per generation. But if we factor in the fact that macro-mutations can change 3-10 fold more nucleotides than all point mutations combined, our final tally of nucleotide changes per person is much greater. Yet even these numbers may *still* be too low. We have not yet considered inversions and translocations. Furthermore, evolutionary theorists are now invoking extremely high conversion rates, which could double these numbers again. At this point, let's recall the beginning of this chapter, where we learned that the Nobel-laureate geneticist Muller considered that a human mutation rate approaching 1.0 or higher per person would doom mankind to rapid genetic degeneration. Although we do not know the precise human mutation rate, there is good reason to believe that there are many more than 1,000 nucleotide changes in every person, every generation (see Table 1).

Of all these mutations, what percent are truly neutral? In the last few years there has been a dramatic shift in the perceived functionality of most components of the genome. The concept of junk DNA is quickly disappearing (Slack, 2006). In fact, it is the "junk" (non-protein-coding DNA) which appears to be *key* to encoding biological complexity (Taft and Mattick, 2003). The Taft and Mattick study strongly suggests that the more "junk" an organism has, the more advanced the organism is. So mutations within "junk" DNA can hardly be assumed to be neutral.

In 2005 it was already established that more than 50% of the human genome is transcribed into RNA (Johnson et al., 2005), and that at least half of this transcribed DNA appears to be *transcribed in both directions* (Yelin et al., 2003). So all of this DNA is not only functional, much of it may be *doubly* functional. While only a small fraction of the genome directly encodes for proteins, every protein-encoding sequence is embedded within other functional sequences that *regulate* the expression of such proteins. This includes promoters, enhancers, introns, leader sequences, trailing sequences, and sequences affecting regional folding and DNA architecture. I do not believe any serious biologist now considers introns (which comprise most of a typical genic region) as truly neutral "junk". In fact, many of the most strongly *conserved* (essential and invariant) sequences known, are found within introns (Bejerano et al., 2004). While a typical protein-coding sequence may only be 3,000 nucleotides long or less, the typical gene that controls the expression of that protein can be in the range of 50,000 nucleotides long. Since there are over 20,000 protein-encoding genes (estimates greatly vary), if we include all their associated nucleotides (50,000 per gene), complete genes could easily account for over 1.5 billion nucleotides. This is fully half the genome. In addition, a whole new class of genes has been discovered which do not encode proteins, but encode functional RNAs. Such genes have escaped recognition in computer searches for protein-coding sequences, and so have been overlooked as true genes. But they are true genes, and they probably comprise a large part of the genome (Mattick, 2001; Dennis, 2002; Storz, 2002).

They are just now being discovered within DNA regions that were previously dismissed as junk. In addition, two independent studies have shown extensive sequence functionality within the large regions *between* genes (Koop and Hood, 1994; Shabalina et al., 2001). Such regions had also previously been assumed to be junk. Pseudogenes, long considered dead duplicated genes, have been shown to be functional (Hirotsune et al., 2003; Lee, 2003). Pseudogenes seem to be designed to make regulatory RNA molecules (see Chen et al., 2004), rather than proteins, so they are not "dead fossils". As I will discuss in more detail elsewhere, there even appear to be diverse cellular functions for the much-maligned "selfish genes", sometimes called "parasitic DNA sequences" (also called "transposable elements"). These elements appear to have multiple important functions within the cell, including the control of chromosome pairing (Hakimi et al., 2002), and DNA repair (Morrish et al., 2002). Repetitive DNA, including satellite DNA, although long considered junk, has been shown to be essential to genome function, and comprises such essential genomic structures as centromeres and telomeres (Shapiro and Sternberg, 2005). Lastly, there are fundamental genome-wide structural patterns, which virtually permeate every portion of the genome, such as isochores (GC-rich areas – Vinogradov, 2003), genome-wide "word" patterns (Karlin, 1998), and nucleosome binding sites (Tachida, 1990; Segal et al., 2006). These genome-wide patterns appear crucial to cell function, and suggest functionality throughout the entire genome. For example, nucleosome binding (crucial to chromosome structure and gene regulation) appears to be specified by dinucleotide patterns that repeat every 10 nucleotides (Sandman et al., 2000). So, one-fifth of the genome may be functional and essential *just for the purpose of specifying nucleosome binding sites* (Tachida, 1990). **It is becoming increasingly clear that**

most, or all, of the genome is functional. Therefore, most mutations in the genome must be deleterious.

On a per person basis, 100 mutations represent a loss of only a miniscule fraction of the total information in our vast genome. However, the real impact of such a high mutation rate will be seen at the population level, and is expressed with the passage of time. Since there are well over six billion people in the world, and each person has added an average of 100 new mutations to the global population, our generation alone has added roughly 600 billion new mutations to the human race. If we remember that there are only three billion nucleotide positions in the human genome, we see that in our lifetime there have been over 200 mutations for every nucleotide position within the genome. Therefore, every possible point mutation that *could* happen to the human genome *has* happened many times over, just during our lifetime. Because of our present large population size, humanity is now being flooded by mutations like never before in history. The consequences of most of these mutations are not felt immediately, but will manifest themselves in coming generations.

As we will see, there is no selection scheme that can reverse the damage that has been done during our own generation, even if further mutations could be stopped. No amount of selection can prevent a significant number of these mutations from drifting deeper into the population and consequently causing permanent genetic damage. Yet our children's generation will add even more new mutations, followed by the next and the next. This degenerative process will continue into the foreseeable future. We are on a downward slide that cannot be stopped.

When selection is unable to counter the loss of information due to mutations, a situation arises called "error catastrophe". If not rapidly corrected, this situation leads to the eventual death of the species – extinction. In its final stages, genomic degeneration leads to declining fertility, which curtails further selection (selection always requires a surplus population, some of which can then be eliminated each generation). Inbreeding and genetic drift then take over entirely, rapidly finishing off the population. The process is an irreversible downward spiral. This advanced stage of genomic degeneration is called "mutational meltdown" (Bernardes, 1996). Mutational meltdown is recognized as an immediate threat to all of today's endangered species. The same process appears to potentially be a theoretical threat for mankind. What can stop it?

2008 Update – In June of 2007 a large international consortium of genome scientists (under the name ENCODE) published their finds in a set of 29 scientific papers. These findings stunned the genetics community (Kapranov et al., 2007). They showed that the human genome is vastly more complex than they had expected, and that essentially all of the genome is transcribed – most of it in both directions. They concluded that most nucleotides are not only functional but are poly-functional, having multiple roles. This means that the genome's functionality exceeds 100% (most of both strands of the DNA are functional). In this light, no mutations should be considered "perfectly neutral", and almost all mutations must be considered deleterious. This means that the real deleterious mutation rate in man is nothing less than staggering – in the ballpark of 100 mutations per person per generation. This is more than two orders of magnitude greater than was previously considered possible.

2014 Update – Since the 2008 edition of this book, Xue et al. (2009) and Lynch (2010), have further confirmed that the human mutation rate is extremely high – in the general ballpark of 100 new mutations per person per generation. Lynch argues that almost all the human genome is junk DNA, so almost all mutations are harmless. Nevertheless, Lynch concludes that the problem of mutation accumulation in man is severe (see Appendix 1).

The latest and most complete analysis of the human germline mutation rate is found in a recent review by Campbell and Eichler (2013). Table 1 of that paper summarizes the findings of numerous studies involving human mutation rates. Some of the estimates in that table only involved a single family, and so are not very reliable. Using the six larger studies that involved at least 20 families, the mean point mutation rate was 1.56 x 10^{-8} per nucleotide, per gamete, per generation. This translates to 93.6 mutations per birth. However the authors of this review state that this is just a lower boundary. They add that these studies excluded the most mutable portions of the genome. They state; "...it is important to note that all of these studies involve substantial filtering of de novo variants to remove false positives and often exclude highly repetitive regions of the genome... studies from targeted sequencing of exomes or other regions have reported higher mutation rates..." Furthermore, most mutational nucleotide changes are not due to the point mutations (see below). Therefore, 100 mutations per person per generation remains a very conservative estimate of the human point mutation rate.

What about the other types of mutation? The same authors point out that in addition to point mutations, there are many types of larger mutational disruptions of the genome. These include microsatellite mutations, mutations in the centromeric repeats, insertion and deletion mutations (indels), and copy number variant mutations (CNVs). They fail to mention mitochondrial mutations, inversions, translocations, or conversions.

The authors of this latest review confirm that macro-mutations are by far *the greatest source of genomic divergence and degeneration. For example they show that CNV mutations alone account for **16,000** to **50,000** base pair changes per birth. Likewise, they show that the rates of insertions and deletions (indels), are higher than previously thought. Whereas indels were previously thought to be only **6%** as frequent as point mutations, newer estimates suggest that this number should be more like **10%** or even **20%**, and that this number will grow as sequencing methods improve. So there may be **20** new indels per birth. Since indels involve multiple nucleotides per event, and can involve thousands or even millions of nucleotides per event, indels can very reasonably be expected to change thousands of nucleotides per person per generation.*

*Wells (2013) exhaustively reviews the emerging literature that shows that most of the genome is functional, which means that deleterious mutations in man must minimally be in the ballpark of **100** per person per generation. This is strongly supported by the massive final report of the ENCODE project (The ENCODE Project Consortium, 2012).*

A very recent paper (Rands et al., 2014), claims that 8.2% of the human genome is evolutionarily "constrained" (i.e., has remained largely unchanged since the earilest mammals evolved). This is based upon the observed similarity in human genomes compared to genomes of other mammals. This is not remarkable. However, evolutionists are now using these calculations to claim that this proves that the rest of the genome (91.8%) must therefore be "junk DNA". This is a very irrational conclusion. It is not suprising that parts of the human genome would be shared by most mammals – such genomic regions must encode functions which most mammals have in common (i.e. mammillary glands, common biochemical functions, etc.). However, it should be obvious, that other parts of the genome must encode those functions that make each mammal unique. A human, a whale, a bat – each has unique capabilities. Large parts of mammal genomes are different because they prescribe functional information that allows a human to do science, a whale to dive a mile deep, and a bat to fly and echolocate.

Mutation Type	Mutations per Person	Nucleotides changed/person
1. mitochondrial mutations[a]	<1	<1
2. nucleotide substitutions[b]	75-175	75-175
3. satellite mutations[c]	75-175	75-175
4. deletions[d]	2-6+	1-3000+
5. duplications / insertions[e]	2-6+	1-3000+
6. inversions / translocations[f]	numerous	thousands?
7. conversions[g]	thousands?	thousands?
total/person/generation[h]	**100++**	**thousands!**

Table 1. Many types of mutations – resulting in a remarkably high human mutation rate.

There are many types of mutations and each acts as a source of heritable genetic change. Unfortunately, every single class of mutation results in a net loss of information. Mitochondrial mutation is the least significant source of human mutation. It produces less than one new mutation per person. Yet even a fraction of one mitochondrial mutation per person has prompted one evolutionist to comment: *"We should increase our attention to the broader question of how (or whether) organisms can tolerate, in the sense of evolution, a genetic system with such a high mutational burden."* (Howell et al., 1996). Now, consider all the types of mutation combined!

[a] *Mitochondrial mutation rate estimates vary, ranging from 0.1-1.0 per person (Parsons et al., 1997; Carter, R., 2007).*

[b] *Kondroshov (2002), Xue (2009), Lynch (2010), Campbell and Eichler (2013).*

[c] *Normal estimates of nucleotide substitutions would not include mutational hotspots such as microsatellites. Microsatellite mutation rates have been estimated to be roughly equal to the point mutation rate.*

[d,e] *Kondrashov (2002) estimated that deletions plus insertions occur at a combined rate of about 4-12% of the point mutations, or about 2-6% each. However, he seemed to limit his estimate to only small inserts and deletions, so the actual number may be higher. Campbell and Eichler (2013) suggest that indels may be 3 times more frequent than Kondrashov's estimate. Because deletions and insertions can be very large, their total effect is believed to be 3-10 fold greater than all point mutations combined in terms of total nucleotides changed.*

[f] *The actual rate of chromosomal rearrangements is unknown. Evolutionary assumptions about the recent divergence of chimp and man require high rates of such changes. These changes can affect very large pieces of DNA, and so for the evolutionary scenario to work, thousands of nucleotides, on average, must move in this way every generation.*

[g] *The actual rate of conversion is unknown, but evolutionary assumptions require extremely high rates of gene conversion between different loci – many thousands per person per generation.*

[h] *The total number of mutations can only be estimated in a very crude way, but it should be very clear that the number of all types of new mutations, including conversions, must be much more than 100 per person per generation. These mutations, which include many macro-mutations, must clearly change thousands of nucleotides per person per generation.*

All-Powerful Selection to the Rescue?

Newsflash – Selection capabilities are very limited.

The consensus among human geneticists is that, at present, the human race is genetically degenerating due to rapid mutation accumulation and relaxed natural selection pressure (Crow, 1997; Lynch, 2010). These geneticists realize that there is presently a continuous accumulation of mutations in the human population and that this is occurring at a much higher rate than was previously thought possible. Geneticists widely agree that these mutations are almost entirely either neutral or deleterious (if any are beneficial, they are considered so rare as to be excluded from consideration). Subsequently, they realize that genetic information is currently being lost, which must eventually result in reduced fitness for our species. This decline in fitness is believed to be occurring at 1-2% per generation (Crow, 1997) (see Figure 4, p. 71) and may be as high as 5% (Lynch, 2010). All this is happening on the genetic level, even while medical and technical advances are increasing our average life spans on the social level. Hence, most human geneticists would probably agree that selection must eventually be increased if we are to stop genetic degeneration. However, there are essentially no public statements to this effect – imagine the profound political ramifications of such statements.

This acknowledged problem raises an interesting question: How much selection would be required to halt genetic degeneration? Or perhaps the question should really be this: Can selection stop degeneration at all?

For many people, including many biologists, natural selection is like a magic wand. There seems to be no limit to what it might accomplish. This extremely naive perspective toward natural selection is pervasive. Even as a plant geneticist, I had an unrealistic concept of how selection was really operating in nature, and I had a very naive idea about how selection might work at the level of the whole genome. For the most part, the only scientists who have actually seriously analyzed what selection can and cannot do on the genomic level are a small number of population geneticists (a very small and specialized group). Population genetics is a field that is extremely theoretical and mathematical. Theoretical mathematicians are completely constrained by their *axioms* (assumptions), upon which they build their formulas. The entire field of population genetics was developed by a small, tightly knit group of people who were radically committed to the Primary Axiom. Today, it is still a very small field, still exclusively populated by "true believers" in the Primary Axiom. These people are extremely intelligent, but are totally and unconditionally bound to the Primary Axiom. For the most part, other biologists do not understand their work and accept their conclusions by faith. Yet it is these *same* population geneticists themselves who have exposed some of the most profound limitations of natural selection (see Appendix 1). Because natural selection is *not* a magic wand but is a very real phenomenon, it has very real capabilities and very real *limitations*. It is not all-powerful.

The Most Basic Problem

The Princess and the Nucleotide Paradox

Natural selection has a fundamental problem. This problem involves the enormous chasm that exists between *genotypic change* (a molecular mutation) and *phenotypic selection* (selection on the level of the whole organism). There needs to be selection for billions of almost infinitely subtle and complex genetic differences on the molecular level. But this can only be done by controlling reproduction on the level of the whole organism. When "Mother Nature" selects for or against an individual within a population, she has to accept or reject a complete set of 6 billion nucleotides – all at once! It is either take all the letters in the whole book, or take none. **In fact, Mother Nature (natural selection) never sees the individual nucleotides.** She only sees the whole organism. She does not have the luxury of seeing, or selecting for, any particular letter. We start to see what a great leap of faith is required to believe that by selecting or rejecting whole organisms, Mother Nature can precisely control the fate of billions of individual misspellings within a population.

The problem of *genotypic change* versus *phenotypic selection* is very much like the problem of the children's story, *The Princess and the Pea.* The royal character of a Princess is discovered, because, even through 13 mattresses, she feels a pea beneath her bed and so can't sleep. Children are entertained by this story because it is so silly. Royalty or not, no one can feel a pea through 13 mattresses. But our genetic problem is actually a much more difficult situation. Our Princess is natural selection on the level of the whole organism – accepting or rejecting individual people. Our Princess essentially needs to read extensive books written in

Braille through a set of mattresses in order to precisely identify which books have the fewest errors in them. It makes a great fairy tale, but who would believe it as the underlying process which explains life? This whole problem can be called the *Princess and the Nucleotide Paradox*, which is whimsically illustrated in Figure 5 (pp. 72-73).

To be fair, there are a few mutations that have a much bigger effect than a single Braille letter in our example. A few rare mutations have profound biological effects, acting more like a bowling ball under the mattress. Natural selection against these types of major mutations is an obvious "no-brainer". But the bowling ball (semi-lethal) mutations are very rare, and such nucleotide sites carry only a miniscule amount of the total information in the genome. Most of the information in the genome is carried by nucleotides whose effects are actually much more subtle than even the Braille letters in our example. It is the origin and maintenance of all *those* nucleotides that we are trying to understand. The essence of this paradox is that Mother Nature (natural selection) has to write the book of life, and continuously proofread the book, without ever seeing any of the letters. In more technical terms – selection is based on phenotype, not genotype.

The gap between a single nucleotide molecule and the whole organism is profound. Part of this gap involves size. If we were to make a nucleotide as big as a pea, a proportionately-sized human being would be roughly 10,000 miles tall. Moreover, standing between a nucleotide and an individual organism are many different *levels of organization*. For example, a single nucleotide may affect a specific gene's transcription, which may then affect mRNA processing, which may then affect the abundance of a given enzyme, which may then affect a given metabolic pathway, which may then affect the division of a cell, which may then affect a certain tissue, which may then affect the whole organism, which may then affect the probability of reproduction, which may then affect the chance for that specific mutation to get passed on to the next generation. Massive amounts of uncertainty and dilution are added at each organizational level, resulting in massive increase in "noise", and loss of resolution. There must be a *vanishingly small* correlation between any given nucleotide (a single molecule), and a whole organism's probability of reproductive success. The nucleotide and the organism are very literally worlds apart. Our Princess (natural selection on the level of the whole organism), has to perceive differences which are just above the *atomic level*.

We do not generally see individual pixels on our television, so imagine the difficulty of trying to select a specific TV set at the store by trying to evaluate the quality of each separate pixel, by eye, on all the various TV sets available. But it's really much worse than this. In a biological system, we are talking about pixels, within pixels, within pixels, within pixels. We are talking about a very long chain of events separating the direct effect of a given nucleotide and very remote consequences on the whole organism level. There is a logarithmic dilution at each step. At each level there is an order of magnitude loss of correspondence. It is like measuring the impact of a butterfly's stroke on a hurricane system a thousand miles away. It is a little like trying to select for a specific soldier, based upon the performance of his army. This whole picture is totally upside down. Yet this is the essence of the Primary Axiom. Advocates of the Primary Axiom see a human genome (6 billion nucleotides), and imagine that each letter is independently selected for (or against), merely based upon a limited amount of reproductive filtering on the level of the whole organism. As we will see, this is impossible.

To better understand the nature of the Princess and the Nucleotide Paradox, let's imagine a new method for improving textbooks. Start with a high school biochemistry textbook and say it is equivalent to a simple bacterial genome. Let's now begin introducing random misspellings, duplications, and deletions. Each student, across the whole country, will get a slightly different textbook, each containing its own set of random errors (approximately 100 new errors per text). At the end of the year, we will test all the students, and we will only save the textbooks from the students with the best scores. Those texts will be used for the next round of copying, which will introduce new errors. Can we expect to see a steady improvement of textbooks? Why not? Will we expect to see a steady improvement of average student grades? Why not?

Most of us can see that in the above example, essentially **none** of the misspellings in the textbook will be beneficial. More importantly, there will be no meaningful correlation between the subtle differences in textbooks and a student's grade. Why not? Because every textbook is approximately equally flawed, and the differences between texts are too subtle to be significant in light of everything else. What do I mean by "everything else"? I mean that a student's grade will be determined by many other important variables, including different personal abilities and different personal situations (teachers, classrooms, other kids, motivation, home life, romantic life, lack of sleep, "bad luck", etc.). All these other factors (which I will call *noise*) will override the effect of a few misspellings in the textbook. If the student gets a high grade on the test, it is not because his text had slightly fewer errors, but primarily for all those other diverse reasons.

What will happen if this mutation/selection cycle continues unabated? The texts *will* obviously degenerate over time, and average student scores *will* eventually also go down. Yet this absurd mutation/selection system is a very reasonable approximation of the Primary Axiom of biology. It will obviously fail to improve or even maintain grades. The most fundamental reason why this type of selection fails is the incredibly weak relationship between individual letters in the text and the over-all performance of the student. The correlation will be essentially zero. Therefore, this is an excellent illustration of the Princess and the Nucleotide Paradox. If this scenario seems absurd to you, try to understand one more thing – the Primary Axiom claims this very same mutation/selection system is actually what *wrote the entire biochemistry textbook in the first place*. There was never any intelligent agent acting as author or even as editor.

The problem of the Princess and the Nucleotide Paradox becomes even greater when we understand the phenomenon of *homeostasis*. Homeostasis is the natural phenomenon wherein all living things *self-regulate* themselves as circumstances change. Such homeostasis further neutralizes the effect of most mutations, making even more mutations invisible to selection. A good example would be a warm-blooded animal in a cold climate. Homeostasis results from an incredibly complex network of sensors and regulators within each cell. Although it is too complex to explain in detail, it is universally agreed that it is both operational and highly effective in all life systems. The phenomenon of homeostasis is a little like having a super-duper, self-adjusting mattress. If a tennis ball is put beneath this mattress, the mattress will automatically adjust itself via a myriad of complex mechanical mechanisms to effectively level the sleeping surface. But in real biology, it is more like we have 13 self-adjusting mattresses, one on top of the other (homeostasis operates at every level of biological organization). This makes things much more difficult for our Princess, who needs to sense the pea (read the Braille) through the mattresses.

When Gregor Mendel's genetic principles were "rediscovered" almost 50 years after Darwin, geneticists realized that there must be large numbers of hereditary units segregating within any given population. They also soon realized they had a problem if the number of hereditary units was very large. Although they did not speak of it as such, it was essentially what I am now calling the Princess and the Nucleotide Paradox. The early population geneticists, who were all philosophically committed Darwinists, realized they had to devise a way to overcome the Princess and the Nucleotide Paradox in order to make Darwinian theory appear genetically feasible*. So they very cleverly transferred the *unit of selection* from the whole organism to the genetic unit (i.e., the gene or nucleotide). To do this they had to redefine a population as being nothing more than a "pool of genes". In this way they could claim real selection was operating at the level of the nucleotide within the gene pool and not really on the individual. Each nucleotide could be envisioned as being independently selected for,

---

* *"Haldane... intended..., as had Fisher... and Wright... to dispel the belief that Mendelism had killed Darwinism... Fisher, Haldane, and Wright then quantitatively synthesized Mendelian heredity and natural selection into the science of population genetics." (Provine, 1971).*

or against, or neither. This made it very easy to envision almost any evolutionary selection scenario, no matter how complex the biological situation. And this effectively removed the mattresses from under the Princess, as if she could suddenly feel each pea, and could even read each Braille letter directly! This was an incredibly effective way to obscure the entire problem. Indeed, Darwinism would have died very naturally at this point in time, except for this major intellectual invention (Provine, 1971).

There is one serious problem with redefining the problem in this way – the new picture is categorically false. Populations are not even remotely like pools of genes, and selection is **never** for individual nucleotides. To justify this radical new picture of life, the theorists had to axiomatically assume a number of things which were all known to be clearly false. For example, they had to assume that all genetic units could sort independently so that each nucleotide would be inherited independently, as though there were no genetic linkage blocks (totally false). Likewise, they had to assume no epistasis, as though there were no interactions between nucleotides (totally false). They also typically assumed essentially infinite population sizes (obviously false). They usually implicitly assumed unlimited time for selection (obviously false). And they generally assumed the ability to select for unlimited numbers of traits simultaneously (which we will show to be false). From the very beginning of population genetic theory, many unrealistic and unreasonable assumptions were needed to make the model appear feasible.

On this false foundation were built the theoretical pillars of modern population genetics. The models did not match biological reality, but these men had an incredible aura of intellectual authority, their arguments were very abstract, and they used highly mathematical formulations which could effectively intimidate most biologists. Furthermore, most biologists were also committed Darwinists and so were in philosophical agreement with the population geneticists. They were more than happy to go along for the ride, even if the story did not quite make sense. In fact, the early population geneticists quickly became the idolized "darlings of science". I remember my own graduate-level classes in population biology, and my own naive and meek acquiescence in accepting the very unnatural redefinition of life as "pools of genes". I remember not quite getting it, and assuming the problem was just with me (although all the other students in my class seemed to have the same problem). Since I *knew* evolution was true, it did not really matter if I was not *quite smart enough* to really grasp the idea of life as pools of nucleotides. If the gurus of population genetics were saying it was true, who was I to argue? Even if their premises were false (such as independent assortment of nucleotides), their conclusions must still doubtless be true – they were geniuses! I was actually one of the more free-thinking students, but I still swallowed the Princess and the Nucleotide story without resistance.

What is the biological reality, apart from ideology? The reality is that selection acts on the level of the organism, not on the level of the nucleotide (see Crow and Kimura, 1970, p. 173). Human genes never exist in "pools". They exist in massive integrated assemblies within real people. Each nucleotide is intimately associated with all the other nucleotides within a given person, and they are only selected or rejected as a set of 6 billion. The phenomenon of linkage is profound and extensive, as we will see. No nucleotide is ever inherited independently. Each nucleotide is intimately connected to its surrounding nucleotides, even as each letter on this page is specifically associated with a specific word, sentence, paragraph, and chapter. This book is not a pool of letters, and it was not produced by a selective system like a giant slot machine where each letter is selected randomly and independently. Each letter was put in place by design, as part of something greater – as part of a specific word, a sentence, a paragraph and a chapter. This is also true of nucleotides. They only exist and have meaning in the *context* of other nucleotides (which is what we call epistasis). We now know that human nucleotides exist in large linked clusters or blocks, ranging in size from 10,000 to a million. These linkage blocks are inherited as a single unit and almost never break apart. This falsifies one of the most fundamental assumptions of the theorists, that each nucleotide can be viewed as an individually selectable unit. Since the population genetics model of life (as pools of genes) is categorically false, the Princess and the Nucleotide Paradox remains entirely unresolved. This should be an enormous embarrassment to the entire field of population genetics. On a practical level, it means natural selection can never create even moderately long strings of nucleotide specifications.

Not only is the Princess and the Nucleotide Paradox unresolved, we now know that the problem is vastly worse than the early population geneticists could have imagined. We have now learned that the size and complexity of the genome (the extent of the Braille books) is vast, that homeostasis (the thickness of the mattresses) is extensive, and there are many more levels of organization (the number of mattresses) separating the genotype from the phenotype. We will have to wait until Chapter 6 to fully understand the problem of biological "noise" (it turns out the mattresses themselves are full of pea-sized lumps). So we should be able to see that the Princess and the Nucleotide Paradox is a show-stopper. The Primary Axiom fails at this first and most basic level. Any child should be able to see it, although many adults are "too well educated" to see it. Yet the paradox of the Princess and the Nucleotide is just the first of many problems with the Primary Axiom. For the purpose of further discussion, and for the rest of this book, I will be happy to give the theorists their model of life as "pools of genes" and the idea of selection on the level of single nucleotides. I agree to do this because, as we will see, there are many other problems which fully discredit the Primary Axiom. For the record, the Princess and the Nucleotide Paradox is in itself sufficient basis for rejecting the Primary Axiom (see Appendix 3).

Three Specific Selection Problems

To understand the basic issues of genomic selection (which will soon become complex), let us first look at this question using a simple case involving a single mutation (instead of millions) and artificial selection (instead of natural selection). Imagine a single point mutation that has accumulated within the human population, to the extent that 50% of all people bear this mutation. What type of artificial selection is required to eliminate this mutation, and what are the critical factors? For simplicity, we will be assuming the mutation is dominant (most mutations are recessive, which makes selection much more difficult). At first glance, the problem seems very easily solved. We could eliminate all these mutants in a single generation if we could 1) afford to lose 50% of the breeding population; 2) if we could clearly identify every person carrying the mutation; and 3) if we could prevent 100% of the carriers from reproductive mating. So what are the problems?

1. Cost of selection. The problem of the "cost of selection" was first described by Haldane (1957), and later validated and expanded upon by Kimura and Ohta (1971), and Kimura (1983). It has been further clarified by ReMine (1993, 2005). All selection involves a biological *cost* – meaning that selection must remove ("spend") part of the breeding population. Selective elimination is the essence of selection. In the current example, we should ask, "Can we really afford to regularly spend 50% of humanity, preventing half the people from reproducing, so that we can make rapid selective progress?" Given humanity's fertility levels (globally less than 3 children for every 2 adults), if we eliminate 50% of our children for the purpose of selection, the population size will be immediately reduced by at least 25%. Obviously, each pair of adults need to have at least two reproducing children to maintain the population size. Furthermore, not all children will go on to reproduce (for reasons like accidental death, personal choice, etc.). Therefore, considerably more than two children for every two adults are needed to keep the population viable. Given our low fertility, if three children per two adults were needed for population continuity, zero selection would be possible. For these reasons, substantially less than one child in three is available to be "spent" for selection purposes. Haldane (1957) believed that only 10% of a typical natural human population could realistically be spent for selection purposes. If 50% of the population *was* regularly removed for purposes of selection every generation, the human population would shrink rapidly, leading to our extinction. Therefore, in the above example, elimination of all the mutant individuals in one generation is not reasonable. However, doing this same amount of selection in two generations *might* be conceivable since only 25% of the population would be spent for selection, per generation.

The purpose of this simple illustration is to show that while selection works, there are clear limits in terms of how intense our selection can be, and we must understand that every selective event has a biological cost. This becomes a major issue when selecting against many different mutations simultaneously. For the human population, it becomes clear that the maximum part of our population which can be "spent" for all selection purposes is much less than 33%, and, according to Haldane, might realistically be in the range of 10%. In contrast, while I was a plant breeder at Cornell University, I could easily "spend" (eliminate) 99% of the individual plants in my breeding populations for selection purposes because of the extreme fertility of plants.

The concept of "cost of selection" is so important that I need to say more about it. The normal reproductive rate of a species must obviously be at least two offspring for every two adults or the species quickly goes extinct. However, every species needs much more reproduction than this just to survive. An *excess* population is needed to "fund" many things, both genetic and non-genetic. For example, there is a huge *random* element to successful reproduction. Many individuals in a population die or fail to reproduce for reasons that have nothing to do with genetics. Being hit by a truck or killed in a war has very little to do with a person's genetic "fitness". This cost of random death is absolute, and must be "paid" before we even consider selection. In some species, this cost may be 50% or more of the total population. In such cases, we need at least 4 offspring per 2 adults just to avoid rapid extinction. But at this point, selection has not yet even begun. When we actually consider the genetic factors that determine reproductive success, there are significant genetic features which are *not* passed on to the offspring. These genetic components are not "heritable". For example, many genes work well in certain combinations, but are undesirable by themselves (this would be true wherever there is heterosis or epistasis). Selecting for such gene combinations is really "false selection", because it does the offspring no good. The gene combinations are broken up in meiosis and are not passed on. Yet such "false selection" must still be paid for, requiring still more reproduction. And we have not yet started to pay for "real" selection! Real selection can take several forms: stabilizing selection, sexual selection, progressive selection, etc. Each form of selection has a reproductive cost. All reproductive costs are additive, and **all costs must be paid**. Total reproductive costs must never exceed the actual reproductive potential of a species. Only if a species is sufficiently fertile, and there is sufficient surplus population to fund **all other costs**, does any type of selection become feasible. In other words, selection is only possible to the extent that there is residual excess population, after all other costs have first been paid. Selection is a little like discretionary spending for a family on a tight budget. The question always comes down to, "Can we afford it?"

Fitness (total biological functionality) is actually the real trait that natural selection always acts upon, and this very fundamental trait is actually *very poorly inherited*. This runs counter to popular thinking. According to Kimura, fitness has low *heritability*, perhaps as low as 0.004 (Kimura, 1983, p.30-31). The concept of heritability is dealt with in more detail in Chapter 6. For now it is sufficient to know that low heritability means that environmental factors are much more important than genetic factors in determining who appears "superior". For Kimura to say that general fitness has very poor heritability is an amazing acknowledgment. It means that, even with intense selection pressure, nearly all of a population's surplus ends up being "spent" to remove non-heritable variations, and thus **most reproductive elimination is unproductive.** In other words, selection for general fitness has minimal impact on the makeup of the next generation. Kimura's statement implies that *only a small fraction of the surplus population is truly available to pay for the elimination of mutations.* Despite this very important fact, I am going to be exceedingly generous for now and will assign all available "selection dollars" (the entire surplus population) to the elimination of deleterious mutations. Unless otherwise specified, I will assume that the entire surplus population is dedicated exclusively to selection for removal of mutations. However, the reader needs to understand that, in reality, only a very small fraction of any population's surplus can honestly be apportioned to mutation elimination (see Chapter 6, Figure 8a-c, pp. 105-107).

I believe one of the most fundamental mistakes that theorists make as they invent their various scenarios, is to ignore selective cost. They spend their selection dollars like a teenager with a credit card. They speculate as if there is always an infinitely large surplus population. Because theorists are usually unconstrained by realistic cost limits, in their minds they imagine they can "fund" any number of simultaneous selection scenarios. They can stack one selection scenario upon another and another. This reminds me of the old westerns where the cowboy would fire his "six-shooter" dozens of times without reloading, or like Legolas, in *Lord of the Rings,* who never runs out of arrows. However, such movies are fantasies, and the movie makers are free to claim "artistic license".

Genetic theorists do not have artistic license, and should be held accountable for how they spend their selection dollars, even as an accountant would be held accountable for where the money goes. Theorists should be assigned a realistic number of selection dollars based upon the reproductive reality of a given species. They should then "spend" this part of their surplus population soberly, and without any deficit spending. If this principle were honestly employed, there would be greatly diminished expectations of what selection can really do.

2. Recognizing obscured ("invisible") mutations. If you want to select against a mutant, you must be able to identify it within the population. But we cannot identify the carriers of a typical point mutation (apart from screening the whole population using very expensive DNA tests). Only those extremely rare point mutations which cause gross physical deformities can normally be identified on a practical level. For most individual point mutations, even though they are destructive and result in loss of information, they are so subtle that they are essentially "invisible". They do not produce a distinct or recognizable effect. To artificially select against a typical point mutation, we would need to do expensive lab analyses for every person on the planet, and this is entirely impractical. Therefore, we can see that there are fundamental problems in terms of identifying "good" versus "bad" individuals for selection. Obviously, when considering millions of mutations simultaneously, this problem becomes mind-boggling. Imagine wanting to buy an encyclopedia set, knowing that each set of volumes has its own unique collection of thousands of misspellings. Could you realistically stand there in the bookstore and sort through all those volumes with the expectation of finding the set of volumes which was least "degraded"? Given two sets, each of which contains its own unique set of 10,000 misspellings, how would you choose which set has the worst mistakes? The choice would become totally arbitrary! This issue of large numbers of silent or "nearly-neutral" mutations was first recognized by Kimura (1968) and Ohta (1973, 1974, 1992, 2002), and its implications have been explored by Kondrashov (1995).

3. Systematic reproductive elimination. The cost of selection and "silent" mutations are both huge problems. The challenge becomes even greater when it comes to preventing mutant individuals from mating. Nowhere on this planet is there a social system that can control human reproduction with high precision. The most infamous example of this occurred in Nazi Germany under Hitler. But that experiment failed catastrophically. Planned Parenthood and modern birth control practices, while effective in reducing average family size, have not been effective in eliminating mutations. In most instances, human mating and reproduction remain essentially random, except for those very rare cases where mutations result in very pronounced genetic defects.

From our very modest illustration above, we must conclude that we are not in a practical position to *artificially* select for even one typical point mutation within the human population. This is very sobering news. When we then go on to consider multiple mutations, the problems escalate exponentially. Even if we were able to identify all the carriers of numerous mutations, and could effectively prevent them all from mating, we would still sooner or later encounter the problem of selective cost, because when we simultaneously try to select against multiple mutations we run into the problems inherent with a rapidly shrinking population size. So we begin to see that selection is not as easy as we thought! Even the simplest selection scenario requires several important factors: 1) maintenance of population size; 2) clear identification of mutants; and 3) effective exclusion of the mutants from the breeding population. As we will see more clearly in the next chapter, when we consider all mutations simultaneously each one of these three requirements becomes utterly impossible.

If artificial selection fails to eliminate the typical point mutation, might *natural selection* come to the rescue? After considering these problems, one possible conclusion might be to have mankind take no action and just let nature do it for us (let the unfit die naturally). The problem is that natural selection, like artificial selection, has exactly the same problems. Natural selection, because of the cost of selection, cannot select against too many mutations simultaneously, or else selection will either become totally ineffective, or will result in a rapidly shrinking population size (or both). Natural selection needs to be able to recognize multitudes of essentially invisible mutations, but cannot. Lastly, natural selection needs to be able to somehow exclude multitudes of mutations from the breeding population, simultaneously, which is logistically impossible because of *selection interference*. These very real constraints on natural selection will limit what we can realistically expect natural selection to accomplish. In fact, artificial selection is vastly superior to natural selection. Artificial selection is based upon artificial truncation (complete elimination) of all the "unfit". Natural selection is based upon "probability selection", which merely reduces the probability that the unfit will be excluded (incomplete elimination – some unfit will still survive).

Genetic selection still works. Please do not misunderstand where I am going with this. I am not saying that selection does not work, for on a limited level it certainly does. My career as a plant breeder involved the use of artificial selection. My colleagues and I were able to regularly breed better plant and animal varieties which have had fundamental importance to modern agriculture. When I later became involved in genetic engineering of plants, we routinely used selection techniques to recover transgenic (genetically engineered) plants. Likewise, natural selection tends to eliminate the worst human mutations. If not, the human race would have gone extinct long ago and we would not be here to discuss any of this. But both natural and artificial selection have very limited ranges of operation, and neither has the **omnipotent power** so often ascribed to them. Selection is not a magic wand. While I will enthusiastically agree that selection can shape some specific allele frequencies, I am going to argue that no form of selection can maintain (let alone create) higher genomes. The simplest way to summarize all this is as follows: **Selection can sometimes work on the level of certain genes, but systematically fails in the big picture – at the genomic level.**

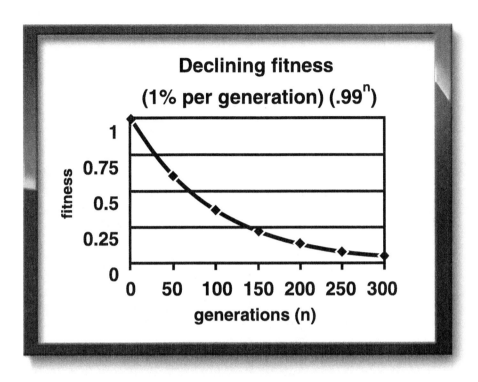

Figure 4. The consequence of genetic entropy.

Dr. Crow (1997) indicated that the fitness of the human race is presently degenerating at 1-2% per generation due to the accumulation of mutations. A 1% decline in fitness per generation (beginning with a fitness of 1) is plotted for a hypothetical human population over a period of 300 generations (6,000-9,000 years). The resulting pattern seen is a classic biological decay curve. This type of progressive loss of fitness would clearly lead to dramatic degeneration of the human race within the historical timeframe.

Figure 5. The Princess and the Nucleotide Paradox.

The Primary Axiom requires that natural selection (the Princess), which occurs on the level of an individual, must recognize billions of individual nucleotide effects (the peas), which only exist on the molecular level. Separating the Princess and the nucleotides is a vast gulf. This gulf is partly due to separation in scale (to picture this, try to realize that if a nucleotide was as big as a pea, a human body would be roughly 10,000 miles tall). This gulf is also the separation by level of organization (there are at least a dozen levels of biological organization between a nucleotide and a human being). No nucleotide affects a human body directly, but acts only through an elaborate labyrinth of nested systems. So the mattresses between the Princess and the nucleotide are many, and they are very thick. To make things still worse, life's self-correcting mechanism (called homeostasis) operates on every biological level, effectively silencing most nucleotide effects, even as modern sound-cancellation technologies use negative feedback to negate noise. For our analogy, we would have to incorporate high-tech internal "auto-correction" machinery into each mattress. But we have to add one more dimension to our analogy to make it accurate. The Primary Axiom does not just ask the Princess to sense if there is a single pea beneath her stack of mattresses. Through these mattresses she must "feel" encyclopedias written in molecule-sized Braille bumps, and decide which volumes have the fewest mistakes!

Can Genomic Selection Problems Be Solved?

Newsflash – Selection cannot rescue the genome.

We began the last chapter by considering the problems associated with selecting for a single mutation within a human population. Traditionally, geneticists have studied the problem of mutations by simply considering one mutation at a time. It has then been widely assumed that what works for one mutation can be extended to apply to all mutations. Obviously, that is senseless extrapolation! This is like saying that if I can afford one car, I can afford any number, or if I can juggle three balls, I can juggle 300. We are learning that the really tough problems are not seen in selecting isolated single genes or single nucleotides, but arise when we consider all genetic units combined (the whole genome). To understand what is needed to prevent genomic degeneration, we must consider the problem of mutation on the whole genome level, and so we must implement what I will call "comprehensive genomic selection".

There are 3 billion nucleotide positions, each with two copies in the genome, and so there are 6 billion possible point mutations (misspellings). The profound difficulties of making mutation/selection work on the genomic level have only been recognized by a few far-sighted geneticists in the past (e.g., Haldane,

Muller, Kimura, Kondrashov), but the whole sticky problem has repeatedly been swept under the rug. This is because it creates insurmountable problems for evolutionary theory. In the last few decades, we have learned that the functional genome is much larger and more complex than anyone predicted. We have learned that the human mutation rate is much higher than was previously thought possible. We are learning that the actual percentage of mutations that are truly neutral is steadily shrinking, and the percentage that actually *add* information is vanishingly small. So not only is the mutation rate very high – but almost all such mutations are deleterious. For all these reasons, we cannot ignore the problem of genomic degeneration, and we must ask, "Can *genomic selection* solve the problem?"

The bottom line is that virtually every one of us is exceedingly mutant. This destructive mutation process has been going on for a long time. In addition to the roughly 100 new mutations we each have added to the human gene pool, we have inherited a multitude of mutations from our progenitors. To put the problem of genomic selection in proper perspective, we have to take the selection problem posed at the beginning of the last chapter (for a single point mutation at a single nucleotide site) and multiply this problem by a factor of at least one billion. Can you start to see that selection against mutations on the genomic level is fundamentally different from our first illustration where we were just selecting against a single mutation?

1. Cost of selection. The fact that all people are mutant makes selection much more difficult. If we were to select against all mutations, no one could reproduce, resulting in instant extinction. Obviously this selection strategy creates a reproductive cost that is too high. It is widely acknowledged that we each inherit many thousands of deleterious mutations from previous generations. Collectively, as a population we carry many *trillions* of deleterious mutations. To make the problem easier, let's limit our attention to just the 600 billion new mutations that entered the human gene pool within our own generation (100 new mutations times well over 6 billion people). Since we cannot simply select against "mutants", we will have to select between individuals who are "more mutant" versus those who are "less mutant". As we will see, recognizing "more mutant versus less mutant" is a huge problem in itself. Due to the cost of selection – we must select away much less than 33% of the population per generation – or we will quickly go extinct.

Let me try to illustrate the extent of the cost problem associated with selecting against 600 billion mutations. If we have a population of over 6 billion people, then much less than one third of them could be "eliminated" (prevented from having children). This is at least 2 billion people. Try to imagine that. This thought should be enough to make even the most cold-blooded eugenicist shudder. Yet what good would this Draconian measure accomplish? Preventing 2 billion people from mating would only eliminate 100 x 2 billion = 200 billion new mutations. This would still leave over 400 billion new mutations as the newly added *genetic burden* for the next generation! Each surviving individual still has about 100 more mutations than their parents. Even if we assume that two-thirds of the remaining mutations are perfectly neutral, we still have at least 133 billion deleterious mutations added to the population. We can't get rid of enough of the mutations and still maintain population size! Even if two-thirds of the mutations are neutral, and in addition we doubled selection intensity (although we certainly cannot afford to "spend" two-thirds of our population on a regular basis without certain extinction), it would still leave over 67 billion new deleterious mutations for the next generation. The cost of selection clearly limits how many mutations we can eliminate per generation, and the known mutation rate for humans is too high to be counteracted by any level of selection. Therefore, mutations will accumulate, and the species must degenerate! Can you see that the cost of selection is rather a mind-boggling problem when viewed on the genomic level?

2. Obscured or "invisible" mutations. Surprisingly, when it comes to selection, lethal and near-lethal mutations are not the real problem, at least not from the whole population's point of view. Such mutations are rare and are self-eliminating. Likewise, absolutely neutral mutations do not matter (if they exist). It is the minor mutations that do the most damage, especially within short time frames (Kimura and Ohta, 1971, p.53). Selection must somehow prevent the accumulation of large numbers of minor mutations, or the species will rapidly deteriorate and fitness will decline. However, even if selection *could* keep minor mutations in check, it appears to be powerless to stop the accumulation of the most abundant class, i.e. the *nearly-neutral* mutations. Therefore, higher genomes must eventually all degenerate in the long run, with or without selection.

2a) Nearly-neutral mutations. *Nearly-neutral mutations* have infinitesimally small effects on the genome as a whole. Mutations at all near-neutral nucleotide positions are only subject to random drift — they are essentially immune to selection. Their fitness effects are so miniscule that they are masked by even the slightest fluctuations, or *noise*, in the biological system (Kimura, 1968; 1983; Kimura and Ohta, 1971). These are the most abundant mutations, as shown in the "near-neutral box" in Figure 3d (p. 35).

Since most mutations should be nearly-neutral, and since they are so subtle as to avoid being selected for, why are they important? They matter because those nucleotide sites contain *meaningful information*, and their mutation contributes to the erosion of information. **Collectively, near-neutral nucleotides must account for most of the information in the genome.** This is just as true as the fact that all the seemingly insignificant letters in this book collectively add up to a clear message. If we start with a very long and complex written message (an encyclopedia, for example), and we start to introduce typographical errors, most of the individual errors will only have an extremely trivial effect on the total message. Individually they are truly insignificant. But if this process is not halted, the message will eventually become corrupted, and will eventually be completely lost. An alternative example would be the rusting of a car. As a car ages we can repair the big stuff, replace tires, and fix dents (akin to selection for major and minor mutations), but we cannot stop the rusting process, which is happening one atom at a time (akin to near-neutral mutations). Each iron atom that oxidizes seems perfectly insignificant, but added up across the entire car, the process is certain and deadly. A third example would be the aging of our bodies. We can repair teeth, do facelifts, even replace hearts. But it is the cumulative aging of the individual cells (principally due to mutations) that places a specific limitation on our lifespan. This is true even though each individual cell is trivial and entirely expendable. Just as the human body "rusts out" due to countless microscopic mistakes (all of which in themselves are insignificant), the human genome must also be "rusting out" due to near-neutral mutations. No selection scheme can stop this process. This is the essence of the near-neutral mutation problem. This whole problem has led one prominent population geneticist to write a paper entitled, "Why have we not died 100 times over?" (Kondrashov, 1995). The problem of the unselectability of near-neutrals is very real.

A large, homogeneous population in a homogenous environment (for example, a typical bacterial culture) is more resistant to genetic entropy because it sees much less noise and experiences much more efficient selection. Such populations usually have simpler genomes, fewer mutations per genome, and far fewer inter-genic interactions. Furthermore, they exist in large numbers and have very high rates of reproduction. Most importantly, because bacteria are single-celled organisms, *every cell is subject to selection, independently, after every cell division*. Selection in such systems is more effective, more precise, and can have much higher resolution. This means that in bacteria, a much smaller proportion of the genome is near-neutral and unselectable. This is why theorists typically prefer to use microbial examples.

Unfortunately, mammals like ourselves have none of the advantages listed above. We are subject to high levels of reproductive noise. We have a large genome, high mutation rates, high levels of gene interaction, and we have very serious constraints on selection. This is why the proportion of mutations which are virtually "unselectable" should be very large in man, and the frequency of such mutations within the population should be entirely due to random genetic drift. All such nucleotide positions will mutate freely, and all information encoded by them will degenerate over time.

2b) Minor mutations and selection breakdown. Minor mutations, by definition, have a small but distinct effect on reproductive potential. These are the mutations immediately to the left of the no selection zone box, in Figure 3d (p. 35). While animal and plant breeders may have a hard time seeing these subtle changes, natural selection (which is really just another way of saying differential reproduction) can generally "see" them, given large populations and deep time. Furthermore, the effects of such mutations are partly additive, so natural selection can select for *numerous* minor mutants simultaneously. In fact, the way natural selection works, it appears to be designed to stabilize life, which would otherwise quickly deteriorate. It appears to be a wonderfully designed system.

However, selection for minor mutations has significant limitations. The orderly elimination of minor mutations is seriously disrupted by noise. Natural selection must *see* the mutants as a significant factor in reproductive probability. But even Mother Nature can have trouble seeing minor mutations. This is because the differences in reproductive fitness caused by minor mutations are subtle, while the effects of other factors can be very large. It is a little like trying to see the ripples produced by a pebble thrown into a stormy sea.

All other variables affecting reproduction, when combined, will significantly interfere with natural selection against any given minor mutation. For example, a high rate of accidental death in a population will override and obscure the subtle effects of minor mutations. Likewise, selection for lethal and near-lethal mutations (which must automatically take precedence) will override the more subtle effects of minor mutations. The fact that most mutations are recessive dramatically masks their negative fitness effects, and greatly hinders selection against them. Likewise, all interactions between genes ("epistasis") will interfere with selective elimination of minor mutations. In smaller populations, the randomness of sexual recombination (chromosome-segregations and gamete-unions are both random and thus fluctuate randomly) can routinely override selection. These effects cause the fundamental phenomenon of *genetic drift*. Genetic drift has been extensively studied, and it is well known that it can override selection against all but the most severe mutations in small populations. Plant breeders like myself know that *all* extraneous effects on an individual's performance will interfere with effective selection. The frequency (abundance) of a single mutation in a population will tend to drift randomly and become immune to selection whenever the net effect of all other factors combined has a greater effect on reproductive probability than does the nucleotide itself.

To put the issue in more familiar terms, selection for very subtle genetic effects is like trying to hear a whisper in a noisy room. Soft whispers, complex messages, and loud background noises will all contribute to the loss of the message. Selection against a minor mutation works best when its fitness effect is still moderately loud, and where there is minimal biological noise. Despite these very significant limitations, selection for numerous minor mutations still works. Thank goodness it works on this level, otherwise we would not be here!

While selection can definitely work for numerous minor mutations, as the **number** of those mutants increases, each mutant's fitness effect becomes less and less significant in terms of total reproductive probability. As the number of minor mutations increases, the individual mutation effects become less and less significant, and the efficacy of selection for each one moves toward zero. Kimura (1983) alludes to this. I have demonstrated it mathematically in Appendix 2, and the results are shown in Figures 6a and 6b (pp. 90-91). Each time we add another trait that needs to be selected for, the maximum selective pressure that can be applied to each trait individually must decline. As the number of traits undergoing selection increases, selection efficiency for each trait rapidly approaches zero, and the time to achieve any selective goal approaches infinity. According to my calculations (see Appendix 2), for a population such as our own, the maximal number of mutations which could be selected for simultaneously is approximately 700. Kimura (1983, p.30) alludes to the same problem, and although he does not show his calculations he states that only 138 sites can undergo selection simultaneously, even for a population with very intense total selection pressure (50% elimination) and weak selective elimination per trait (s=0.01). Trying to select simultaneously against more than several hundred mutations should clearly lead to cessation of selective progress. Yet even in a small human population, millions of new mutations are arising every generation and must be eliminated! In the big picture, we really need to be selecting against billions, not hundreds, of mutations. Even in the very limited case of selecting for just a few hundred mutations, although it is theoretically possible to do this, it is noteworthy to point out that such highly diluted selection per trait greatly affects the rate of selective progress, which essentially grinds to a standstill. As the number of loci under selection increases, the rate of selective progress (per trait) slows very rapidly, approaching zero. The resulting rate of genetic change would be glacial at best, requiring hundreds of thousands of generations of selection to significantly affect even this very limited number of nucleotide positions.

In a sense, as we select for more minor mutations, each mutation becomes noise for the others. At a distance, a room full of whisperers is full of noise and devoid of net information. As each mutation's effect becomes less and less significant, its individual whisper gets softer, and so the problem of overriding noise gets worse. Even under the best of selection conditions, each individual whispered message cannot be discerned. The effect of any given mutant becomes totally insignificant in light of all other reproductive factors. At this threshold point, the mutation becomes effectively neutral, and all selection for it ceases. As we select for more and more minor mutations, we must always reach a threshold point where selection should largely break down. Above a certain number, all minor mutations should become unselectable, even when conditions are ideal and noise is minimal. Simultaneous selection against too many minor mutations should lead to zero selective progress, and genetic drift takes over. In essence, selecting for too many minor mutations simultaneously makes them all behave as *near-neutrals*, as described in the section above. We have now shown this using numerical simulations (see Chapter 11).

Haldane (1957) and Kimura (1983, p. 26) both agree that it is not possible to simultaneously select for a large number of traits due to the cost of selection. This simple reality makes any type of global genomic selection virtually impossible.

3. Reproductive elimination. We have learned we cannot stop genomic degeneration because of the high number of mutations occurring in the human population and the prohibitive reproductive cost of eliminating each one. Even more, we have learned we cannot stop genomic degeneration because most mutations are near-neutral and their effects are obscured and essentially undetectable above biological noise. This makes them immune to selection and subject only to drift and degeneration. Furthermore, we have learned that if we try to select against too many minor mutations simultaneously, they effectively all become like near-neutrals. They also become unselectable and subject to random drift. Lastly, I would like to argue that we cannot stop genetic degeneration because we cannot effectively enforce the reproductive elimination of large numbers of mutants simultaneously, for logistical reasons. I have called this problem *selection interference*. This problem has not been addressed sufficiently, but has simply been recognized as a factor interfering with selection (Haldane, 1957; Lynch, Conery, and Burger, 1995; Kondrashov, 1995). When attempting simultaneous selection for tens of thousands – or millions – of different mutants in the genome, the problem of selection interference becomes absolutely overwhelming.

Selection interference occurs when selection for one trait interferes with selection for another trait. For example, a desirable trait will routinely be found along with an undesirable trait within the same individual. To select against the *undesirable* trait automatically means that you are also unintentionally selecting against the associated *desirable* trait (we have to accept or reject the whole person). This association between traits can be very tight (both traits coded for by the very same gene, or two genes side by side on the same chromosome), or the association can be loose (two genes somewhere within an individual's genome). Even if mutations are only loosely associated in the individual, the two traits are still linked for that single generation. Any mutant must always be temporarily linked to thousands of other mutants in every individual and in every generation. Therefore, selection can never operate on a given mutation in isolation. To select for any given beneficial mutation will always automatically multiply a host of associated deleterious mutations. The problem is inescapable.

To illustrate this, let us imagine selecting between two individuals in a population. Because the genes are drawn from the same "gene pool", any two individuals will have about the same number of mutations and these two sets of mutations will have approximately the same net deleterious effect. When contrasting two such individuals to discover who is more fit, we may find that each has roughly 10,000 different mutations, so there are 20,000 differences between them. Each will have about 10,000 "bad" genic units (mutations) and about 10,000 "good" genic units (non-mutant nucleotides). Due to averaging, the actual difference in genetic fitness between them will be small and will hinge on just a few *major-impact* nucleotide differences. Who will actually be reproductively favored? Because of their high degree of overall similarity in genetic fitness, reproductive success will depend more on random chance and noise factors than on true genetic fitness. But even if the "better" individual is favored in reproduction, almost no selective progress will be made. The individual that is favored will have just as many mutations as the rejected individual. We will have *selected away* the 10,000 bad mutations in one individual, but at the same time we will have *multiplied* another 10,000 bad mutations in the other individual. Almost all selection is canceled out; 10,000 steps forward and 10,000 steps backward. The only net gain is for those few "major" mutations which actually made the real difference in fitness. In higher genomes, selection can only be effective for a limited number of "significant" nucleotide differences. The vast bulk of mutations will be minor or near-neutral, will cancel each other out, and will be unselectable. On the genomic level, even if we could have perfect control over the reproduction of individuals, we would still fail to effectively prevent the propagation of the vast bulk of deleterious mutations. This problem, to my knowledge, has not been adequately addressed by others, although it is often alluded to by population geneticists.

4. Selection interference due to physical linkage. The most obvious and extreme form of selection interference is when there is tight physical linkage between beneficial and deleterious mutations. This results in an irreconcilable problem referred to as "Muller's ratchet". One of the most obvious requirements of natural selection is the ability to separate good and bad mutations. This is not possible when good and bad mutations are physically linked. Essentially all of the genome exists in large linkage blocks (Tishkoff and Verrelli, 2003), so this problem applies to virtually every single building block of the genome. If we refer back to Figure 3d (p. 35), we can see that mutations are overwhelmingly deleterious, but there should be a few extremely rare beneficial mutations. These very rare beneficial mutations might seem to leave a slight glimmer of hope for forward evolution, but this hope would not be rational because such beneficials will be overwhelmingly nearly-neutral (and thus unselectable) and because the accumulating deleterious mutations will always outweigh the beneficials. Yet as long as those rare beneficials are on that graph, they seem to offer a glimmer of hope to the hopeful. The problem of physical linkage erases those beneficials from our graph because the linkage block which contains the rare beneficial mutation carries many deleterious mutations, so the net effect of that block is still negative (Figure 7, p. 92). This should completely eliminate *any* trace of rational hope for forward evolution.

Within any given physical linkage unit, there should be, on average, thousands of deleterious mutations accumulated before the first beneficial mutation would even arise. Therefore, there would seldom arise any linkage group within the whole genome that could realistically experience a net gain of information. Every single beneficial mutation would always be inseparably tied to a large number of deleterious mutations. This can be visualized graphically (Figure 7, p. 92). In Figure 3d (p. 35), we mapped the distribution of the effects of single mutations. We can do the same thing in terms of the mutational effects of linked mutation clusters. Because these clusters never break apart, the net effect of any cluster of mutations will be inherited as if it were a single mutation, and the effect of any mutation cluster would simply be the net affect of all its component mutations. By the time at least two mutations per linkage block have accumulated, nearly every beneficial mutation will have been canceled out by a linked deleterious mutation. At this point, the distribution will already show essentially zero linkage blocks with a net gain of information (see Figure 7). To illustrate this point further, if only one mutation in a million is beneficial, the probability of a linked pair of mutations with both having a net beneficial effect becomes too small to even consider (10^{-12}). As more time passes, the average number of mutations per linkage group will increase such that the net loss of information per linkage group will increase, and the complete disappearance of net-gain linkage groups will approach *absolute certainty*. The human genome is a composite of roughly 100,000-200,000 linkage blocks. Based upon the logic provided above, we can know that almost every single one of these "building blocks of evolution" is deteriorating.

Based upon numerous independent lines of evidence, we are forced to conclude that the problem of human genomic degeneration is real. While selection is essential for slowing down degeneration, no form of selection can actually halt it. I do not relish this thought any more than I relish the thought that all people must die. **The extinction of the human genome appears to be just as certain and deterministic as the death of organisms, the extinction of stars, and the heat death of the universe.**

2008 Update – In 2006 a paper was published showing that the natural operation of "Muller's ratchet" should theoretically be lethal to the human race within an evolutionary time scale. This is especially significant because that author only considered a single linkage unit – the mitochondrial chromosome. But this is only one out of roughly 200,000 linkage groups in the human genome, so the author understated the linkage problem in man by a factor of about 200,000 (Loewe, 2006).

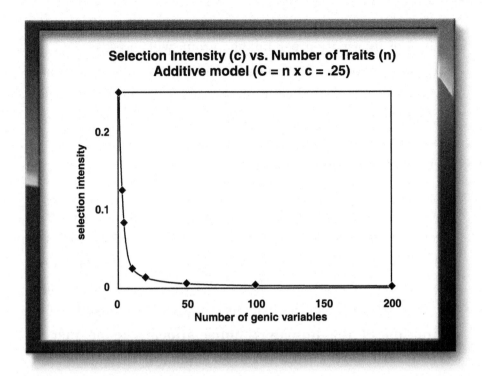

Figure 6a. Selection interference

Selection always involves a reproductive cost (C), meaning that some individuals cannot reproduce. Total selection cost must be substantially less than a species' excess reproduction, or the population will rapidly shrink and face extinction. As more traits are under selection (n), the total cost attributable to each trait (c) must diminish rapidly, so that the total cost does not exceed the population reproductive potential. To visualize the problem of selection threshold, I have plotted maximal allowable selection intensity per trait (c) against number of traits under selection (n), for a population which can afford to lose 25% of its individuals for elimination of mutations (C=0.25). As can be seen, the allowable selection pressure per trait plummets rapidly as the number of traits increases. Selection pressures will obviously approach zero very rapidly and a threshold point will be reached where each trait is effectively neutral. This curve is based on an additive model, following the formula C = n x c (see Appendix 2). Appendix 2 shows that nearly identical results are observed doing the same analysis using the multiplicative model.

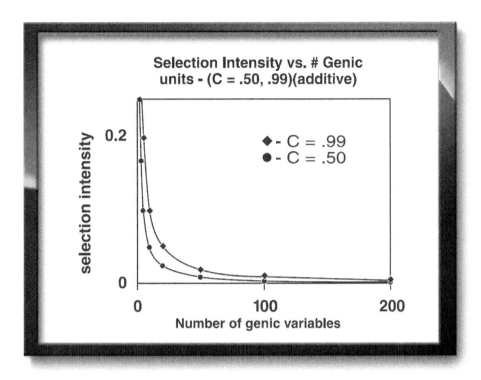

Figure 6b. Selection interference for extremely fertile populations.

Even if we assume an extremely fertile human population, such that 50% of the people can be selectively eliminated every generation (C=0.5), it does not significantly reduce the problem shown in Figure 6a. Even for extremely fertile species, such as plants, where C may be 0.99 (100 offspring per plant with selection removing 99%), the problem of selection threshold is still very real. Selecting for many traits simultaneously decreases selection efficiency for each individual trait, until selection reaches a point where it is entirely ineffective. These curves follow the additive formula: C = n x c.

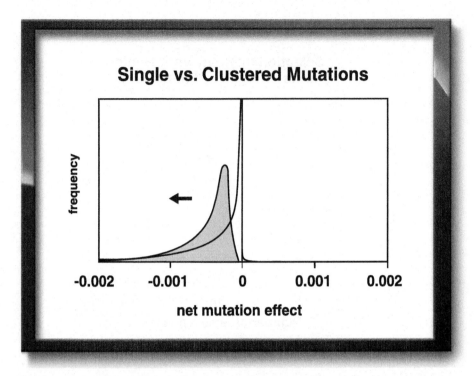

Figure 7. Mutations arise in physically linked clusters.

Mutation clusters must be almost 100% deleterious. In Figure 3d (p. 35), we saw that the distribution of individual mutations is skewed toward neutral, and that while there are many deleterious mutations, there are vanishingly few beneficial mutations. These rare beneficial units largely disappear when we analyze mutations as they actually occur – within physically linked clusters. The actual distribution of the effects of linked mutation clusters (the shaded distribution curve), will be strongly shifted to the left when compared to individual mutations. Any linked mutation cluster will be inherited as a single genetic unit and the effect of that mutation cluster will simply be the net effect of all of its component mutations. The fitness effect of any cluster can be calculated to be the *average effect of its individual mutations times the number of mutations within that cluster*. Any rare beneficial will be quickly cancelled out by much more abundant linked deleterious mutations, with high certainty. By the time there are at least two mutations per cluster, almost every beneficial mutation effect will have been cancelled out by a linked deleterious mutation. As more mutations arise in that cluster, the net effect will be increasingly deleterious (progressively moving the cluster's fitness distribution to the left in the figure above).

Chapter 6

A Closer Look at Noise

Newsflash – The problems are much worse than you think!

If you want to receive a radio message, you need to limit the amount of "noise" or static. If there is a strong interfering signal, the message will be lost. It is for this reason that governments can "jam" radio programs they do not want their people to hear. Likewise, if governments do not regulate the allowable bandwidth for each radio station, stations very soon become noise *for each other*. Radio static can arise from many sources: other radio stations, solar flares, cosmic radiation, radio waves being reflected by cloud cover, electric motors running in the neighborhood, local walkie-talkies, etc. Regardless of the source, noise results in loss of information.

A very weak signal is easily destroyed by any amount of noise. The weaker the signal and the greater the noise, the more certain is the loss of information. A low signal-to-noise ratio always ensures loss of information. When we receive a signal plus noise, *amplification* does not help us. Turning up the volume on your radio does not help overcome static. We just wind up amplifying the static as much as the signal. To ensure minimal loss of information, there must be a favorable signal-to-noise ratio.

The reason that most nucleotides must be unselectable is because of consistently low signal-to-noise ratios. Likewise, the reason we cannot select for many nucleotides simultaneously is because of rapidly shrinking signal-to-noise ratios. When we apply selection to the entire genome, the signal-to-noise ratio quickly approaches zero. Hence, noise will consistently outweigh the effects of individual nucleotides in the big picture. This is a primary reason why selection works on the level of the gene, but fails on the level of the genome.

In genetics, the signal-to-noise ratio is often expressed in terms of "heritability". Heritability is the important difference between genotype and phenotype. If a trait has high heritability, most of the variation observed for that trait is genetically heritable, and it will be easy to select for. The essence of this concept of heritability is simply the ratio of heritable versus non-heritable variation. Non-heritable variation is largely due to variation within an organism's individual environment, and is the source of phenotypic noise. So a genetic heritability value for a trait is essentially equivalent to a signal-to-noise ratio. For example, any observed difference in the intelligence of two people will be partly due to heritable genetic differences (genic differences which can be passed from parent to child), and partly due to environment (i.e., nutrition, the quality of training, etc.). So intelligence is determined partly by *nature* (inherited capabilities), and partly by *nurture* (non-inherited characteristics). This is equally true for height, speed, weight, etc. In a sense, heritability can be understood as a reflection of the ratio of nature to nurture. When heritability is "1" for a trait, that trait is 100% hereditary (i.e., blood type), and it is not affected by environment at all. If heritability is "0" for a trait, that trait is not inherited; it is entirely environmental in nature (i.e., a tattoo). A simple trait such as height is usually quite highly heritable ($h^2 = 0.3$). This specifically means that for such a trait, 30% of the phenotypic variation is heritable (selectable) variation. Unfortunately, for very complex traits such as fitness, heritability values are low (even as low as 0.004), and approach zero (Kimura, 1983, pp. 30-31). This is because *total fitness* includes all the different types of *noise* from all the different aspects of the individual and their environments.

Studies by Merila and Shelton (2000), and Kruuk et al. (2000), confirm that heritability values for total fitness are typically too small to measure in natural populations. They also show that such low heritability values are largely due to interference from non-heritable noise factors. Historically, it was assumed that near-zero heritability values were because selection was so extremely efficient that there was no genetic variation in such populations – hence no heritable variation. That naive view is no longer viable – we now know that higher life forms have very high mutation rates, and that selection fails to eliminate a wide spectrum of deleterious mutations, ensuring high genetic variance. This is further born out by countless molecular studies that show that natural populations are typically very diverse genetically. It is not a lack of genetic variation, but rather ubiquitous biological noise that causes fitness heritability values to routinely be too low to measure.

When Kimura says that fitness heritability is generally very low, he means that almost all variation for individual fitness is due to non-heritable (non-selectable) influences. Thus, almost all selection for fitness will be *wasted*. **Low heritability means**

that selecting away bad *phenotypes* does very little to actually eliminate bad *genotypes*. Consider seeds falling off a tree. Some seeds will land on fertile ground ideal for growth. But most seeds will land on places that are too dry, too wet, too many weeds, too much shade, too many people, etc. The result will be great diversity in the health and vigor of the resulting trees, and huge differences in their survival and reproduction. But almost all of this apparent "natural selection for the fittest" will really only be selection for the *luckiest*, not the genetically superior. Hence, in most natural situations, most phenotypic variation in fitness will only be due to non-genetic noise, and will have very little to do with heritable differences. This is what we mean by low heritability. Low heritability largely neutralizes the effectiveness of selection. Like an automobile with a racing motor but a broken transmission, there can be lots of selection happening, yet almost no genetic progress.

Let us further consider what is involved in non-heritable variation for fitness by referring to Figure 8a (p. 105). The largest source of phenotypic variation is due to different individuals being exposed to different environments. Obviously, variation in environment can create major differences between individuals. It is often estimated that most (over 50%) of phenotypic variation is due to just environmental variation. If one plant is growing better than another plant in the same field, there is a high probability it is growing better just because it sits on a slightly more favorable piece of soil. This aspect of phenotypic variation is shown in sector 1 in Figure 8a. This type of variation strongly interferes with effective selection by adding to non-heritable noise and diminishing the signal-to-noise ratio.

The second largest part of phenotypic variation is called "environment-by-genotype" interaction. This is often estimated to represent about 25% of all phenotypic variation. Given two plants in the field, if we change the environment by irrigating the field, the extra water may be good for one plant but bad for the other, depending on their genotype. This type of variation is not consistently heritable. Like environmental variation, this aspect of phenotypic variation adds to the noise and interferes with selection. This is shown as sector 2 in our pie-chart.

The third largest part of phenotypic variation is non-heritable genetic variation. That may sound like a contradiction, but it is not. A large part of genetic variation is due to factors that are not passed down consistently from generation to generation. These factors include epigenetic effects (sector 3), epistatic effects (4), dominance effects (5), and genetic effects subject to cyclic selection (6). To make a long story short, most genetic variation is not heritable, at least not in a linear and selectable manner.

The only fraction of genetic variation that is heritable (and therefore potentially selectable) is what is called additive genetic variation (sector 7). Very simply, additive genetic variation is where a given trait (or nucleotide) is unambiguously and consistently better than an alternative trait (nucleotide) within the population. For a complex trait such as fitness, this type of additive genetic variation makes up a very small part of the total phenotypic variation. If Kimura is correct that fitness heritability can be as low as 0.004, then as little as 0.4% of such phenotypic variation would be selectable. This represents a signal-to-noise ratio of about 1:250. One way of expressing this is that 99.6% of phenotypic selection for fitness will be entirely *wasted*. This explains why simple selection for total phenotypic fitness can result in almost no genetic gain.

If we have a trait, such as fitness, which has low heritability (Figure 8a), and we have a species of low fertility such as man (Figure 8b, p. 106), we can see that only a tiny part of a population can be used for effective selection (Figure 8c, p. 107). If we can only selectively eliminate about 16.7% of a population, and only 0.4% of that selection is actually effective, then only 0.07% of that population can be employed for truly *effective* selective elimination. In other words, less than 1 person in 1,000 is available for the *effective* elimination of all deleterious mutations, and for the *effective* fixation of any possible beneficial mutations.

The heritability for a single *trait* such as total fitness can be remarkably small, yet the heritability of a typical *nucleotide* is infinitesimally smaller. Let us consider the heritability of an average single nucleotide mutation (an unorthodox but useful application of the concept of heritability). The "signal" (i.e., the heritable additive fitness value of such a nucleotide) is inherently too small to measure. But the "noise" is astronomical. It is the combined effect of all the non-heritable components of variation plus the effects of all the other segregating nucleotide positions! In a typical population there are millions of other segregating nucleotides. So the effect of an average single nucleotide will consistently be lost in an *ocean of noise*, with signal-to-noise ratios consistently less than one to one million. The heritability of such a nucleotide is not significantly different from zero, explaining why most nucleotides are inherently unselectable and must be termed nearly-neutral by Kimura's (and Ohta's) definition (see Chapter 2).

Another major source of noise is probability selection, not truncation selection. As a plant breeder I would score hundreds of plants for their phenotype (yield, vigor, disease resistance, etc.), and then I would rank them from best to worst. I would decide what fraction of the population I wished to eliminate, drawing a line through the ranking at the desired level and keep only those plants above the mark. This is a form of artificial selection and is called "truncation selection" and is used by breeders because it is especially effective. However, this type of selection never happens in nature. Natural selection is always based only upon differential probability of reproduction. Mother Nature does not tabulate for each member of a population some fictional "total fitness value" based upon total phenotypic performance for all traits combined. Mother Nature does not then rank all the individuals. Lastly, Mother Nature does not draw an arbitrary line and eliminate all individuals below that line. Instead, the phenotypically inferior individuals simply have a slightly lower probability of reproduction than the others. Very often, by chance, the inferior individual will reproduce, and the superior individual will not. In fact, there is only some modest correlation between phenotypic superiority and reproductive success. The more reproductive noise (i.e., random survival/mating), the weaker the correlation becomes, and the less certain it becomes that a superior individual will actually be favored in reproduction. This is how real natural selection operates – it is called "probability selection", and it is very fuzzy and very inefficient. If we invoke realistic probability selection and disqualify all types of artificial truncation selection from the evolutionary model, the result is the addition of a whole new level of noise, which further reduces the effectiveness of selection.

The general impotence of true natural selection (probability selection) can easily be illustrated. Picture a population of shrimp swimming *en masse*, and a whale comes and swallows half the population in one bite. Is this an example of survival of the fittest among the shrimp? Was there a precise ranking of most fit to least fit, followed by a strict cut-off type of selection? Alternatively, picture a large mass of frog eggs in a river. A large number of eggs are eaten by fish, even before they hatch. A large number of tadpoles are picked off by birds, a boat is launched and squishes a few hundred more, many more are swept over a waterfall. Many maturing adults burrow into a mud bank which is later removed by a dredging operation, and most of the surviving adults are picked off by more predators. Almost all the elimination has been random. We are seeing survival of the *luckiest*. So where is the systematic sorting by phenotype? It is largely absent. There is a huge element of noise, not just in determining who has the best phenotype, but also in terms of differential survival and reproduction. Reproductive noise affects success *in spite of phenotype* and this noise is *over and above* the noise we have considered in the heritability section above. Perhaps 50% of reproductive failure is independent of phenotype (Figure 8b, p. 106).

There is a third level of genetic noise called gametic sampling. This is the statistical variation associated with small population sizes which causes random genetic drift. If you toss a coin many times, you will predictably get about 50% heads and 50% tails. However, if you toss the coin just 10 times, there is a good chance you will *not* get 50/50. The frequency of each possible outcome is readily predicted by using probability charts. This same type of statistical variation occurs when a gene or nucleotide is segregating within a population. Gene segregations tend to be highly predictable in very large populations, but they will fluctuate very significantly in smaller populations, just like the outcomes of a series of coin tosses. Such statistical fluctuations result in what is called genetic drift. This means gene frequencies can change regardless of the presence or absence of selection. This simple probability element of fluctuating gene frequencies is well studied.

Classically, population geneticists have dealt with genetic noise only on the level of this last type of noise, gametic sampling (probability fluctuations), which is very sensitive to population size. Random genetic drift is very strong and can override the effects of even substantial mutations in small populations. This is why the populations of endangered species are especially subject to what is called *mutational meltdown*. In small populations, natural selection is largely suspended. It is on the basis of gametic sampling that Kimura first defined his near-neutral mutations. It is for this same reason that Kimura calculated the size of his no-selection box (Figure 3d, p. 35) as a simple function of population size (either plus or minus $1/2N_e$). It is very attractive for the genetic theorist to limit consideration of noise to just gametic sampling. This is because one can conveniently cause the noise from gamete sampling to largely disappear simply by imagining larger populations. At the same time the theorist can make selection itself periodically "go away" by invoking high-noise episodes associated with small population *bottlenecks* (e.g., the Out-of-Africa theory).

Gametic sampling is only a minor part of total genetic noise, and the other two important aspects of genetic noise (noise affecting phenotype and noise affecting success in reproduction) *are only partially diminished in large populations.* We cannot make noise "go away" by invoking larger population sizes. Noise is *always* present, and at much higher levels than is normally acknowledged by population geneticists. In fact, very large populations invariably have *enhanced* noise. This is due in part to population substructure (many smaller sub-populations, each with its own gametic sampling fluctuations). It is also because larger populations extend over a wider range of environments, becoming subject to even more environmental variation. Large population size does not reduce the random elements of reproduction, nor does it reduce the phenotypic masking of genotype. Noise *always* remains a severe constraint to natural selection. Under artificial conditions, plant and animal breeders have been able to very successfully select for a limited number of traits. They have done this by employing their intelligence to deliberately minimize noise. They have used blocking techniques, replication, statistical analysis, truncation selection, and highly controlled environments. Natural selection does none of this. It is, by definition, a blind and uncontrolled process, subject to unconstrained noise and unlimited random fluctuations.

What are the genetic consequences of all this noise? When we realize that high levels of biological noise are unavoidable, we realize we cannot wave away the no-selection box in Figure 3d (p. 35), not even by invoking larger population sizes. As we come to appreciate that there are two entire levels of noise above and beyond gametic sampling, we realize the no-selection box must be corrected (see Figure 9, p. 108). Kimura's no-selection box must be greatly expanded, based on the imperfect correlation between genotype and phenotype, and based upon the imperfect correlation between phenotype and reproductive success. The result of these two weak correlations is that the number of near-neutral (unselectable) nucleotide positions is vastly greater than commonly realized, and is not simply dependent on population size. Small population size certainly aggravates the noise problem, but large population size does not eliminate this problem (for more detailed discussion see Appendix 5).

The pervasive existence of serious genetic noise amplifies virtually all my previous arguments regarding the limits of selection. Kimura's no-selection box gets much bigger (Figure 9) because huge numbers of otherwise minor mutations become nearly-neutral and unselectable. The selection threshold problem, wherein simultaneous selection for too many traits results in a complete cessation of progress, will happen much sooner because of high levels of noise. Lastly, the noise problem will result in most "selection dollars" being completely wasted (Figures 8a-c, pp. 105-107). This greatly increases the actual cost of selection, and severely increases the very real limits that "cost" places upon any selection scenario.

To get a more intuitive understanding of the noise problem, we can return to some of our visual analogies. In terms of our evolving red wagon, try to imagine a situation where wagon performance was influenced much more by *workman errors* on the assembly line than by the *typographical errors in the assembly manual*. Can you see that the quality control agent would mostly be wasting his time and resources by selecting for "non-heritable" variations? In terms of our Princess, the noise problem is like having innumerable pea-sized lumps within her mattresses. Wouldn't that make her problem worse? In terms of our biochemistry textbook, the noise problem is like swapping students textbooks mid-term. This would further reduce the already vanishingly small correlation between typographical errors and student scores. In all these examples, when we add any reasonable level of noise, these already absurd scenarios just become even more impossible.

The late Stephen Jay Gould, like Kimura, argued against the strict selectionist view of evolution. In terms of the survival of entire species, he recognized the importance of natural disasters, "survival of the luckiest", and noise. **What Gould and Kimura both seem to have failed to realize is that if noise routinely overrides selection, long-term evolution is impossible and guarantees genetic degeneration and eventual extinction.**

2014 Update – Since the early editions of this book, my colleagues and I have been doing detailed studies regarding the role of noise in limiting the efficacy of natural selection. We have used the program "Mendel's Accountant" to do numerical simulation studies. We have shown that realistic levels of biological noise dramatically increase the size of Kimura's no-selection zone. The no-selection zone increases in width by roughly 1000-fold, both for deleterious and beneficial mutations. Population geneticists who do not take into account the profound effects of biological noise are deceiving themselves and their readers. See Gibson et al. (2013), and Sanford et al. (2013).

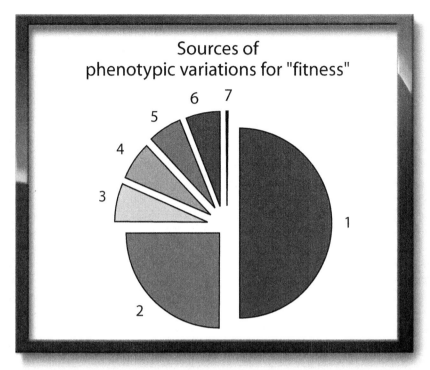

Figure 8a. Sources of phenotypic variation.

The primary source of phenotypic variation is environmental variation (sector 1). This variation is not heritable and interferes with selection. The second major source of variation is the interaction of the environment with the genotype (2). This variation is also not heritable and interferes with selection. Within the genetic component of variation, there is variation due to: epigenetics (3), epistasis (4), and dominance (5). None of these genetic components are heritable and all of them interfere with true long-term selection. There are other genetic components which would otherwise be selectable but are "neutralized", either by homeostatic processes or such things as cyclic selection (6). All these non-heritable components account for the vast bulk of all phenotypic variation. This leaves additive genetic variation as a relatively insignificant component of phenotypic variation (7). For a very general phenotypic trait, such as reproductive fitness, additive variation can account for less than 1% of total phenotypic variation (Kimura, 1983, p.30-31). In other words, more than 99% of any selective elimination based upon phenotypic superiority is *entirely wasted*. All variation that is not due to additive genetic variation is "noise" and actually works very powerfully *against* effective selection.

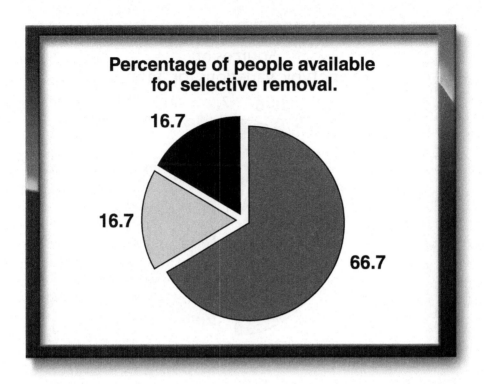

Figure 8b. How many people can be selectively eliminated?

Only a limited proportion of any population (the *population surplus*) can be selectively eliminated. Given the current global rate of human reproduction (three children per couple), two-thirds of all children must reproduce for simple replacement. This maximally leaves one-third of the children available for selective reproductive elimination. However, a significant fraction (perhaps half) of the population's surplus will fail to reproduce due to random causes such as war, accidents, and choice, which have nothing to do with phenotype. So less than one-sixth (16.7%) of the human population is actually available for any potential selective elimination. This is in keeping with Haldane's estimate that only about 10% of a human population is actually available for selection.

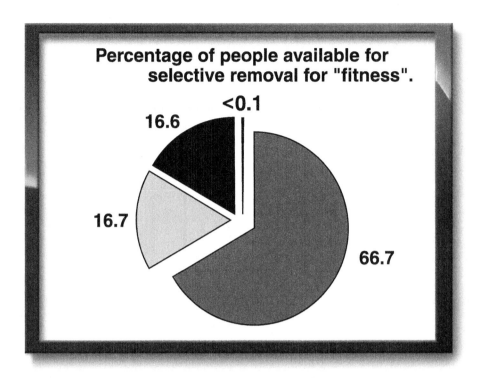

Percentage of people available for selective removal for "fitness".

<0.1
16.6
16.7
66.7

Figure 8c. How many people who were selectively removed, were actually better genetically?

Selective elimination within human populations based on phenotypic fitness (a very general trait) has an effectiveness approaching zero. This is seen when we combine Figures 8a and 8b. Of the 16.7% of the human population theoretically available for selective removal based upon phenotypic inferiority, as little as 0.4% of such removal will result in any heritable effect on succeeding generations. This means less than 0.1% (16.7% x 0.4% = 0.07%) of the total population would be available for effective selection. This is too small a fraction to show accurately in this type of graph. In a sense, this means that less than one person in a thousand can be removed for truly *effective, selective, reproductive elimination.* Even if someone like Hitler were to "kill off" as many phenotypically "inferior" human beings as possible every generation, it would result in insignificant selective progress for something as general as "fitness". This conclusion is a logical extension of low human fertility rates and the extremely poor heritability of a trait as complex as fitness (Kimura, 1983, p.30-31).

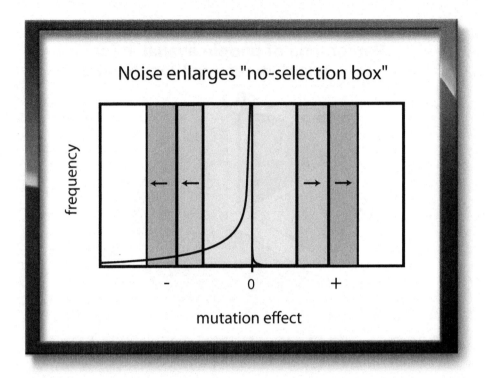

Figure 9. Realistic levels of biological noise greatly expand Kimura's "no-selection zone".

Kimura's no-selection box, as shown in Figure 3d (p. 35), is based upon a minimal estimate of noise (i.e., only that attributable to gamete sampling). This is the classic near-neutral model, but this view fails to recognize all sources of noise. So Kimura's classic no-selection box is too small. We need to first expand our no-selection box because of poor heritability, which arises from the imperfect correlation between genotype and phenotype (more than 99% of phenotypic variation can be non-heritable [Figure 8a]). We then need to expand our no-selection box further in order to account for the imperfect correlation between phenotype superiority and reproductive success that arises from the random aspects of reproduction (Figure 8b). These are the primary sources of noise. When we consider **all** sources of noise, we realize that the real "no-selection box" is large, and that it cannot be dismissed by simply invoking large population sizes.

Artificial Rescue Mechanisms?

Newsflash – Contrived "rescue mechanisms" fail reality test.

Is the net information within the genome increasing or decreasing? We can, at best, wave our hands when we speculate about how selection might synthesize *new* information. It is inherently hypothetical. In a sense it becomes a philosophical question and is not easily subjected to scientific analysis. Strong arguments can be made against mutation/selection creating new information, but theorists can always speculate to the contrary (it is very difficult to prove something can never happen). However, I believe the "going down" aspect of the genome is subject to actual scientific analysis. It is for this reason that I have focused on the issue of the degradation of information. I believe it is subject to rigorous scientific analysis. Such analysis persuasively argues that *net* information must be declining. If this is true, then even if it could be shown that there were specific cases where new information *might* be synthesized via mutation/selection, it would still be meaningless – since such new information would promptly then begin to degenerate again. The net direction would still be *down*, and complex genomes could never arise spontaneously.

If the genome is actually degenerating, it is bad news for the long-term future of the human race. It is also bad news for evolutionary theory. If mutation/selection cannot *preserve* the information already within the genome, it is difficult to imagine how it could have *created* all that information in the first place. We cannot rationally speak of genome-building when there is a net-loss of information every generation. Halting degeneration is just a small prerequisite step before the much more difficult question of *information-building* can reasonably be opened for discussion (see Chapter 9).

In the last several decades, concerns about the mutation rate have been growing among geneticists as it has become more and more clear that the rate of deleterious mutations must be much higher than one per person per generation (Neel et al., 1986). One way for theorists to dismiss this problem has been to claim that most DNA is actually *non-information*, hence most mutations are perfectly neutral in effect. By this logic, if the actual rate of nucleotide substitution was 10 per person, then by defining 98% of the genome as junk DNA, the *effective* mutation rate must be only 0.2 per person. So the number commonly quoted in the media and textbooks would then be 0.2, not 10. However, as the known rate of mutation is clearly much greater than 10, and as the recognized percent of functional DNA is vastly greater than 2%, even this type of rationale has failed to explain away the problem of genetic degeneration. At this point, two primary "escape mechanisms" were invented in the hopes of rescuing neo-Darwinian theory. The first mechanism can be called the "mutation-count mechanism", and the second can be called the "synergistic epistasis mechanism".

The mutation-count mechanism

Dr. Crow (1997) popularized an argument first developed by Muller. Crow acknowledged that in any population, when the rate of deleterious mutations approaches 1 per individual, such mutations must begin to accumulate and population fitness must decline. However, as the total number of accumulated mutations per person becomes quite large, he realized that some individuals would have significantly more mutations than others (due to chance). He proposed that by focusing selection against such individuals, one could sweep away a disproportionate number of mutations. The consequence would be that more mutations in the population would be eliminated at less "cost" to the population (see Appendix 1). Eventually, the number of mutations per person might then be stabilized, and the decline in fitness might taper off. Crow's proposed mechanism can be called the "mutation-count mechanism" (MCM), because it requires Mother Nature to count each individual's mutations and then focus all selection against the high mutation-count individuals.

As mentioned earlier, we are all highly mutant, so selection must be between "more mutant" versus "less mutant" individuals. There are two ways of deciding who is more mutant. The first, of minor importance, is the question, "Who has the most mutations?" The second, of primary importance, is the question, "Who has the worst mutations?" The model described by Crow only considers the former, while ignoring the latter. The Crow model is an unrealistic mental construct which was designed to obscure a major theoretical problem.

Because each of us has a genome that represents a more or less random sampling of the human "gene pool", we should each have roughly the same total number of accumulated mutations per person. The actual difference in total number of mutations between two people will be quite trivial, only representing sampling variation (i.e., minor variations from the population's average mutation count). We know this because these mutations have been accumulating and mixing within the "gene pool" for many generations. Such mutations have grown very abundant, and mutation count per person should be quite uniform. Thus "mutation-count" will be a very minor variable in terms of differences in fitness between individuals.

The genetic differences in fitness we see between human beings are not due to an individual's number of mutations. Rather, substantial differences in fitness are due to the specific effects of relatively few high-impact genetic differences. Just one major mutation can overshadow the effects of thousands of near-neutral mutations. One person may have several thousand fewer mutations than another, yet just one specific mutation can still make that person much less fit. Therefore, the idea of counting the total number of mutations per individual, and then selecting away high-count individuals is not a reasonable or an honest mechanism to get rid of mutations. This concept appears to have been invented as a mathematical trick to attempt to rationalize how to get rid of more mutations, using less selection cost. Although this process may be operating to a very limited extent in nature, it is very clearly *not* what is generally happening.

The mutation-count mechanism has now been rigorously falsified by means of numerical simulation experiments (Brewer et al., 2013a). Given any parameter settings which are even remotely realistic biologically, mutation count per individual increases linearly over time, and fitness declines continuously (Figure 10a).

The synergistic epistasis mechanism
The second rescue mechanism is the "synergistic epistasis mechanism". This mechanism is very similar to the mutation

count mechanism in that selection is artificially focused against high mutation-count individuals. However, the mechanism is more convoluted, and presumes that as deleterious mutations accumulate, mutations amplify each others' deleterious effect (this is what "synergistic epistasis" means). This would logically be expected to accelerate genetic degeneration. However, some imagine that as mutational damage to the genome accelerates, selection might somehow become more effective, being more specifically directed against the higher mutation-count individuals. The synergistic epistasis mechanism has all the appearance of representing *deliberate obfuscation*. Fancy terminology is often used to hide a problem. Synergistic epistasis means that mutations interact such that several mutations cause more damage collectively, than would be predicted on the basis of their individual effects. This type of interaction between mutations can happen, but it is the exception to the rule – all population geneticists agree that normally mutations interact either additively or multiplicatively. There is no reason to think that on a genomic level, the primary mode of interaction between mutations could involve synergistic epistasis. At least one paper provides experimental evidence against generalized synergistic epistasis (Elena and Lenski, 1997). To the extent there is a substantial amount of synergistic epistasis happening, it makes the genetic situation worse, not better. We have *always* known that genic units interact, and we know that such *epistasis* is a huge impediment to effective selection. This fact is normally ignored by most geneticists because selection scenarios become hopelessly complex and unworkable unless such interactions are conveniently set aside. But now, when genetic interactions can be used to cloud the problem of error catastrophe, the modified version of the concept is conveniently brought forth and used in an extremely *diffuse and vague* manner, like a smoke screen. But let's look through the smoke. If multiple mutations really *do* combine to create damage in a non-linear and escalating manner, then error catastrophe would happen much sooner and populations would spiral out of control and into mutational meltdown much faster. We would already be extinct! We are looking at a conceptual "sleight of hand", which clearly does not apply to the real world, and which is only aimed at propping up the Primary Axiom.

The synergistic epistasis mechanism has now been formally falsified using numerical simulation experiments (Baumgardner et al., 2013). What is seen is that even when there is very strong synergistic epistasis, it fails to curb deleterious mutation accumulation. Instead, it causes accelerated genetic degeneration and rapid extinction – just as logic would suggest (See Figure 10b).

Both of the two primary escape mechanisms which theorists have traditionally used to rescue the Primary Axiom are artificial, contrived, and are profoundly unrealistic biologically. They have now both been rigorously falsified (Brewer et al., 2013a; Baumgardner et al., 2013). Logic and careful numerical simulation experiments show that most deleterious mutations must escape purifying selection. This leads to a linear increase in mutation count over time, and a continuous decline in fitness. This has now been extensively documented using biologically-realistic numerical simulations (i.e., see Gibson et al., 2013). Likewise, most beneficial mutations escape positive selection, except for a few very rare beneficials that have high impact (Sanford et al., 2013). These isolated high-impact beneficials allow for adaptive episodes, but these rare anomalies happen even while the rest of the genome is undergoing systematic degeneration.

By now we should clearly see that the Primary Axiom is not "inherently true", nor is it "obvious" to all reasonable parties, and so it is very clear that it should be rejected as an axiom. What is left is just the "Primary Hypothesis" (mutation/selection might hypothetically create and maintain genomes). The "Primary Hypothesis" is actually shown to be indefensible. In fact, multiple lines of evidence indicate that the "Primary Hypothesis" is clearly false and must be rejected.

2014 Update – Three recent papers claim to have solved the high mutation rate problem (Lesecque et al., 2012; Charlesworth, 2013; and Qui et al., 2014). As shown below – their claims are not credible. Moreover, none of these papers address the much more profound problem of near-neutral mutations, which are mutations with fitness effects below the selection threshold – which must accumulate without limit. Even if these authors could solve the high mutation rate problem, the near-neutral mutation problem would still result in genetic entropy.

The paper by Qui et al. involved numerical simulations very similar to our own work. However, numerical simulations do not produce realistic results unless realistic parameter settings are used. Their analysis assumed artificial truncation selection, perfect heritability, and zero biological noise. This set of parameter settings grossly misrepresents biological reality. Based upon our own analyses, we know this combination of settings will yield a selection threshold that is roughly 1000-fold too low (compared to natural probability selection). These authors then combined these unrealistic settings with an extremely unrealistic rate of beneficial mutation (10%). The result was that most deleterious mutations were eliminated by strict truncation selection and then enough beneficial mutations could be amplified to counterbalance the still-accumulating deleterious mutations. If they go back and examine the mutation-counts in their experiment, I am quite sure that deleterious mutations still greatly outnumbered beneficial mutations. If I wanted to do a numerical simulation that would misrepresent biological reality and make the mutation problem seem to go away – I would use exactly the same parameter settings they used. But these parameter settings do not reflect biological reality. To be honest, these authors need to go back and do the same experiments with realistic settings (i.e., using probability selection and a much lower rate of beneficials). This should produce results very similar to our own simulations, validating the reality of genetic entropy.

The two papers by Charlesworth and by Lesecque et al. begin by clearly establishing that population geneticists really do have a very major theoretical problem associated with deleterious mutation accumulation. They then set out to try and solve that problem. Unfortunately they formulate the problem in the context of traditional "genetic load" calculations which are poorly correlated to reality, and which require a long list of unrealistic simplifying assumptions. Both papers follow the long-standing tradition of trying to force-fit complex population dynamics into a few over-simplified algebraic formulas. Their papers do NOT actually explain how selection might eliminate deleterious mutations as fast as they accumulate. Instead they skirt the primary issue (accumulation of genetic damage), by deliberately clouding the definitions of fitness, mutation effects, and selection. In this way the genetic entropy problem seems to disappear in the resulting cloud of ambiguity.

Both papers resort to the biologically unrealistic concept of "soft selection" (which is better named "soft mutation"), which was developed roughly 25 years ago by Wallace. Wallace wanted to deal with the traditional problem of "genetic load" (a concept akin to genetic entropy – but more limited), and so he contrived an extremely unrealistic model of reality. In his imaginary world, a population's fitness is fixed (depending only on available ecological resources), and deleterious mutations do not involve objective losses of function – they only affect relative competitive standing within the current population (i.e., sexual selection). These two fundamental assumptions (fixed fitness and mutational effects that are only relative), are both categorically false. It is upon this delusional foundation that Wallace based his arguments 25 years ago, and the current authors are now basing their calculations.

To get a sense of the un-reality of what is claimed – "soft selection" assumes: 1) population fitness is fixed – being constant regardless of accumulating mutations; 2) all mutations are just "relative" (neutral in terms of total biological functionality), and do not cause any objective genetic damage; 3) all mutations only affect social standing (for example – sexual selection). The paper by Lesecque et al. further explains their assumptions: a) number of mutations per individual is static and predictable (U/s); b) average allele frequency is static and predictable (u/s); c) all mutations are fully-selectable and all have the identical fitness effect (s). They also assume no linkage and only multiplicative mutation interactions. These types of models have no correspondence to the real biological world.

The soft selection model was intended to be a smoke screen when it was first invented by Wallace. Soft selection is still being used as a smoke screen by these authors today. "Soft selection" diverts attention away from the hard reality of accumulating genetic damage. In some rare cases this type of soft selection does happen for certain isolated traits. For example in a culture where blond hair is preferred – blonds may reproduce more than brunettes. In this instance accumulating mutations that affect hair color obviously do not threaten species extinction. Isolated cases of soft selection have nothing to do with the problem of genome-wide genetic degeneration and the need for massive amounts of purifying selection.

These authors must know that "hard" (real) selection is needed to deal with accumulating deleterious mutations. They are using mathematical abstraction to create a make-believe world where genetic degeneration is not even feasible. They are using conceptual sleights of hand, not to resolve a problem – but to hide it. They seem to be committed to rescuing the Primary Axiom at any cost. The obvious un-reality of these recent models make it clear that the field is grasping at straws.

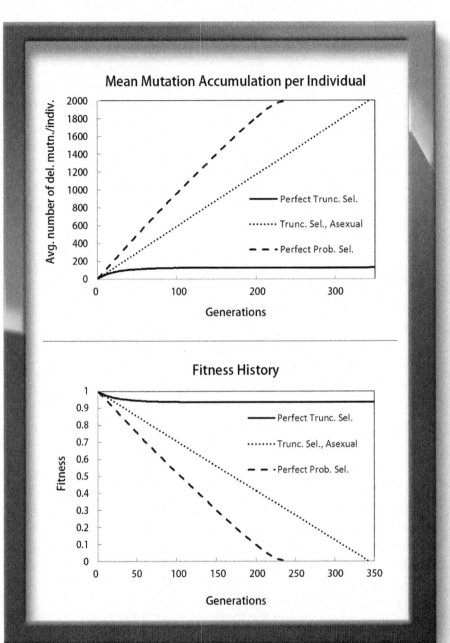

Figure 10a. Numerical simulation experiments test the validity of the "mutation-count mechanism" (MCM).

From Brewer et al., 2013a. Mean mutation accumulation per individual (top) and fitness history (bottom) for three MCM experiments. Phenotypic fitness depended solely upon mutation count, that is, mutations all had the same effect (-0.001), and no environmental noise was added. Selection modes were a) perfect truncation selection; b) perfect probability selection, and c) truncation selection but without sexual recombination. Given realistic probability selection (long dashes), mutations accumulated at constant rate, and fitness declined continuously – to the point of extinction. The same was seen with artificial truncation selection (when assuming asexual reproduction). However, mutation count and fitness stabilized quickly when truncation selection was combined with uniform fitness effects of all mutations, due to the MCM effect. The MCM works, but only under *extremely* un-realistic conditions. Any level of biological realism abolished the MCM effect – leading to continuous genetic decline. Any of the following will inactivate this highly artificial device: a) a natural mutation-effect distribution (including near-neutrals), or b) probability selection, or c) asexual reproduction. Probability selection is what happens in nature – while truncation selection is what happens in artificial breeding. All this proves that MCM is not operational under realistic conditions and can only operate under very artificial circumstances (Brewer et al., 2013a).

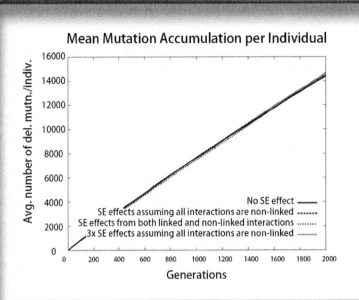

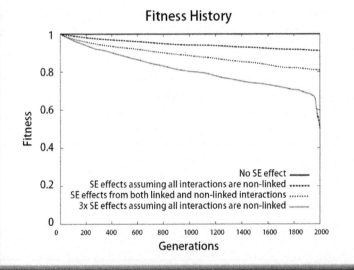

Figure 10b. Numerical simulation experiments test the validity of the "synergistic epistasis mechanism".

From Baumgardner et al., 2013. Mean mutation accumulation per individual (top) and fitness history (bottom) for 4 synergistic epistasis (SE) experiments. All four experiments employed extremely exaggerated selection pressures and extremely exaggerated SE interactions. The four experiments involved: (1) no SE effect, (2) SE effects assuming all interactions are non-linked, (3) SE effects from both linked and non-linked interactions, and (4) SE effects assuming all interactions are non-linked, but with a scaling factor three times larger. All cases applied truncation selection, perfect genotypic heritability, and a fertility of 2.0 (which implies 50% of the offspring in each generation are selected away). Even under these optimal conditions, the SE mechanism did nothing to halt mutation accumulation, but only accelerated fitness decline. If the SE mechanism had been effective, mutation count per individual would have stopped increasing, and fitness would have stopped declining (Baumgardner et al., 2013).

Chapter 8

Man to the Rescue?

Newsflash – Eugenics cannot stop degeneration, and cloning makes the mutation problem worse.

Most informed geneticists would acknowledge that there is a fundamental problem with genetic degeneration of the human genome due to reduced selection pressure. They would probably acknowledge this problem extends to many other species and certainly to any endangered species. They would probably also acknowledge the theoretical difficulties of establishing an effective selection scheme to stop the accumulation of genetic damage within the human population. As the problem becomes more advanced genetic damage will increase, leading eventually to a run-away (meltdown) situation developing. Hedonists who live only for today will say – "So what?" But for those idealists who pin all their hopes on the survival and advancement of the human race, this should be alarming. They are likely to turn hopeful eyes to science and technology. Can human intervention triumph over this threat? The nature of genetic degeneration is such that accumulating damage is inherently diffused throughout the genome. It cannot be dealt with one gene at a time. It should therefore be obvious that the laser-like precision of genetic engineering has nothing to offer. However, we might reasonably ask if artificial selection, or the emerging capacity to clone human beings, might not solve the problem.

Eugenics to the rescue?

The general perception that man is degenerating is found throughout modern and ancient literature. All cultures have legends about "men of old" who were smart, powerful, and long-lived. Darwin's book, *The Origin of Species by Means of Natural Selection, or The Preservation of Favoured Races in the Struggle for Life*, introduced the new idea that strong and continuous selection might halt this perceived degenerative trend. He pointed to human efforts in animal and plant breeding as evidence. In his book *The Descent of Man*, Darwin went further, contending that there is a need for "superior" races (i.e., the white race) to replace the "inferior" races. This ushered in *modern* racism, which came to a head in Hitler's Germany (Weikart, 2004). Before World War II, many nations, including America, had government-directed eugenics programs. These programs included forced sterilization of the "unfit" and aggressive promotion of abortion/fertility-control for the underclass. Ever since the time of Darwin, essentially all of his followers have been eugenicists at heart, and have advocated the genetic improvement of the human race. The philosophers and scientists who created the "modern synthesis" of evolutionary theory were uniformly eugenicists. However, after the horrors of WWII, essentially all open discussions of eugenics were quietly put aside.

In light of a deteriorating genome, should eugenics be re-examined? Unfortunately, this is already happening, but it is neither morally nor scientifically defensible. The thesis of this book cannot logically be used to support eugenics, but strongly argues against it. The eugenicist's vision is an insidious delusion. No form of selection can stop genomic degeneration. It would be physically, socially, and politically impossible to attempt to artificially increase selection intensity globally. Only a ruthless, world-wide, authoritarian "power elite" could possibly dictate the standards for selection, deciding who could and could not reproduce. Even if such an insidious plan could effectively be implemented, it would not stop genomic degeneration. Any potential genetic "progress" would be superficial, and would not be sufficient to offset the overall degeneration of the genome. "Inferiority" versus "superiority" is an ambiguous and very poorly inherited characteristic, and is largely influenced by non-genetic (environmental) factors (see Chapter 6). Selection for non-genetic trait results in zero selective progress. Even selection for more "heritable" traits would largely be ineffective, because of all the genetic arguments I have just presented. "Fitness" is a very general term, has very low heritability, and is affected by countless nucleotides – most of which are minor or near-neutral. As we have been learning, effective selection can only act upon a limited number of "significant" genetic units. It is true that we could artificially select for virtually any single human trait to make people taller or shorter, lighter or darker, or fatter or skinnier. But we could not effectively select for *superior*, which inherently is subjective, and involves thousands of genes and hundreds of millions of nucleotides.

Any possible *benefit* of enhanced or artificial selection in man would be a slight improvement of a very limited number of very specific traits. But the genome would still be "rusting out" at about the same overall speed. The *cost* of eugenics would be a social and moral upheaval on a level that would be catastrophic. Eugenics was a racist concept at its inception, and has always been driven by the Primary Axiom. Eugenics is not genetically sound. Furthermore, it is tightly linked with authoritarian government, elitist philosophy, suppression of personal rights, and violation of human dignity. Eugenics cannot rescue us from genomic degeneration. If eugenicists foolishly try to rescue the genome in this way, who will then rescue us from the eugenicists?

Cloning to the rescue?

To clone a human being means to take a cell from a mature (presumably superior) individual and to use that cell to produce one or more copies of that individual. The consequence of cloning would have profound genetic consequences. While I was still an evolutionist and was very concerned about the genetic degeneration of man, I naively believed that cloning might be the answer. I hoped that cloning might halt genomic degeneration, and might even allow rapid improvement of the human population.

In plant genetics, when a species is easily propagated, clonal selection provides the surest and fastest way to improve a population. Given this knowledge, perhaps it is surprising that clonal selection for man has not been more vigorously advocated. However, even apart from the moral and social problems associated with cloning, the best-case scenario for cloning would involve only short-term gains and would guarantee long-term genetic degeneration.

An unspoken theme of this book is that what is already known for clonal populations also applies to sexual populations. The proof that all clonal populations must degenerate genetically was first shown by Muller, and has been termed "Muller's ratchet" (Muller, 1964; Felsenstein, 1974). Within any clonal line, mutations will accumulate over time. Even selection within a clonal line for the *best sub-clones* does not stop the decline because every subclone must be more mutant than its parent clone. The "ratchet" only works one way and all change must be downward. Each cell division adds mutations and there is no mechanism to take mutations away within a clone. Even allowing for some beneficial mutations, each beneficial mutant is always linked to many more deleterious mutations. Within clones, there is no mechanism to break this linkage between rare beneficial mutations and abundant deleterious mutations. The deleterious mutants will always grow in number faster than the beneficials, and they will always drag any beneficials down with them. **Therefore, within clones, net information must always decline**. To repeat, this applies to even the best, most highly selected sub-clones. The certainty of genomic degeneration in clonal populations is well known among geneticists. The reason there are still many populations of clonal plants (and some animals), appears to reflect the fact that there has not yet been enough time for such populations to degenerate to the point of extinction.

Preliminary animal cloning experiments indicate the cloning of animals cannot even produce short-term genetic gains. Cloned animals routinely display immediate and severe genetic damage. Why is this? Cloned animals routinely show evidence of mutational damage as if they are "pre-aged" (Hochedlinger et al., 2004). There are probably multiple reasons for this (genetic and epigenetic), but one major reason involves the fact that mutations continue to build up within somatic cells. Normal reproductive cells are "designed" to undergo the least possible cell divisions between generations, thereby minimizing mutation accumulation per generation. It is for such reproductive cells that we have the minimal estimate of "just" 100 point mutations per person per generation. For somatic cells (at least for the continuously-dividing stem cells), the number of cell divisions is much higher than in the germline, and so the somatic cell mutation rate should also be very much higher (at least 10-fold higher), and sharply increasing with age. As we grow and then begin to age, every cell in our body becomes genetically more mutant and more "unique". It is impossible to keep a large genome unchanged, even within a clone. New mutations occur in every cell, at the rate of roughly *1-3 new mutations every cell division*. Therefore, essentially every single cell in our body is unique. For these reasons every human clone will always be inferior to the mature "source individual" from which they were cloned. Such a clone will in a sense be *pre-aged*, having the original mutational load of the zygotic source individual, plus the mutational load that has accumulated during that person's growth and aging. Because of the many cell divisions during somatic development and stem cell maintenance, a human clone will be roughly comparable, in terms of degeneration, to individuals many sexual generations into the future. In this sense such a clone is like a foreshadowing of where the species is going. It is going down, not up (Figure 11).

There are powerful moral, social, and genetic arguments against cloning. Cloning can be viewed as a very high-tech form of eugenics with all its technical and moral problems. Eugenics in general, and cloning in particular, are definitely not solutions to genomic degeneration.

Figure 11. Degeneration of the genome, degeneration of man, and degeneration of mankind.

We experience it on a personal level, and we see it all around us. It is "genetic entropy", and there is nothing man can do to halt it. It is biologically inevitable. It is part of why species go extinct, and it is why we are all individually in the process of dying.

Can Natural Selection Create?

Newsflash – Mutation / selection cannot even create a single gene.

We have been examining the problem of genomic degeneration and have found that deleterious mutations occur at a very high rate. Natural selection can only eliminate the worst of these, while all the rest accumulate – like rust on a car. Might beneficial mutations at other sites in the genome compensate for this continuous and systematic erosion of genetic information? The answer is that beneficial mutations are much too rare, and are much too subtle to keep up with such relentless and systematic erosion of information. This is carefully documented by Sanford et al. (2013), and Montañez et al. (2013). It is very easy to systematically destroy information, but apart from the operation of intelligence it is very hard (arguably impossible) to create information.

This problem overrides all hope for the forward evolution of the whole genome. However, some limited traits might still be improved via mutation/selection. Just how limited is such progressive ("creative") mutation/selection? By now it should be clear that random spelling errors in an instruction manual could never give rise to an airplane component (say a molded aluminum part), which then resulted in a significantly improved overall performance of a jet plane. Not even with an unlimited number

of flight trials/crashes and an unlimited budget. So it is certainly
reasonable to ask the parallel biological question, "Could mutation/
selection create a single functional gene from scratch?"

A gene is like a book, book chapter, or an executable program
– and minimally consists of a text string with 1,000 characters.
Mutation/selection could not create a single gene because of the
enormous preponderance of deleterious mutations, even within
the context of a single gene. The net information must always still
be declining, even within a single gene or linkage block. Even if a
gene was 50% established, deleterious mutations would degrade
the completed half of the gene much faster than beneficials could
create the missing half of the gene. However, to better understand
the limits of forward selection, let us for the moment *discount
all deleterious mutations* and only consider beneficial mutations.
Could mutation/selection *then* create a new and functional gene?

1. Defining our first desirable mutation. The first problem we
encounter in trying to create a new gene via mutation/selection
is defining our first beneficial mutation. By itself, no particular
nucleotide (A, T, C or G) has more value than any other, just as no
letter in the alphabet has any particular meaning outside of the
context of other letters. So selection for any single nucleotide can
never occur except in the context of the surrounding nucleotides
(and in fact, within the context of the whole genome). A change
of a single letter within a word or chapter can only be evaluated
in the context of the surrounding block of text. This brings us to
an excellent example of the principle of "irreducible complexity"
within the genetic realm. In fact, it is irreducible complexity
at its most fundamental level. We immediately find we have
a paradox. To create a new function, we will need to select for

our first beneficial mutation, but we can only define that new nucleotide's value in relation to its neighbors – and we are going to have to be changing most of those neighbors also. We create a circular path for ourselves. We will keep destroying the "context" we are trying to build upon. This problem of the fundamental inter-relationship of nucleotides is called *epistasis*. True epistasis is almost *infinitely complex*, and virtually impossible to analyze, which is why geneticists have always conveniently ignored it. Such bewildering complexity is exactly why language and information (including genetic language and genetic information) can never be the product of chance, but always requires intelligent design. The genome is literally a book, written literally in a language, and short sequences are literally sentences. Having random letters fall into place to make a single meaningful sentence, by accident, would require more tries (more time), than earth history can provide (i.e., "methinks it is like a weasel" would take 27^{28} tries – that is 10 followed by 40 zeros). The same is true for any functional string of nucleotides. If there are more than a dozen nucleotides in a functional string, we know that realistically they will *never* just "fall into place". This has been mathematically demonstrated repeatedly. But as we will soon see, neither can such a sequence arise by selecting one nucleotide at a time. A pre-existing "concept" is required as a framework upon which a sentence or a functional sequence must be built. Such a concept can only pre-exist within the mind of the author. Starting from the very first mutation, we have a fundamental problem even in trying to define what our first desired beneficial mutation should be.

2. Waiting for the first mutation. Let's assume we can know the first desired mutation. How long do we have to wait for it to happen?

Human evolution is generally assumed to have occurred in a small population of about 10,000 individuals. The mutation rate for any given nucleotide, per person per generation is exceedingly small (very roughly about one mutation per 30 million individuals, for a given nucleotide site). Within a population of 10,000, one would have to wait 3,000 generations (at least 60,000 years) to expect a specific nucleotide to mutate. But two out of three times, it will mutate into the "wrong" nucleotide. So to get a specific desired mutation at a specific site just in one individual will take three times as long, or at least 180,000 years. Once the mutation arises in one individual, it has to become *"fixed"* (such that each individual in the population will eventually have a double dose of that mutation). Because a newly arisen mutation arrives in a population as just a single copy, it arrives on the brink of extinction. The vast majority of new mutations soon drift back out of the population, even the ones that are beneficial. So any specific desired mutation must arise many times before it "catches hold" in the population. Only if the mutation is dominant and has a very distinct benefit does selection have any reasonable chance to rescue it from random elimination via drift. According to population geneticists, apart from effective selection, in a population of 10,000, our given new mutant has only one chance in 20,000 (the total number of non-mutant nucleotides present in the population) of **NOT** being lost via drift. Even with some modest level of selection operating, there is a very high probability of random loss, especially if the mutant is recessive or is weakly expressed (we actually know that most mutations will be both recessive and nearly neutral). Therefore, even a beneficial mutation will be randomly lost due to genetic drift most of the time. Our numerical simulations suggest a weakly beneficial mutant will be lost about 99 out of 100 times.

So a typical mildly-beneficial mutation must happen about 100 times before it is likely to "catch hold" within the population. So on average, in a population of 10,000 we would have to wait 180,000 x 100 = 18 million years to stabilize our first desired beneficial mutation, to begin building our hypothetical new gene. So, in the time since we supposedly evolved from chimp-like creatures (6 million years), there would not be enough time to realistically expect our first desired mutation to go to fixation in the genomic location where our required gene is hopefully going to arise. A vast amount of mutations would arise during 18 million years, but only once would that specific nucleotide mutate to that specific new nucleotide – such that it's not lost due to genetic drift and is fixed.

3. Waiting for the other mutations. After our first desired mutation has been found and fixed, we need to repeat this process for all the other nucleotides encoding our hoped-for gene. A gene is minimally 1,000 nucleotides long. More realistically, a human gene is on average about 50,000 nucleotides long, when regulatory elements and introns are included. To be extremely generous we will only consider a gene of 1,000 nucleotides (and we assume each nucleotide is by itself selectable). If this process was a straight, linear, and sequential process, it would require about 18 million years x 1,000 = 18 billion years to create the smallest possible gene. This is more than the time since the reputed Big Bang! So it is a gross understatement to say that the rarity of desired mutations limits the rate of evolution. Furthermore, single nucleotides do not carry any information by themselves, and cannot be selectively favored. Specified information requires many characters (minimally, a sentence or similiar text string is needed). Like any message, a genetic message which specifies some life function requires many nucleotides to reach its "functional threshold". Functional threshold is the minimal number of characters (or nucleotides) needed to convey a meaningful message. Below the functional threshold, individual letters or nucleotides have no benefit and cannot be favored by selection. This means that realistically, waiting time will be much, much longer – because no selection can happen until the minimum string of nucleotides falls into place by chance. If the functional threshold for selection is 12 (no selection until all 12 letters are in place), the waiting time in our hypothetical human population becomes trillions of years.

4. Waiting on "Haldane's dilemma". Once that first mutation destined to become fixed within the population has finally occurred, it needs time to undergo selective amplification. A brand new mutation within a population of 10,000 people exists as only one nucleotide out of 20,000 alternatives (there are 20,000 nucleotides at that site, within the whole population). The mutant nucleotide must multiply gradually within the population, either due to drift or due to natural selection. Soon there might be two copies of the mutant, then four, then 100, and eventually 20,000 (two copies per individual). How long does this process take? For dominant mutations, assuming very strong unidirectional selection, the mutant might conceivably grow within the population at a rate of 10% per generation. At this very high rate, it would still take roughly 105 generations (2,100 years) to increase from 1 to 20,000 copies ($1.1^{105} = 20,000$). However, mutation fixation takes much longer than this because selection is generally very weak, and most mutations are recessive and very subtle. When the mutation is recessive, or when selection is not consistently unidirectional or strong, this calculation is much more complex, but it is obvious that the fixation process would be dramatically slower. For example, an entirely recessive beneficial mutation, if it could increase fitness by as much as 1%, would still require at least 100,000 generations (2 million years) to reach fixation (Patterson, 1999).

Haldane (1957), calculated that it would take (on average) 300 generations (more than 6,000 years) to select a single new mutation to fixation, given what he considered a "reasonable" mixture of recessive and dominant mutations. Selection at this rate is so slow that it is essentially the same as no selection at all. This problem has classically been called "Haldane's dilemma", for at this rate of selection, one could only fix 1,000 beneficial nucleotide mutations within the whole genome in the time since we supposedly evolved from chimps (6 million years). This simple fact has been confirmed independently by Crow and Kimura (1970), ReMine (1993, 2005) and most recently by Rupe and Sanford (2013). Furthermore, the nature of selection is such that selecting for one nucleotide reduces our ability to select for other nucleotides (selection interference). For this reason, *simultaneous selection for many weakly beneficial mutations is largely ineffective.*

At first glance, the above calculation seems to suggest that one *might* at least be able to select for the creation of one *small* gene (up to 1,000 nucleotides long) in the time since we reputedly diverged from chimpanzee. There are two reasons why this is not true. First, Haldane's calculations were only for independent, unlinked mutations. Selection for 1,000 *specific and adjacent* mutations (to create a 1,000-letter string) could not happen in 6 million years because that specific sequence of adjacent mutations would never arise, not even after trillions of years (see calculations above). One cannot select for a letter string that has never happened. Second, the vast bulk of a gene's nucleotides are near-neutral and cannot be selected at all – not in *any length of time*. The bottom line of Haldane's dilemma is that selection to fix new beneficial mutations occurs at glacial speeds, and the more nucleotides under selection, the slower the progress. This severely limits progressive selection. Within reasonable evolutionary timeframes, we can only select for an extremely limited number of unlinked nucleotides. In the last 6 million years, selection could maximally fix about 1,000 unlinked beneficial mutations, creating less new information than is on a typical page of text. There is no way that such a small amount of information could transform an ape into a human.

5. Waiting for recombination? Because sexual species (such as man) can shuffle mutations to a limited extent every generation, it might be thought that all the needed mutations for a new gene might be able to occur simultaneously within different individuals within the population, and then all the desirable mutations could be "spliced together" via recombination. This would mean that the mutations would not have to occur sequentially, thus shortening the time needed to create the hoped-for gene (so we might need less than billions of years). There are two problems with this. First, when we examine the human genome, we consistently find the genome exists in large blocks (20,000-40,000 nucleotides) within which no recombination has occurred *since the origin of modern man* (Gabriel et al., 2002; Tishkoff and Verrelli, 2003*)*. This means that virtually no meaningful shuffling is occurring on the level of local nucleotide strings. Only large gene-sized blocks of DNA are being shuffled. To further clarify, no actual shuffling is happening on the nucleotide level! Second, even if there were effective nucleotide shuffling, the probability of getting all the mutants within the population to shuffle together into our hoped-for sequence of 1,000 is astronomically remote, and then all that shuffling would tear apart such strings faster than it could create them. Extensive shuffling of strings would require even *more* time than is needed for the sequential approach. If there really *were* a type of nucleotide level shuffling that could create a new gene in this way, it would be torn apart again by the same extensive nucleotide shuffling in the very next generation. In poker, it is not likely a player would be dealt a royal flush. If one was, what are the odds he would then get that very same hand dealt to him again after the cards are reshuffled? Recombination does not help us create a nucleotide string of 1,000.

6. Endless fitness valleys. Evolutionists agree that the creation of a new gene requires a great deal of "experimentation". During the construction phase of developing a new gene, we have to expect a period of time when the experiment reduces a species' fitness. This is a *fitness valley*. A half-completed gene is neither beneficial nor neutral. It is going to be deleterious. In a sense, the species has to get worse before it can get better. It is easy to imagine a species surviving fitness valleys if they are brief and if they are rare.

Deep and frequent fitness valleys are likely to lead to extinction. The rarity of good mutations, in combination with Haldane's dilemma, should make fitness valleys indefinitely long and deep. Continuous evolutionary innovation would make a species' fitness decline with no end. Life would be just one fitness valley upon another. The super-highway of evolution would always be under construction, and total fitness would always be declining rather than increasing. The concept of a species passing through fitness valleys makes evolutionary sense only when individual traits are considered. However, when the whole genome is considered, the concept of indefinitely numerous and indefinitely long fitness valleys argues strongly against the evolution scenario.

7. Poly-constrained DNA. Most DNA sequences are *poly-functional* and so must also be *poly-constrained*. This means that DNA sequences have meaning on several different levels (poly-functional) and each level of meaning limits possible future change (poly-constrained). For example, imagine a sentence which has a very specific message in its normal form but with an equally coherent message when read backwards. Now let's suppose that it also has a third message when reading every other letter, and a fourth message when a simple encryption program is used to translate it. Such a message would be poly-functional and poly-constrained. We know that misspellings in a normal sentence will not normally improve the message, but at least this would be *possible*. However, a poly-constrained message is fascinating, in that it cannot realistically be improved. It can really *only* degenerate (see Figure 12, p. 151). Any misspellings which might possibly improve the normal sentence form will be disruptive to the other levels of information. *Any change at all* will diminish total information with nearly absolute certainty. My colleagues and I have demonstrated this mathematically in a recent paper (Montañez et al., 2013).

There is abundant evidence that most DNA sequences are poly-functional, and are therefore poly-constrained. This fact has been extensively demonstrated by Trifonov (1989). For example, most human coding sequences encode for two different RNAs that read in opposite directions (i.e., both DNA strands are transcribed; Yelin et al., 2003). Some sequences encode for different proteins, depending on where translation is initiated and where the reading frame begins (i.e., read-through proteins). Some sequences encode for different proteins based upon alternate mRNA splicing. Some sequences serve multiple functions simultaneously (i.e., as a protein-coding sequence and as an internal transcriptional promoter). Some sequences encode for both a protein coding region and a protein-binding region. Alu-elements and origins of replication can be found within functional promoters and within exons. Basically all DNA sequences are constrained by isochore requirements (regional GC content), "word" content (species-specific profiles of di-, tri-, and tetra-nucleotide frequencies), and nucleosome binding sites (because all DNA must condense). Selective condensation is clearly implicated in gene regulation, and selective nucleosome binding is controlled by specific DNA sequence patterns that must permeate the entire genome. Lastly, probably all sequences also affect general spacing and DNA-folding/architecture, which is clearly sequence-dependent. To explain the incredible amount of information which must somehow be packed into the genome (given the extreme complexity of life), we really have to assume that there are even higher levels of organization and information encrypted within the genome. For example, we know there is another whole level of organization at the epigenetic level (Gibbs, 2003). There also appears to be extensive, sequence-dependent, three-dimensional organization within chromosomes and within the whole nucleus (Manuelidis, 1990; Gardiner, 1995; Flam, 1994). Trifonov (1989) has shown that probably all DNA sequences in the genome encrypt multiple codes (up to 12). In computer science, this type of data compression can only result from the highest level of information design and results in maximal information density. These higher levels of genomic organization/information content, greatly multiply the problem of poly-constrained DNA. Every nucleotide interacts with many other nucleotides, and everything in the genome seems to be context-dependent. The problem of ubiquitous, genome-wide, poly-constrained DNA seems absolutely overwhelming for evolutionary theory. Changing *anything* seems to potentially change *everything*! The poly-constrained nature of DNA serves as strong evidence that higher genomes cannot evolve via mutation/selection except on a trivial level. Logically, all poly-constrained DNA had to be designed.

8. Irreducible complexity. The problem of irreducible complexity has been brilliantly presented by Behe (1996). He has illustrated the concept of irreducible complexity in various systems that have multiple components, such as a mousetrap design which requires a handful of independent parts, or a bacterial flagellum having several dozen component parts. His idea is that each *part* has no value except within the context of the *whole* functional unit, and so irreducible systems have to come together all at once and cannot arise one piece at a time. In the case of a mousetrap, all the pieces may have been sitting next to each other on the inventor's workbench but they would not have come together by chance, or by any realistic evolutionary progression. They came together as a *synthesis*, simultaneously, in the mind of the inventor. It is in the realm of *mind* that deep complexity comes together and manifests integrated functionality.

In our example of the evolution of transportation technology, the simplest first improvement we might imagine might be the occurrence of misspellings that would convert our red wagon into a blue tricycle. It is indeed easy to imagine a misspelling that might cause the paint code to be changed (although the blue paint would have to already be available, and coded). Likewise, a misspelling could certainly cause a wheel to fall off. However, a three-wheeled wagon is not a tricycle. It is a broken wagon. To convert a wagon to a tricycle would require extensive reworking of the instruction manual and radical changes in most of the component parts. There would be no intermediate functional steps to accomplish these complex changes, and so no prospect for our quality control agent to selectively help the process along. In fact, he would be selecting against all our desired misspellings and changes. So the correct combination of misspellings would have to arise simultaneously by chance, all at the same time, which would never happen. Obviously, a tricycle could only arise from a wagon by way of intelligent and extensive reworking of the design and a thorough re-writing of the instruction manual (see Figure 13, p. 152).

Although a wagon or tricycle may have dozens of component parts, a protein is much more complex, having hundreds of component parts, and achieving a level of irreducible complexity profoundly greater than that illustrated by our wagon analogy. As the number of components of a design increases linearly, the number of *interactions* (hence the complexity) increases exponentially.

As complex as proteins are, underlying every protein is a genetic system comprising even higher levels of irreducible complexity. The molecular machinery underlying the coding, transcription, and translation of a protein is phenomenal. Ignoring all the other accessory proteins involved, just the design of the DNA/RNA sequence is mind-boggling. Although a protein has a few hundred component parts, the underlying gene that produces it has thousands of component parts. All of these parts are interacting and mutually-defining. Each nucleotide has meaning only in the context of all the others. The gene's DNA sequence defines regional 3-D chromatin structure, local protein binding, uncoiling, transcription, and also defines one or more RNA sequences. The RNA sequence defines RNA stability, RNA variable splicing, RNA processing, RNA transport, transcription efficiency, and protein sequence.

When we consider the full complexity of a gene, including its regulatory and architectural elements, a single gene has about 50,000 component parts. Presumably, this is more component parts than are found in a modern automobile. *Yet a single gene is just a microscopic speck of irreducible complexity within the universe of irreducible complexity comprising a single cell. Life itself is the very essence of irreducible complexity, which is why we cannot even begin to think of creating life from scratch. Life is layer upon layer of irreducible complexity.* Our best biochemical flow charts, of which we are so proud, are just childish cartoons of true biological complexity. It is a tribute to the mind of man that we have started to understand how even a single gene works, and that we can now design and build very small artificial genes. But we still cannot design a new gene for a new and unknown protein, which could then precisely integrate into the integrated complexity of a cell within a higher life form. If we cannot do this, why would we think that random mutations, combined with a very limited amount of reproductive sieving, could accomplish this? For the reader's interest, Appendix 3 expands upon the idea of irreducible complexity with the concept of *Integrated Complexity*.

9. Almost all beneficial mutations must be nearly-neutral. We have already discussed at length the difficulty of selecting against near-neutral deleterious mutations, and this problem is begrudgingly acknowledged by most population geneticists. However, there is an important flip side to this problem that I almost *never* hear acknowledged. As we have already discussed in Figure 3d (p. 35), the problem of near-neutrality is much more severe for beneficial mutations than for deleterious mutations. Almost *every* beneficial mutation must fall within Kimura's "no-selection zone". All such mutations can *never* be selected for. This problem multiplies all of the problems outlined above. Our hoped-for new gene will certainly have a *few* nucleotides that have major effects. For example, the ones that specify the active site of an enzyme. But such nucleotides can only have major effects within the context of the whole protein and the whole gene sequence. The whole protein/gene is constructed primarily with components that individually have only a small impact on the whole unit, and have only a miniscule impact on the fitness of the whole individual. Without them the "important nucleotides" are meaningless. Yet they are all individually unselectable. So how can we establish them and keep them in their respective places during gene construction? Obviously, the answer is that we cannot. And apart from these "insignificant masses" of nucleotides the elite "important nucleotides" cannot be selected for either. Because of the near-neutral problem, we cannot even get to first base in terms of building our hoped-for new gene. The entire framework of the new gene is defined by the near-neutrals, but there is no way to either put them or hold them in place. The near-neutral nature of beneficial mutations is strong evidence that every gene had to be designed, and that there is simply no conceivable way to build a gene one nucleotide at a time via selection.

10. Putting bad mutations back in the picture. We have briefly considered a variety of powerful arguments about why progressive mutation/selection must be very limited in its scope. These arguments have temporarily excluded from consideration deleterious mutations. However, in reality, progressive selection must occur in the real world, where deleterious mutations vastly outweigh beneficial mutations. To be honest, we must now re-introduce deleterious mutations.

> **a) Muller's ratchet** – As mentioned earlier, when we study the human genome, we see that large blocks of DNA have essentially no historical evidence of recombination via "crossing over" (Gabriel et al., 2002; Tishkoff and Verrelli, 2003). Recombination appears to be primarily between genes rather than between nucleotides. So within any local gene sequence there is essentially no recombination. Any such block of DNA that does not have recombination is subject to "Muller's ratchet" (Muller, 1964; Loewe, 2006). This means that the good mutations and the bad mutations cannot be separated. Since we know that the bad mutations overwhelmingly outnumber the good, we can be certain that any such stretch of DNA must degenerate. The hordes of bad mutations will always drag the rare good mutations down with them. While we are waiting for a rare beneficial mutation, bad mutations are piling up throughout the region. Even if we could succeed in accumulating perhaps a hundred "good" mutations within a region, and were waiting for the next one to come along, we would start to

see many of our good mutations start to back-mutate into the bad. Time is our enemy in this situation. The more time, the less information. Muller's ratchet will *kill* an emerging gene long before it can become functional.

b) Too much selective cost – In previous chapters we have discussed the *cost of selection*. Haldane's dilemma only considers progressive selection. But we can only afford to "fund" progressive selection for beneficial mutations after we have paid for all other reproductive costs, including all costs associated with eliminating bad mutations. As we have already seen, there are so many bad mutations we cannot afford even to pay the reproductive cost of eliminating *them*. Since we cannot afford to stop degeneration, we obviously have nothing left over in terms of surplus population to fund progressive selection. There is just one way around this. In the short run, we *can* fund progressive selection for a very limited number of traits if we borrow "selection dollars" from our long-term struggle against bad mutations. However, we need to understand that this means that any short-term adaptive progress in terms of specific beneficial mutations is paid for by faster genomic degeneration in the rest of the genome.

c) Non-random mutation – As it turns out, mutations are not entirely random. Can this help us to create new genes? No, it makes our problem much worse! For example, we now know that some nucleotide positions are much more likely to mutate than others ("hotspots"), and that certain nucleotides are favored in substitutions. Mutational "hot spots" will give us the mutant we want sooner in that location, but while we then wait for the complementary mutations within the "cold spots", the hotspots will proceed to back-mutate again. We are forced to keep re-selecting our good mutations within the hot spots, while we wait for even the first good mutation to occur within the cold spots.

This makes things worse, rather than better. The greater tendency to mutate to a certain nucleotide, (let's say T), will help us in positions where T is desired, but it will slow us down whenever G, C, or A is desired. Therefore, *75% of the time the bias toward T mutations will slow down progressive selection.* "Non-random mutation" sounds good from the point of view of building information, but unfortunately we are not talking about the non-randomness of *design*. Rather, we are talking about a type of non-randomness which (ironically) is antithetical to information building.

d) Extinction of both human and chimp lineages – Although we have temporarily suspended deleterious mutations from consideration, it is fair to note that, since the hypothetical time when human and chimps diverged, geneticists believe that many thousands of deleterious mutations should have been fixed via genetic drift (Kondrashov, 1995; Crow, 1997; Eyre-Walker and Keightley, 1999; Higgins and Lynch, 2001). The logical conclusion is that we have significantly degenerated from our ape-like ancestors. The power of this logic is overwhelming. In fact, we know man and chimp differ at more than 150 million nucleotide positions (Britten, 2002), due to at least 40 million hypothetical mutation fixations. Therefore, if we assume man evolved from a chimp-like creature, during that process there must have been about 20 million nucleotide fixations within both the human and chimp lineages, but natural selection could only have selected for about 1,000 of these. All the rest would have had to have been fixed by random drift, resulting in millions of nearly-neutral deleterious substitutions. The result? A maximum of 1,000 beneficial fixations and millions of deleterious fixations. This would not just make us inferior to our chimp-like ancestors, in 6 million years it would obviously have killed us!

We have reviewed compelling evidence that, even when ignoring deleterious mutations, mutation/selection cannot create a single gene within the evolutionary timescale. When deleterious mutations are factored back in, we see that mutation/selection cannot create a single gene *ever*. This is overwhelming evidence against the Primary Axiom. In my opinion, this constitutes what is essentially a logical proof that the Primary Axiom is false.

In conclusion, the genome, and each of its genes, must have been designed and could not have evolved. Yet we all know that micro-evolution (adaptive selection) *does* happen. How can this be? Most adaptation is due to fine-tuning, not creation of new information. Furthermore, most adaptation is not due to newly arising random mutations – but is due to pre-existing variation. To use the terminology of our earlier chapters, mutations are the dings, scratches, and broken parts of life. Reasonably, we can conclude that most useful variations are designed variations. When we see adaptive selection occurring, we are usually witnessing segregation and recombination of useful variants of genes and gene components that were designed to segregate and recombine in the first place. We are not usually seeing the result of random mutations, which are consistently deleterious. In this case, selection favors the most desirable recombinants and segregants of the designed variation. For example, a single human couple, if they contained designed and functional heterozygosity at only a tiny fraction of their nucleotides, would produce (via recombination and segregation) an essentially unlimited range of useful diversity. It is this type of designed diversity that natural selection can act upon most effectively. All such designed variants

would be expected to be created within useful linkage groups, and
would have originated at high allelic frequencies. For example,
in the case of an initial single human couple where there could
be only four initial sets of chromosomes, all initial nucleotide
variants would have a frequency of at least 25%. Functional
linkage groups and high initial allele frequencies greatly enhance
selection efficiency, thus enabling rapid local adaptation. Like an
ordered deck of cards, the net information in such a scenario would
be greatest at the beginning, but diversity would be greatest only
after many cycles of shuffling. Except at the beginning, no new
functional information would be required.

*2008 Update – In 2007 Michael Behe published his second book "The
Edge of Evolution". While his first book was based largely on theoretical
considerations, this second book reviews massive amounts of empirical
molecular data associated with three medically important microorganisms
(the AIDS virus, the Malaria pathogen, and the E. coli bacterium). These
systems are known to be highly mutable and undergo massive numbers
of selection cycles, and are cited as powerful examples of "evolutionary
systems". Behe shows that while these organisms rapidly adapt to new
external conditions, they do not innovate any new internal functions.
Even within these "ideal evolutionary systems", the type of change being
documented only represents "fine-tuning", not true innovation. Although
scientists have tracked these model systems through a vast number of
reproductive cycles (many more than could occur even through "deep time"
for higher organisms), all the observed changes have been merely "stop-
gap measures". Behe powerfully demonstrates that the Primary Axiom
cannot create irreducible complexity, even on the simplest level. Behe's
new book has been very harshly attacked, but recent new data has strongly
validated his analysis (see http://www.evolutionnews.org/2014/07/so_
michael_behe087901.html).*

Figure 12. Poly-constrained information and poly-constrained DNA.

Like puns, palindromes, and other word puzzles, DNA contains poly-functional letters, words, and phrases. Such sequences can only arise by very careful *design*. Once they are created, they cannot be "mutated" to make them better. An excellent example is the painstakingly crafted poly-functional Latin phrase shown above (see Ohno and Yomo, 1991). This ancient word puzzle (dating back to 79 AD) has a translation something like, "THE SOWER NAMED AREPO HOLDS THE WORKING OF THE WHEELS." It reads the same, four different ways: left to right, up to down, and starting at the lower right, down to up, right to left. Any single letter change in this system destroys all four messages simultaneously (all four of which happen to be the same in this example). Similarly, a simple sentence palindrome would be: ABLE WAS I ERE I SAW ELBA, which reads the same forward or backwards. Any letter change destroys both messages. A simple example of a poly-functional word would be *LIVE*, which backwards is *EVIL*. To change *LIVE* to *HIVE* might be desirable, but it turns *EVIL* which has meaning, to *EVIH*, which is meaningless. So this dual-meaning word, like the other examples above, is poly-constrained, precisely because it is poly-functional.

Figure 13. Irreducible complexity.

In our red wagon example, the simplest improvement one might imagine would be some misspellings that would convert our red wagon into a blue tricycle. This seemingly small evolutionary step forward could never happen by chance because it requires creation of many new components, each of which represents "irreducible complexity". It is not hard to imagine a misspelling that would change the paint code or cause a wheel to fall off. However, to make an operational tricycle that actually works requires extensive re-working of most of the components. Just one new component – the pedal apparatus – illustrates this. Creation of an operational pedal apparatus for our little red wagon could not arise from a few misspellings. Several entirely new chapters in the manual would be required for manufacturing and assembling the various components. But the new pedal apparatus would still not work without a place for one to sit and a place for one's legs. Very obviously, the corruption of a wagon's assembly manual via random misspellings (even with the help of our quality control agent) could never result in a shiny new blue tricycle. It could only lead to a run-down and broken wagon.

Are the Downward Curves Real?

Newsflash – All evidence points to genetic degeneration.

The nature of information and the correctly formulated analogy of the genome as an instruction manual, with mutations being word processing errors, help us see that the genome must degenerate. This common sense conclusion is supported by information theory (Gitt, 1997; Gitt et al., 2013). The very high rate of human mutation indicates that man must be degenerating. The prohibitive cost of selecting for large numbers of mutations simultaneously indicates that man must be degenerating. The problems of near-neutral mutations, selection threshold, and selection interference, all indicate that man must be degenerating. State-of-the-art numerical simulations are now conclusively showing that we must be degenerating (Sanford et al., 2007b; Gibson et al., 2013).

Going back to Figure 4 (p. 71) we can see what genetic entropy should look like – it should be a classic biological decay curve. This figure plots human genetic degeneration over several thousand years, assuming a 1% rate of fitness decline per generation – as has been claimed by Crow (1997). According to the newer study by Lynch (2010), the actual rate of decline is probably much higher – conceivably 5% per generation. Similar fitness decay curves are seen in numerous places in this book (Figures 4, 10a, 10b, 14, 15,

16). Some of these are simply based upon genetic theory, some are based upon numerical simulations, some are based upon biological data, and some based upon historical data. But they all show the same basic curve – a clear biological decay curve. They all agree.

Given the deeply engrained assumptions about the ubiquity of forward evolution, it seems hard to believe this type of rapid genetic degeneration could be possible. However, for the last 60 years the leaders in the field of population genetics have repeatedly expressed serious reservations, essentially asking "How can genetic theory honestly preclude this type of reverse evolution?" (see Appendix 1). Building on their work, I have spent more than a decade of study, further advancing understanding in this area. Arguably, I have studied the specific problem of genetic entropy more than any other scientist. My research has included careful analysis of how the processes of mutation and selection actually operate, combined with simple logic and mathematical formulation. Most importantly, during the last decade, my colleagues and I have developed the state-of-the-art in numerical simulation programming which realistically models the mutation/selection process. Our numerical simulation program simultaneously and comprehensively takes into account all the relevant biological factors that affect mutation/ selection. Because we can now do biologically realistic numerical simulations, we can actually see how the mutation accumulation process unfolds (see Chapter 11). This work clearly reveals that genetic entropy is a very real problem, and is much more severe than previous population geneticists have admitted. Realistic numerical simulations consistently show a biological decay curve almost identical to the theoretical fitness decline of Figure 4 (p. 71). The fitness trajectory is consistently down – not up.

In addition to all these evidences, there is now strong biological evidence of genetic entropy in RNA viruses such as the influenza virus (Figure 15). All three strains of influenza which caused major human pandemics in the 20th century displayed evidence of rapidly declining virulence correlating with mutation accumulation.

For decades evolutionary biologists have insisted on a philosophical level that natural selection is the counterforce to entropy in biological systems, and must be able to reverse biological degeneration. However, all of the best studies contradict that philosophical assumption. Mutational entropy appears to be so strong, especially within large genomes, that selection should not be able to reverse it. This makes eventual extinction of such genomes inevitable (unless there is some undiscovered counterforce apart from selection). I have termed this fundamental problem *Genetic Entropy*. Genetic entropy is not a starting axiomatic position, rather it is a logical conclusion derived from careful analysis of how the mutation/selection process actually operates.

If mutation/selection can't prevent the degeneration of the genome, then the Primary Axiom is wrong. It is not just implausible. It is not just unlikely. It is absolutely dead wrong. It is not just a false axiom. It is an unsupported and discredited hypothesis, and can be confidently rejected. It is now clear that mutation/selection cannot stop the loss of genomic information – so mutation/selection clearly could not *create* the genome. How can this be true? It is true because selection occurs on the level of the whole organism. It cannot stop the loss of information (which is immeasurably complex) due to mutation accumulation, which is happening on the molecular level. **It is like trying to fix a computer with a hammer. The microscopic complexity of the computer chip makes**

**the hammer largely irrelevant. Likewise, the microscopic
complexity of genomic mutation makes selection on the
level of the whole individual largely irrelevant.**

In our first chapter we considered a parallel scenario, wherein we
tried to advance transportation technology. We proposed using
a robotic, nearly-blind "scribe" who makes misspellings within
instruction manuals at the beginning of a car-manufacturing plant.
We then added a robotic, nearly-blind "judge" who does quality
control at the other end of the assembly line. No human beings *ever*
enter the plant. We asked, "Will the cars coming off the assembly
line get progressively better or worse?" Will the cars evolve into
spaceships? Everything we have been considering should make it
obvious. The cars will not evolve into spaceships. In fact, they will
become progressively inferior cars. The quality control robot can at
best delay the inevitable failure of the enterprise. Does more time
help in this scenario? No, infinite time would just give us infinite
certainty that the system would fail. But our factory has neither
infinite time nor infinite resources. Real life is like a business, and
it must continually "pay all its costs" or go out of business (die).

Despite massive amounts of mental conditioning of the public by
the intellectual elite, I believe most people can still instinctively
see that the relentless accumulation of random misspellings
within assembly manuals cannot transform a car into a spaceship.
Our quality control agent will *never* see a deviant car that has
a rocket engine, no matter how long he waits, nor how many
misspellings occur in the manual. This is because of probability
and because of the problem of irreducible complexity, as described
by Behe (1996). Even if the judge *did* see a deviant car with a

rocket engine, he (it) would have to reject it because a car with a rocket engine is still not a better means of transportation. Our judge (natural selection) has an I.Q. of zero, has zero foresight, and has no concept of what a spaceship might be. Therefore he (it) has no conception of the deviations needed to make a car more like a spaceship, nor would he (it) ever select such deviations. The only possible way he (it) could select toward a *spaceship* would be by selecting for better *cars,* which is clearly paradoxical. Even if our judge *could* begin to select for more "spaceship-like" cars (most emphatically he cannot), it would take such an astronomically huge number of misspellings to create a functional spaceship that it would essentially take forever. But remember, our car factory cannot afford to take forever. It has to pay its bills today. In fact, those cars that might be more "spaceship-like" would likewise be less "car-like". In other words, they would be dysfunctional products, analogous to biological monstrosities. Bankruptcy is just around the corner for any such commercial enterprise. Careful analysis, on many levels, consistently reveals that the Primary Axiom is absolutely wrong.

Would any one of you care to invest your life savings in a new company that had decided to use the mutation/selection manufacturing scheme? Its promoters say that it will be all robotic. No human agents will be needed at the plant, and they assure us that the plant will just keep making better and better products. Remember, we are not talking about a separately-funded research and development program. We are talking about a revenue-generating, boom or bust assembly line! Any buyers? You and I would certainly dismiss this as a fraud. Despite glossy brochures and VIP endorsements, we know that any such scheme could only make deteriorating cars, and could never produce a revolutionary new spaceship.

If the genome is degenerating, then our species is degenerating. There appears to be a close parallel between the aging of a species and the aging of an individual. Both seem to involve the progressive accumulation of mutations. Mutations accumulate both within our somatic body cell lines and our reproductive cell lines. Either way, the misspellings accumulate until a threshold is reached when things rapidly start to fall apart. This results in a distinct upper range for our lifespan. Human life expectancy presently has an average of about 70 years with a maximum near 120. However, when first cousins marry, their children have a serious reduction of life expectancy. Why is this? It is because inbreeding exposes the genetic mistakes within the genome (recessive mutations) that have not yet had time to "come to the surface". Inbreeding is like a sneak-preview of where we are going genetically as a species. The reduced life expectancy of inbred children reflects the overall aging of the genome, and reveals the hidden reservoir of genetic damage (recessive mutation) that has been accumulating. If all this genetic damage were exposed suddenly (if we were all made perfectly inbred and homozygous), it would be perfectly lethal. We all would be dead. Our species would instantly become extinct. **Genetic damage results in aging, and aging shortens lifespan. This is true for the individual and for the population**.

The Bible records a limited time when people had extremely long lives, and when inbreeding was entirely benign. In fact, the life expectancies recorded in the book of Genesis seem unbelievable. According to the Bible, in the beginning, people routinely lived to be more than 900 years old. From where we stand now, that seems absurd. But our perspective and our understanding are so very limited. *We still do not know* why most mammals have a maximal lifespan of less than 20 years while man's is about 120 years. Even chimps have a maximal life-expectancy less than half that of man. However, we *know at least this much: mutation is clearly implicated in aging.* So if there were initially no mutations, wouldn't you expect the maximal human age to be much longer? From this perspective, apart from mutations, human ages of hundreds of years would not be so crazy. It would be logical. Indeed, why would we die sooner?

A paper by a mathematician and a theologian presents some fascinating data (Holladay and Watt, 2001). Their paper compares the lifespan of early Biblical characters to how long they were born after the patriarch Noah. This Biblical data (recorded thousands of years ago) clearly reveals an exponential decay curve. The curve can only be described as biological. My colleagues and I have done a more complete analysis, producing more striking results (Figure 16).

This unexpected pattern in the Biblical data is amazing. We are forced to conclude that the authors of the books of Genesis, Exodus, Joshua, and other books, either faithfully recorded an exponential decay of human life spans – or they collaborated in fabricating the data using sophisticated mathematical modeling. To fabricate this data would have required an advanced knowledge of mathematics, as well as a strong desire to show exponential decay. But without knowledge of genetics (discovered in the 19th century), or mutation (discovered in the 20th century), why would these authors have wanted to show a biological decay curve? It does not seem reasonable to attribute this data to some elaborate fraud thousands of years ago. The most rational conclusion is that the data are real, and that human life expectancy was once hundreds of years, but has progressively declined to current values. The most obvious explanation for such declining life spans, in light of all the above discussions, would be genetic degeneration due to mutation accumulation. The downward curve is especially steep in the early generations, suggesting that there may have been a substantially elevated mutation rate at that time.

My colleagues and I have done thousands of numerical simulations to better understand genetic degeneration in human populations. Using the known mutation rates and other biologically reasonable parameter settings, we consistently see that; a) most deleterious mutations are not selectively eliminated, and so they accumulate linearly and without limit; b) beneficial mutations are too rare and generally too subtle to significantly compensate for the accumulating deleterious mutations; c) fitness declines continuously, manifesting a biolgical decay curve which follows a trajectory very similar to the Biblical data shown in Figure 16.

Many lines of evidence indicate that the downward curve is very real. We are dying – both as individuals and as a species. The Primary Axiom is wrong. Apart from intelligent intervention, information always decays. Apart from some counterforce much more effective than natural selection, genomes must decay. Life should not be going up, up, up. It should be going down, down, down. Selection does not create information, and at best it can only slow its decay.

Information theory clearly indicates that information and information systems arise only through intelligent means and are only preserved by intelligence (Gitt, 1997; Gitt et al., 2013).

Computers and computer programs do not arise spontaneously. They are painstakingly designed. Even computer viruses, contrary to the public's perception, do not arise spontaneously. They are painstakingly and maliciously designed. The emergence of the Internet has created a vast experiment to see if information can organize itself. It does not. Everything happening on the Internet, even the bad stuff, is designed.

It is the fundamental nature of information to degenerate. This reality is reflected all around us, from the illustration of the room full of whisperers, to systems involving chains of command, to the routine crashing of our computer systems. The reason our information systems do not degenerate even *more* rapidly is because of elaborate, intelligently-designed systems created to stabilize and preserve that information. Yet even the best designed information systems, apart from intelligent maintenance and the *continual intervention* of intelligence, will always eventually breakdown. Computers are typically junk within 5-10 years.

The genetic systems of life can be seen as intelligently designed information systems, and natural selection can be seen as an intelligently designed stabilizing mechanism. Even though these systems appear to be superbly designed, they are still degenerating, apart from the intelligent intervention of their designer.

What is the mystery of the genome? Its very existence is its mystery. Information and complexity which surpass human understanding are programmed into a space smaller than an invisible speck of dust. Mutation/selection cannot even begin to explain this. It should be very clear that our genome could not have arisen spontaneously. The only reasonable alternative to a spontaneous genome is a designed genome. Isn't that an awesome mystery – one worthy of our contemplation?

*2008 Update – The term "entropy" has several uses. I am using the term entropy as it is most commonly used, i.e., **the universal tendency for things to run down or degrade apart from intelligent intervention.** Genetic entropy specifically means entropy as it applies to the genome. It reflects the inherent tendency for genomes to degenerate over time apart from intelligent intervention. Genetic entropy is directly related to physical entropy, as this term is formally used by engineers and physicists. Mutations are the result of physical entropy being manifested on the molecular level. It is due to random atomic forces and imperfect operation of the "nanomachines" affecting DNA replication and DNA repair. Natural selection itself can be viewed as a type of mechanical apparatus that reduces mutational entropy by filtering out certain mutations. Like all machines, the bio-machinery affecting DNA replication, DNA repair, and selective elimination, all operate at less than 100% efficiency (mechanical inefficiency is also a measure of entropy). Therefore, traditional entropy, in its most formal sense, lies at the root of both "mutational entropy" and "selection inefficiency", and together these lie at the root of genetic entropy.*

The term "Shannon entropy" will be used by some to confuse the issue of genetic entropy. Shannon entropy is an unfortunate and misleading term which was coined to refer to certain statistical properties of potential information. It is a way to measure the "surprise value" of a letter within a string of letters. Any simple repeating pattern reduces a string's Shannon entropy value. A high Shannon entropy value can reflect either a randomized set of letters or a carefully written poem. In other words, high Shannon entropy values can reflect either intelligent design or random chaos. It is not a useful term in the context of this discussion. High Shannon entropy merely says, "there is no simple repeating pattern here." It is a term which is used in a very limited and specific sense and is not productively applied to biological information systems. It can only be used to deliberately cloud our understanding of the genome and its decay. Shannon himself warned against applying his terminology to biological systems.

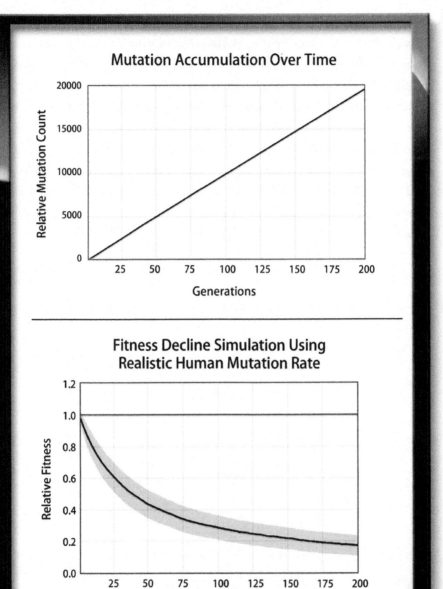

Figure 14. Biologically realistic numerical simulation of the mutation/selection process within the human population.

This numerical simulation employed a mutation rate of 100, a population size of 10,000, and assumed minimal "junk DNA". It was assumed that one mutation in 1,000 was beneficial.

Above: Deleterious mutation count per individual over time is shown (accumulating beneficial mutations were too rare to be seen in this figure). As can be seen, only a small fraction of the deleterious mutations can be eliminated even with intense selection. Genetic damage accumulates at a constant rate.

Below: Fitness decline relative to the starting population is shown. On the left axis is shown fitness, while time (generations) is plotted along the bottom axis (200 generations approximates 4,000-6,000 years). Reducing the mutation rate by half or increasing population size ten-fold did not fundamentally change the observed downward trajectory. The trajectory shown in this numerical simulation experiment is remarkably similar to Figures 4, 10a, 10b, 15 and 16. The shaded area reflects the standard deviation of the population fitness.

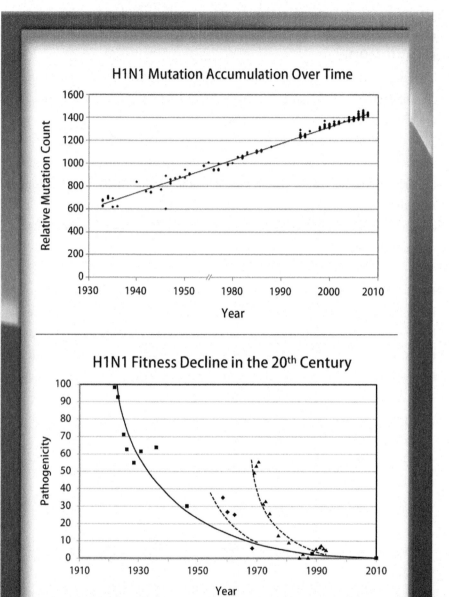

Figure 15. Actual biological data, showing mutation accumulation and fitness decline in human influenza virus.

Above: This graph shows the accumulation of mutations within the H1N1 strain, subsequent to the 1918 pandemic (over 10% of the viral genome mutated). As can be seen, mutations accumulated at a remarkably constant rate, just as our logic and our numerical simulations predicted. See Carter and Sanford (2012).

Below: This graph illustrates the pathogenicity (i.e., fitness) of the H1N1 strain (solid line), as well as the other two pandemic-causing influenza strains (dashed lines), during the last century (from Simonsen, et al., 1998). All three strains (H1N1, H2N2 and H3N2) show exponential decline. The human version of H1N1 apparently went extinct in 2009. Figure courtesy of Dr. Rob Carter.

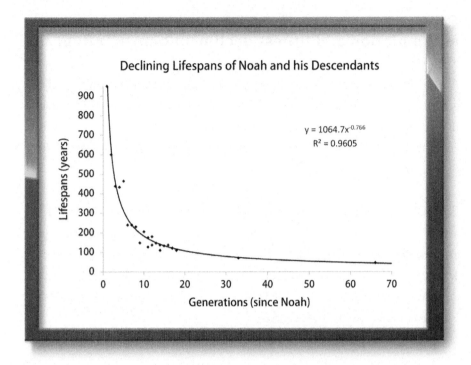

Figure 16. Human lifespans in early history, as recorded in the Bible.

When Biblical lifespans (scale on left) are plotted across generations after Noah, we see a dramatic decline in life expectancy. The pattern of decline reveals a very clear biological decay curve. Fitting the data to the "line of best fit" reveals an exponential curve following the formula $y = 1064.7x^{-0.766}$. The curve fits the data very well, with a coefficient of determination of 0.96 (1.0 would be a perfect fit). It seems highly unlikely this Biblical data could have resulted from an ancient fabrication. The curve is very consistent with the concept of genomic degeneration caused by mutation accumulation. The curve is very similar to the theoretical curves shown in Figures 4, 10a, 10b, 14, and the biological data in Figure 15. For more information on this analysis of the patriarchs and their ages, see LogosRA.org (article entitled "Genetic Entropy Recorded in the Bible?").

Summary of Major New Scientific Developments.

Newsflash - The case for genetic entropy is now much stronger...

Since this book's first publication in 2005, there have been numerous new scientific findings that strongly support the thesis of this book. These new scientific developments indicate that the problem of genetic entropy is profound, and that the Primary Axiom is no longer defensible. Some of these evidences come from other labs, but most of the evidences come from research that I have been doing in collaboration with a network of other scientists. I have touched upon these new scientific developments in previous chapters, but here I wish to bring all the new developments into a single summary chapter (please excuse some redundancy).

New experimental evidences from my collaborators and myself

1. Validation of Genetic Entropy using numerical simulation: During the last 10 years, my colleagues and I have developed the world's most advanced numerical simulation program for studying the mutation/selection process (Sanford et al., 2007a, 2007b; Sanford and Nelson, 2012). This biologically realistic computer simulation program ("Mendel's Accountant"), has been used to do a series of empirical experiments which strongly confirm all the logically-deduced conclusions of this book. The Mendel program faithfully simulates a biologically realistic virtual population, and creates a biologically realistic array of mutations that are added to individuals every generation. Mendel then realistically simulates recombination, reproduction, and the generation of progeny. Among the progeny, a specified fraction is selected away based upon fitness, and the process is repeated generation after generation. All of the relevant circumstances (variables), that affect selection efficiency and mutation accumulation can be specified by the program user. Mendel is not programmed to produce any specific result – it simply simulates the mutation/selection process as biologists understand it to be operating in nature. The outcome of any particular simulation experiment depends on the exact biological circumstances that the user specifies. Using any set of biologically reasonable circumstances, genetic entropy (i.e., continuous deleterious mutation accumulation and subsequent fitness decline) is seen. Forward evolution is only observed using settings that are biologically very unrealistic.

1a) Most deleterious mutations accumulate without limit

When Mendel is used to do simulation experiments that employ biologically reasonable settings, it consistently reveals the following: i) Only the worst mutations are effectively selected away, while the rest (roughly 90%) accumulate at a remarkably constant rate (Gibson et al., 2013); ii) There is a measurable "selection threshold" where selection becomes ineffective for lower-impact deleterious mutations (Gibson et al., 2013); iii) Any and all types of biological and genetic noise result in an increase in the observed selection threshold, such that more and more of the deleterious mutations accumulate (Gibson et al., 2013).

1b) Beneficial mutations, for the most part, fail to amplify

In regard to beneficial mutations, Mendel simulation experiments consistently show the following: i) There is also a measurable "selection threshold" for beneficial mutations, wherein selection becomes ineffective for the lower-impact mutations (Sanford et al., 2013); ii) Any and all types of biological and genetic noise cause an increase in the observed selection threshold for beneficial mutations, such that more and more of the beneficial mutations fail to be selectively amplified (Sanford et al., 2013); iii) Under realistic settings, more than 98% of the beneficial mutations fail to be amplified (Sanford et al, 2013); iv) Rare high-impact beneficial mutations are strongly amplified by selection and go to rapid fixation, but when this happens it strongly interferes with selection for weaker beneficials. This leads to a higher selection threshold and a lower number of total beneficial mutations being fixed. Fitness always declines, except when very high rates of beneficial mutations are provided, and where high-impact beneficials are included. Even given a generous and continuous supply of beneficial mutations combined with very intense selection, the ratio of good to bad mutations that accumulate is not reversed. This results in continuous reduction in the functional genome size (number of accumulating deleterious mutations always exceeds beneficials). Given enough time, this must invariably lead to extinction (Sanford et al., 2013).

1c) Invalidation of the two primary "rescue devices"

In response to the well-established (but generally unspoken) problem of deleterious mutation accumulation, two rescue mechanisms have been invoked (see Chapter 7). Without an effective rescue mechanism, the Primary Axiom cannot stand.

The first rescue mechanism is the mutation-count mechanism (MCM). The concept is to direct natural selection so that it acts based upon the number of deleterious mutations per individual (rather than based upon fitness). This requires artificially strong selection being focused on those individuals with slightly more deleterious mutations than the other individuals. The key to this rescue mechanism is simple – it artificially and arbitrarily assumes all mutations are essentially equal in their deleterious effect. Conveniently, by using this artificial mental construct, nearly-neutral mutations go away and the near-neutral mutation problem disappears. This model does not even remotely resemble reality. The mechanism requires "Mother Nature" to line up all the individuals, count their mutations, and with high precision select away the higher-count individuals. This simply does not happen. We have investigated this mechanism in great detail, using numerical simulation experiments. Even if all mutations are made equal in effect (obviously not true in nature), our numerical simulations clearly show that the MCM fails completely whenever realistic probability selection is operational. This is reported in a recent scientific publication (Brewer et al., 2013a). See Figure 10a on pages 118-119. The MCM rescue mechanism has now been invalidated with a very high degree of certainty, and can no longer honestly be invoked.

Recent papers that claim to have solved the problem of a very high human mutation rate appear to be unintentionally establishing conditions that allow the activation of the artificial mutation-count mechanism (see Chapter 7). This effect is an artifact of over-simplified models, and instantly disappears under realistic conditions.

The second rescue mechanism is the synergistic epistasis mechanism (SE). This rescue mechanism is similar to the first, but involves more obfuscation and mental gymnastics (see Chapter 7). Again, selection is focused against the individuals with higher numbers of mutations, compared to the other individuals. Mutations are not assumed to have equal effects. Instead, each individual mutation becomes increasingly harmful as the individual's mutation-count increases. The hope is that this will effectively amplify selection against high mutation-count individuals. This type of negative interaction between mutations is called "synergistic epistasis". It is well known that this is not generally how mutations interact. This fancy-sounding term is invoked by population geneticists for the sole purpose of trying to create an alternative rescue mechanism which might appear credible. We have done extensive numerical simulation experiments to see if this artificial mechanism actually works. Even using the most generous settings, the synergistic epistasis rescue mechanism fails to halt deleterious mutation accumulation. Instead of slowing fitness decline, this mechanism actually accelerates degeneration and extinction (as is logically expected, and as predicted in the earlier editions of this book). This is reported in a recent scientific publication (Baumgardner et al., 2013). See Figure 10b, pages 120-121. This second rescue mechanism has also now been invalidated with a very high degree of certainty, and can no longer honestly be invoked. There are no other credible rescue mechanisms being proposed – making the Primary Axiom entirely *indefensible*.

1d) Invalidation of Avida

The program called Avida was developed for the purpose of demonstrating "digital evolution". It has been claimed that this program shows that mutation/selection systems can generate new information within a virtual context. Avida is not a true numerical simulation – it is more like a computer game simulation that can randomly create and select variant strings of computer commands. This has obvious parallels to evolution and it is said to prove the validity of the Primary Axiom. At first glance, experiments using Avida appear to contradict what Mendel's Accountant simulations reveal. For this reason we have compared and contrasted these two computer programs.

Compared to Mendel's Accountant, which is the most biologically realistic simulation of the mutation/selection process developed to date, Avida is not even remotely faithful to biological reality. The most important artificial Avida feature is the nature of its selective reward/penalty system. A single "mutational change" which is determined to be beneficial within Avida, is programmed to instantly double reproductive rate (Avida's "fitness"). A single mutational change which is defined as deleterious is programmed to instantly reduce reproductive rate by half. When there are multiple mutations, Avida's rewards/penalties increase multiplicatively. Given these grossly exaggerated reward/penalties, which are many orders of magnitude too high, selection within Avida is extremely effective. Just a handful of favorable mutational changes can amplify fitness a million-fold. Interestingly, when Mendel is assigned similar selective rewards/penalties, the same explosive evolution is seen, resulting in the amplification of fitness by more than a million-fold. Both programs show explosive evolution when given these types of extremely unrealistic settings. But such settings do not match reality, and such explosive fitness increases have never been seen in the biological realm. When Avida settings are modified to reflect biologically-realistic selective rewards/ penalties – suddenly there is zero forward evolution (see Nelson and Sanford, 2011). Not a single beneficial mutation is selected. Not a single binary bit of information is created. So what happens when starting an Avida population using the default settings (extremely large rewards and penalties) – and then later we adjust the settings to be biologically realistic? Using the unrealistic settings we can amplify all possible beneficial mutations and eliminate all possible deleterious mutations. The result is that fitness quickly increases more than a million-fold. When the settings are then adjusted to be realistic, all gained functions are rapidly lost. This is essentially equivalent to extinction – the newly created "information" reverts to zero. Amazingly, Mendel and Avida both prove the reality of genetic entropy whenever biologically realistic settings are applied. This is reported in two separate scientific publications (Nelson and Sanford, 2011; Nelson and Sanford, 2013). When biologically realistic settings are used, Avida affirms the reality of genetic entropy. Avida very effectively disproves the Primary Axiom.

1e) Validation of "Haldane's Dilemma"

In the 1950s, just after DNA was discovered, a leading population geneticist (one of the founding fathers of the Primary Axiom), realized there was a problem. Haldane realized that even if there was an abundant and continuous supply of beneficial mutations, natural selection must be very limited in its ability to amplify such mutations to the point of where they are "fixed" within a sizeable population. He calculated that for a mammalian population such as man, given an evolutionary population size of 10,000, only about 1,000 beneficial mutations could be selectively fixed within 6 million years (this happens to be the current estimated time it took for apes to evolve into man). In light of genomic data, we now know that the human genome is profoundly different from apes. There would need to be tens or even hundreds of millions of beneficial mutations that arose and went to fixation during this timeframe. That scenario would require roughly 1,000 independent beneficial fixations *per generation*. Haldane said this was impossible; he estimated that at best there should be only about 1 fixation every 300 generations. This problem came to be know as "Haldane's Dilemma". This problem has been extensively investigated by Walter ReMine, who has used an entirely independent mathematical formulation of the problem and has reached exactly the same conclusions (ReMine, 2005). We have now used a third approach to the problem, using numerical simulation experiments. Our experiments strongly validate the work of Haldane and ReMine. We see that, depending on the specific settings, only a few hundred to a few thousand selective fixations can realistically occur during 300,000 human generations (about 6 million years) (Rupe and Sanford, 2013). We are very confident that our numerical simulation experiments are the best way to understand this problem. Between Haldane, ReMine, and our own work, the matter is clearly settled. This means the ape-to-man story is not even remotely feasible.

1f) On-going research

We have numerical simulation experiments underway which will continue to establish the reality of genetic entropy and the collapse of the Primary Axiom. Work which is underway will bring clarity to several important issues. Our work is showing that there is an insurmountable "waiting time problem" for the creation of specific sets of nucleotides (information does not just require letters, but requires specific strings of letters, comparable to sentences). Our work is also showing there is strong and quantifiable "selection interference" which further limits the potential selection of many beneficial mutations simultaneously. We will also soon show that the accumulation of deleterious mutations which are recessive, happening at millions of sites throughout the genome, must lead to an extreme fitness crisis. As such mutations drift to high enough frequencies, homozygotes start to arise and contribute to a lethal genetic load. Lastly, we will soon show that group selection cannot explain altruistic behavior.

All of these empirical simulation experiments have produced (and continue to produce) results that were predicted in the earlier editions of this book. This shows that the logic of this book is sound and predictive. Numerical simulation experiments have consistently validated all of the logical deductions described in this book (Baumgardner et al., 2008; Baumgardner et al., 2013; Brewer et al., 2013a; Brewer et al., 2013b; Gibson et al., 2013; Nelson and Sanford, 2013; Rupe and Sanford, 2013; Sanford et al., 2007a; Sanford et al., 2007b; Sanford et al., 2008; Sanford and Nelson, 2012; Sanford et al., 2013).

Comprehensive numerical simulation of the mutation/ selection process should revolutionize the field of population genetics. For the first time ever, we can actually see how the mutation/selection process plays out, for any specific set of conditions. We are no longer limited to abstract mathematical formulations based upon many layers of unreasonable simplifying assumptions. This growing realization should eventually turn the field of population genetics on its head. To quote another research group doing comprehensive numerical simulation of the mutation/selection process (Qui et al., 2014):

> *"Computer modeling of genetic processes may be considered as an advanced branch of cellular automata, named by Wolfram... 'as a new kind of science.' ...Wolfram demonstrated that any system of interacting elements creates patterns within their arrangements, which are hard to predict mathematically yet trivial to reproduce and study computationally."*

This is exactly what we have been seeing in our own numerical work. The "big picture" questions of population genetics cannot be answered until we stop trying to force-fit complex, dynamic biological population systems into ridicuously over-simplified mathematical formulas. Only through comprehensive numerical simulation can we bring clarity to the big questions. The entire field needs to make a fresh start.

2. Validation of Genetic Entropy in real populations:

Numerical simulation experiments should agree with real-world biological observations. This is difficult to document, because genetic entropy should only become clearly manifested after very many generations have passed. This is obviously a problem when speaking of long-lived organisms such as mammals, where a genetic entropy experiment would have to minimally last many hundreds of years. Even in bacteria this is generally true, because although bacteria have short generation times, they also have very low mutation rates per generation. To expect to see evidence of genetic entropy within a biological setting, one needs an experimental organism that has both a short generation time and a relatively high mutation rate. RNA viruses are uniquely suited for this purpose.

2a) Documentation of genetic degeneration of H1N1 influenza strain
We have documented entropic genetic degeneration within the human strain of the influenza virus that caused the great pandemic of 1918 (Carter and Sanford, 2012). Before examining the historical evidence of the genetic degeneration of the viral genome, preliminary numerical simulation experiments were done. Mendel's Accountant was used to model mutation accumulation within a hypothetical RNA virus similar to the influenza virus (Brewer et al., 2013b). These initial numerical simulation experiments strongly indicated that RNA viruses should rapidly accumulate deleterious mutations at a steady rate, causing the virus to run down and go extinct in a reasonably short timeframe. On this basis we predicted that this same pattern would be evident for the human H1N1 influenza virus strain. H1N1 entered the human population roughly 100 years ago, and in its first pandemic, it caused the death of 50-100 million people. H1N1 viral samples had been collected over the decades, and all these genomes have been sequenced during the last 10 years. Given the reconstructed genome of the original 1918 strain, we were able to compare the original strain to all subsequent genotypes, allowing us to test our prediction by analyzing mutation accumulation in this viral strain over the last century (Carter and Sanford, 2012). The result of this analysis was very rapid and remarkably constant accumulation of mutations. The increase in mutations correlated tightly with continuously declining "fitness" (pathogenicity) – leading to eventual strain disappearance in 2009 (after more than 10% of the viral genome had mutated). These results are summarized in Figure 15 (pp. 166-167). These remarkable results simultaneously validate the reality of genetic entropy in a real biological population, and validate the reliability of Mendel's Accountant to accurately predict genetic degeneration of a real biological population.

2b) Reexamination of the famous Lenski experiment involving Escherichia coli bacteria

Since 1988, Lenski and colleagues have been running a long-term experiment aimed at documenting forward evolution of the *E. coli* bacteria within a test-tube environment (Barrick et al., 2009; Lenski, 2011). Several decades is a very short time – even though more than 50 thousand cell division cycles have occurred. The claim that this experiment somehow involves "deep time" or reflects macro-evolution is not accurate or reasonable. Over a period of a few decades, a strain of *E. coli* bacteria became slightly better-adapted to an artificial nutrient medium. This is not unexpected or remarkable in any way. It merely reflects fine-tuning. It is still the same type of bacterium – *E. coli*. Because the Lenski experiment has only been running for a fraction of the time as the H1N1 population, and because the mutation rate per nucleotide in bacteria is at least 1,000-fold lower than for the influenza virus, the influenza population reflects much "deeper time" than Lenski's bacterial populations. In the Lenski populations, a few hundred mutations have accumulated per cell, while in the influenza population nearly 2,000 mutations accumulated per viral particle. More than 10% of the viral genome mutated, while the change in the bacterial genome was trivial (a few hundred mutations within a genome of over 4 million base pairs). The Lenski experiment needs to run many centuries before we can expect to see extreme manifestations of genetic entropy as observed in the H1N1 virus.

However, when viewed more carefully, Lenski's own data still reveals clear evidence of genetic degeneration (Rupe and Sanford, in preparation). When we examine the specific genetic changes that enabled adaptation to the artificial environment, we see in every case, that the adaptation was accomplished by means of either loss-of-function or loss-of-regulation mutations (and hence loss of information). Because more than half the *E.coli* genome involves functions not relevant to the static artificial environment of Lenski's experiment, the silencing of these temporarily "expendable" genes and the elimination of all non-relevant functions will continue indefinitely until the bacterial genome is stripped down to its minimal functionality. This should take several centuries. In this way the maximal energy efficiency will be accomplished – allowing the bacteria (due to its greatly reduced functional genome) to grow at maximal speed within the fixed artificial environment. But this is not forward evolution. It is *adaptive degeneration,* or *reductive evolution* – it is really a form of genetic entropy. The "evolving" strains are degenerating toward the point where they can only grow in a specific, extremely limited, and entirely artificial environment. In reality, such strains are becoming increasingly disabled, and will be increasingly unfit to survive in the real world. While a handful of loss-of-function mutations have been demonstrated to increase adaptation to the artificial environment, these are greatly outnumbered by other mutations that have been accumulating relentlessly, apart from selection, and which have no visible effect. Very reasonably, most of these can be assumed to be nearly-neutral mutations which are slightly deleterious. Over hundreds of years, Lenski's "evolving" strains of bacteria must logically go extinct (if they could be maintained in the artificial environment that long). Nearly-neutral deleterious mutations will inevitably cause the bacterial genome to "rust out" (Gibson et al., 2013; Sanford et al., 2013).

3. Other lines of research, from my collaborators and myself, supporting the thesis of this book:

3a) Overlapping codes

There is now strong evidence that within any given stretch of genomic DNA, there are multiple overlapping messages. This is a little like getting an email, reading useful information from it, and then discovering that part of it, when read backwards had another useful message, and when reading every-other-letter in another part provides a third overlapping message with useful information. We now know that over half the human genome is read backwards as well as forwards. A given gene produces roughly 7 overlapping transcripts, having different start and stop positions. The resulting transcripts are then differentially-spliced, such that any given transcript can give rise to many possible proteins. We have shown that these types of overlapping codes profoundly effect the probability of mutations arising that are truly beneficial. Most "beneficial" mutations, while they may improve one message, will disrupt one or more overlapping messages. Such mutations are not truly benefical but are at best ambiguously beneficial. In this light, biologists must adjust their estimated rates of truly beneficial mutations downward very dramatically (Montañez et al., 2013). Mutations that are both unambiguously beneficial and also impactful enough to be selectable, must be vanishingly rare.

3b) Invalidation of "Fisher's Theorem"

We are now in the process of preparing a publication which will formally disprove Fisher's "Fundamental Theorem of Natural Selection". Fisher and his theorem were pivotal in establishing neo-Darwinian theory. Fisher's primary error was his belief that the net effect of mutations would be neutral. He thought beneficial mutations might be just as common, and just as impactful as deleterious mutations. At that time it was not understood that genes contain information just like an instruction manual, and that mutations are random typographical errors within those instructions. Therefore, Fisher did not understand that new mutations must overwhelmingly be deleterious, and that any possible beneficial errors that might arise will typically have a very small degree of benefit. Since the net effect of mutation is negative, Fisher's central premise was wrong, invalidating his entire thesis. Fisher's theorem is not applicable to real-world biology. This means that one of the first and most foundational cornerstones of neo-Darwinian theory is verifiably false.

New evidences from other scientists

1. The book "Biological Information – New Perspectives" is the most important new publication heralding the collapse of neo-Darwinian theory.

This book is the proceedings from a recent Cornell symposium and contains the research findings of 29 well-credentialed scientists. These authors, representing many different scientific disciplines, unanimously agreed that the Primary Axiom can't explain the origin of genomes or the origin of any of the other types of biological information systems within living cells (see Marks et al., 2013). See Sanford (2014) for a synopsis of the proceedings.

2. The massive ENCODE results (2007, 2012) are the product of the highest level of mainstream biological research.

ENCODE, the biological equivalent of the NASA space research program, embodies the collective research findings of hundreds of mainstream scientists. ENCODE chronicles the collapse of the "junk DNA" paradigm. Overwhelming evidence is presented showing that most of the human genome is functional. This means that most human mutations are not neutral, but are deleterious. This is another powerful evidence that sounds the death knell of the Primary Axiom. ENCODE also shows that there are extensively overlapping codes, which means unambiguously beneficial mutations must be vanishingly rare. All this means there is much more information that needs to be explained, and much less potential for the Primary Axiom to explain it.

3. Another major paper confirms that the human genome is rapidly degenerating.
A recent paper by Lynch (2010), details the nature of human mutations, and the subsequent manifestation of genetic entropy within the human genome. The author acknowledges the severity of this problem, even though he contends that most of the genome is junk DNA (see Appendix 1).

Final Summation – When I wrote the first edition of this book, I could not have imagined that in less than a decade so much evidence would materialize supporting every aspect of my thesis. I find this both amazing and sobering.

Postlude

What Hope?

Newsflash – There is a hope.

As you have so diligently stayed with me all the way through this book, and have now reached its end, perhaps you will not be offended if I diverge from what has been a scientific discussion and touch upon the philosophical. I would like to humbly put before you my own personal conclusion regarding where our hope lies.

When I was young, I accepted the fact that I was going to die, and that all of the people I loved were going to die. I accepted it, but it robbed me of joy, to say the least. I was taught that there was still one hope: that the world was getting better. Science was advancing. Culture was advancing. Even mankind was getting better. Through our efforts, we could make the world a better place. Through evolution, we could evolve into something better. Through *progress,* we might eventually defeat death itself. Perhaps we might someday even reverse the degeneration of the universe! My personal hope was that I might in some small way contribute to such progress. I believe that this basic hope was shared, to a large extent, by my entire generation[1].

I now believe this was a false hope. I still believe we should diligently apply ourselves to making this a "better world", and to be responsible stewards of the world we have been given. But I see our efforts as a holding action at best. While science can reasonably hope to prolong life, it cannot defeat death. Degeneration is certain. Our bodies, our species, and our world are all dying. It is simply not in our power to stop this very fundamental process. Isn't this obvious when we look around us? So where is the hope? If the human genome is irreversibly degenerating, we must look beyond evolution in order to have a hope for the future.

One of my reviewers told me that the message of this book is both terrifying and depressing. He suggested that perhaps I am a little like a sadistic steward on board the Titanic, gleefully spreading the news that the ship is sinking. But that is not correct. I hate the consequences of entropy (degeneration). I hate to see it in my own body, in the failing health of loved ones, or in the deformity of a new-born baby. I find it all absolutely ghastly, but also absolutely undeniable. Surely a real steward on the Titanic would have a responsibility to let people know that the ship was sinking, even if some people might hate him for it. I feel I am in that position. Responsible people should be grateful to know the *bad news*, so they can constructively respond to it. If we have been putting all our hope in a sinking ship, would it not be expedient to recognize this and abandon the false hope? It is only in this light that we

---

[1]*Kimura, 1976: "Shall we be content to preserve ourselves as a superb example of living fossils on this tiny speck of the universe? Or, shall we try with all our might, to improve ourselves to become supermen, and to still higher forms, to expand into the wider part of the universe, and to show that life after all is not a meaningless episode?"*

can appreciate bad news. Only in the light of the *bad news* can we really appreciate the *good news* – that there is a lifeboat.

Even as we cannot create life, we cannot defeat death. Yet I assert there is One who *did* create life and who designed the genome. I do not know how He did it, but somehow He surely made the hardware, and He surely must have written the original software. He is called the Author of Life (Acts 3:15 – NIV). I believe the Author of Life has the power to defeat death and degeneration. I believe this is the **Good News**.

It is my personal belief that Jesus is our hope. I believe that apart from Him there is no hope. He gave us life in the first place, so He can give us new life today. He made heaven and earth in the first place, so He can make a *new* heaven and earth in the future. Because He rose from the dead, we can be raised from death, even the death which is already enveloping us. In these profound yet simple truths, I believe there is a true hope. I believe this hope is unshakable, because I believe it is founded on the One who is eternal. It is a hope that has withstood the attacks of time and the corruption of religion. It is a hope freely available to anyone who would receive it today. I humbly put before you this alternative paradigm for your consideration – Jesus is our one true hope.

More Resources

1. Genetic Entropy Website

The website **GeneticEntropy.org** provides this book at a greatly reduced price. It also carries updates, supplemental materials, useful links, and a 'comments' section. Translations in other languages will become available. This book is also available at Amazon.com as either a hard-copy or in e-book format.

2. Biological Information - New Perspectives

The new book *Biological Information – New Perspectives* (Marks et al., 2013) is a must-read for anyone interested in compelling new evidence against neo-Darwinian theory. It is available at amazon.com, but is also available at much lower cost at **BINP.org**. Its individual chapters are also available free of charge (worldscientific.com). The booklet *Biological Information - New Perspectives, a Synopsis and Limited Commentary* is a much shorter and more accessible summary of the proceedings. It is availble for free as a PDF at BINP.org. The same synopsis is available as a Kindle book at Amazon.com.

3. Mendel's Accountant

The simple logic described in this book strongly refutes neo-Darwinian theory. However, the Primary Axiom is now so deeply entrenched in people's minds that some will require evidence beyond a straight-forward logical analysis. But apart from logic, how can we objectively and empirically test neo-Darwinian theory to the satisfaction of reasonable people?

There is only one empirical and definitive method to objectively analyze neo-Darwinian theory. That method is called "numerical simulation". In real populations, millions of mutations are arising and segregating simultaneously. This makes the mutation/ selection process amazingly complex. Because of this complexity, the only way to understand the process is to systematically track every mutation that occurs within a population (in the same way an accountant uses a spreadsheet to track every dollar that flows through a large corporation). This is the essence of what is called "numerical simulation". When applied to genetic systems, numerical simulation can be termed "genetic accounting".

The computer program *Mendel's Accountant* was developed for this purpose. It is the first comprehensive, biologically-realistic, forward-time numerical simulation program for population genetics. This new program is a powerful research and teaching tool. When any reasonable set of biological parameters are used, *Mendel's Accountant* provides overwhelming empirical evidence that genomes degenerate over time and that all of the apparent flaws inherent in evolutionary genetic theory are real. Honest numerical simulations effectively falsify the Primary Axiom with a degree of certainty that should satisfy any open-minded person.

Mendel's Accountant is a program that can be run using a Mac or PC. It can be downloaded along with a detailed description and set of instructions free of charge at **MendelsAccountant.info**.

Appendix 1

A Deeply Entrenched Ideology

"It is obvious that the omnipotent power of natural selection can do all things, explain all things...."

The above statement came from an early Darwinist, but I have lost the source. The ubiquitous nature of the philosophy underlying this statement makes its source irrelevant. It could have come from just about any Darwinist. In fact, 15 years ago I might have said it myself. More than 100 years after this "statement of faith" originated, the Primary Axiom still captivates the minds and loyalties of most scientists. This is especially true among geneticists. However, when we look at numerous quotes from some of the most prominent population geneticists who ever lived, it appears that their commitment to the Primary Axiom is not based upon evidence, but is fundamentally an ideological commitment. Repeatedly, their own detailed analyses run counter to the Axiom. They seem to remain bound to the Axiom, not in light of their evidence, but in spite of their evidence. Hence they continuously need to explain why the Axiom can run counter to both common sense and their own data and yet still must be considered axiomatically true.

All the following quotes are from leading evolutionary geneticists (except for Hoyle, who was a prominent physicist). I hold these scientists to be highly competent, but I contend that they have built their work (perhaps their very lives?) upon a false axiom. I have extracted specific statements from their papers, which do not reflect their own philosophy, but which point to the problems I am raising.

Few university-based geneticists today would choose to openly discuss the weaknesses of the mutation/selection theory. Indeed, I suspect most geneticists have never even seriously considered such weaknesses (although I am aware of numerous skeptics who choose to remain quiet). Most university geneticists have never seriously questioned the Primary Axiom. This is because by faith they have always accepted it as axiomatically true, even as I once did myself. So they have not even bothered to examine the full extent of the problems with an open mind or an open heart. Every single study, every single paper, seems to be designed to "make the paradigm work". The ideological commitment to the Primary Axiom among geneticists is tremendous. However, among some (I think the ones most secure in their faith in the Axiom) there has been open acknowledgement of specific problems. These acknowledged specific problems, when combined, powerfully argue against the Primary Axiom. The following quotes illustrate this (all emphases are mine).

Muller's Fear

Muller, H.J. 1950. Our load of mutations. Amer. J. Human Genetics 2:111-176.

"It would mean an ever heaping up of mutant genes... degradation into utterly unrecognizable forms, differing chaotically from one individual of the population to another... it would in the end be far easier and more sensible to manufacture a complete man de novo, out of appropriately chosen raw materials, than to try to fashion into human form those pitiful relics which remained. For all of them would differ inordinately from one another, and each would present a whole series of most intricate research problems... if then the eliminated 20% failed involuntarily... the remaining 80%, although they had contrived to reproduce would on the whole differ... but slightly... practically all of them would have been sure failures under primitive conditions... it is very difficult to estimate the rate of the degenerative genetic process..." (pp. 146-7).

"...the open possibility that the deterioration consequent on the present relaxation of selection may after all be a good deal more rapid than has commonly been imagined... it is evident that the natural rate of mutation of man is so high, and his natural rate of reproduction so low, that not a great deal of margin is left for selection... if u has the minimal value of 0.1... an average reproductive rate of 2.4 children per individual would be necessary... without taking any account whatever of all the deaths and failures to reproduce for non-genetic causes... it becomes perfectly evident that the present number of children per couple cannot be great enough to allow selection to keep pace with a mutation rate of 0.1... if, to make matters worse, u should be anything like as high as 0.5..., our present reproductive practices would be utterly out of line with human requirements." (pp. 149-50).

At the time of this writing, Dr. Muller is the only population geneticist to recieve the Nobel Prize. Muller calculated that the human fertility rate of that time (1950) could not deal with a mutation rate of 0.1. Since then, we have learned that the mutation rate is at least 1,000-fold higher than he thought. Furthermore, fertility rates have since declined sharply.

"...the present genetic load is a serious one... increasing it by only 25%...

would be a matter of grave consequence, while its doubling would be calamitous... if u should rise above 0.5, the amount of selective elimination required... would, as we have seen, be greater than the rate of effective reproduction of even primitive man would have allowed... genetic composition would deteriorate continuously, while the population would meanwhile diminish in numbers, all the way to the point of disappearance."

In 1950, Muller concluded that if the mutation rate was as high as 0.5 early man could not have evolved. Man would have degenerated and become extinct. But known mutation rates are roughly 200-fold higher that this!

"...in many civilized nations, the birth rate is held down to an average of not much more than two per family, the upper mutation rate, that beyond which equilibrium is impossible, must be much lower than 0.5 and, as we have seen, perhaps lower than 0.1, even if selection were to be given full scope." (p. 155).

"If we now postulated that the conditions of raised mutation rate, low birth rate... it would be very problematic whether or not this decline would eventually be arrested." (p. 156).

To clarify, Muller is saying that even if we establish the most severe selection scheme, modern fertility levels would not be high enough to stop genetic deterioration – if mutation rates are as high as 0.5. Since 1950, we have learned that our actual mutation rate is approximately 100.

Haldane's Dilemma

Haldane, J.B.S. 1957. The cost of natural selection. J. Genetics 55: 511-524.

"It is well known that breeders find difficulty in selecting simultaneously for all the qualities desired in a stock... **in this paper I shall try to make quantitative the fairly obvious statement that natural selection cannot occur with great intensity for a number of characters at once..."**

"I doubt if such high intensities of selection have been common in the course of evolution. I think n = 300 (300 generations), which would give I = 0.1 (10% total selective elimination in the population), is a more probable figure."

"If two species differ at 1,000 loci, and the mean rate of gene substitution, as has been suggested, is one per 300 generations, it will take at least 300,000 generations (6 million years)..."

"Even the geological time scale is too short for such processes to go on in respect to thousands of loci... *can this slowness be avoided by selecting several genes at a time? I doubt it..."*

"...the number of deaths needed to secure the substitution by natural selection of one gene... is about 30 times the number of organisms in a generation... **the mean time taken for each gene substitution is about 300 generations."**

"...I am convinced that quantitative arguments of the kind put forward here should play a part in all future discussions of evolution."

Haldane was the first to recognize there was a cost to selection which limited what it could realistically be expected to do. He did not fully realize that his thinking would create major problems for evolutionary theory. He calculated that, in man, it would require 6 million years to select just 1,000 mutations to fixation (assuming 20 years per generation). He could not then have know that the number of actual genetic units is

3 billion, and that at least 1 million new mutations would be entering any hypothetical pre-human population each generation, most of which would require selection. Man and chimp differ by at least 150 million nucleotides, representing at least 40 million hypothetical mutations (Britten, 2002). If man evolved from a chimp-like creature, there were at least 20 million mutations fixed within the human lineage (40 million divided by 2), yet natural selection could only have selected for 1,000 of those. All the rest would have had to have been fixed by random drift, creating millions of nearly-neutral deleterious mutations. This would not just have made us inferior to our chimp-like ancestors, it would surely have killed us. Since Haldane's paper, there have been repeated efforts to sweep Haldane's dilemma under the rug, but the problem is still exactly the same. ReMine (1993, 2005) has extensively reviewed the problem, and has analyzed it using an entirely different mathematical formulation, obtaining identical results. Rupe and Sanford (2013), have now conclusively settled the matter and validated Haldane's dilemma using numerical simulation experiments.

Muller's Ratchet

Muller, H.J. 1964. The relation of recombination to mutational advance. Mutation Research 1:2-9.

"There comes a level of advantage, however, that is too small to be effectively seized upon by selection, its voice being lost in the noise, so to speak. This level would necessarily differ greatly under different circumstances (genetic, ecological, etc.), but this is a subject which has as yet been subjected to little analysis... although deserving of it."

Muller anticipated the problem of near-neutral mutations, but failed to see the profound problems they create for evolutionary theory. He did realize that many diverse circumstances (not just population size) would amplify this problem.

"It might appear as though a species without recombination would be... subject to genetic degeneration... This might be thought to be the case... However, this conclusion, which was misleadingly stated by the present author in a recent abstract, is only valid for the artificial conceptualization... nevertheless... **an asexual population incorporates a kind of ratchet mechanism, such that... lines become more heavily loaded with mutation.***"*

How extremely reticent Muller was to acknowledge the very problem which soon came to bear his name ("Muller's ratchet"). Throughout his career, Muller had a deep concern for radiation-induced mutation and human genetic degeneration and was a leading advocate of eugenics. However, even as he wanted to warn the public of the problem of genetic deterioration, he appeared to be extremely careful not to make any statements which might detract from the "certainty" of evolutionary theory (apparently this reflected where he placed his highest loyalty). His statements about the problem of genetic degeneration within asexual species (for which he became famous) are so cautiously worded that one can hardly discern his message.

Muller argued that his "ratchet" was of only limited relevance because he thought mutations were extremely rare. Therefore, he thought each mutation could be dealt with as a discrete and distinctly-selectable unit being eliminated one at a time. We now know that mutations are numerous and diffuse, thwarting any possible "one-at-a-time" elimination mechanism.

If we combine Muller's recognition of near-neutral (i.e., unselectable) mutations with his recognition of mutational advance we see that no selection system can stop Muller's ratchet, even in sexual species. In asexual species, every clone must become more mutant every generation. Even if we select the best clone in the population and multiply it, the sub-clones will be more mutant than the initial clone. Hence, the information can only degenerate. It is a unidirectional (ratcheted) process. Each new generation the average mutation count per organism will be higher than in the previous generation. Ironically, we should realize this is not just true in asexual species. It is also true in sexual species. The "ratchet" works because every rare beneficial mutation is physically linked to a host of deleterious mutations. Selection cannot separate the few good from the many bad, because they are in large linkage blocks. They cannot be teased apart. Therefore, each part of the genome (each linkage block) must individually degenerate due to Muller's ratchet.

Kimura's Quandary

Kimura, M. 1968. Evolutionary rate at the molecular level. Nature 217:624-626.

"...in the evolutionary history of mammals, nucleotide substitution has been so fast that, on average, one nucleotide pair has been substituted in the population roughly every two years. This figure is in sharp contrast to Haldane's well-known estimate... a new allele may be substituted in a population every 300 generations...." "and *"... at the rate of one substitution every two years...* **the substitutional load becomes so large that no mammalian species could tolerate it...**" and *"This brings us to the* **rather surprising conclusion... the mutation rate per generation for neutral mutations amounts to roughly... four per zygote...** *"*

Kimura's estimate of the actual mutation rate was 25-100 fold too low. But it is amazing how easily evolutionary theorists can accommodate any new data. They seem to have an infinitely flexible model, allowing continuous and unlimited development/revision of their many scenarios.

Kimura, M. 1983. *The Neutral Theory of Molecular Evolution.* Cambridge University Press. p.26.

"This formula shows that as **compared to Haldane's formula the cost is larger by about 2...** *under the assumption that the majority of mutation substitutions at the molecular level are carried out by positive selection...* **to maintain the same population number and still carry out mutant substitutions... each parent must leave... 3.27 million offspring to survive and reproduce.** *This was the main argument I used when I presented the neutral mutation-random drift hypothesis of molecular evolution...."*

Kimura realized that Haldane was correct, that selection must occur extremely slowly, and that it can only affect a limited number of mutations simultaneously. He further realized that all the evolutionists of his time were evoking too much selection for too many loci, leading to absurd costs (for example, the need for more than 3 million offspring selected away for every adult). He developed his neutral theory in response to this overwhelming evolutionary problem. Paradoxically, his theory led him to believe that most mutations are unselectable, and therefore most genetic sequences must be irrelevant, and most evolutionary change must be independent of selection. Because he was totally committed to the Primary Axiom, Kimura apparently never considered the possibility that his cost arguments could most rationally be used to argue against the Primary Axiom itself.

Neel's Realization

Neel, J.V. et al. 1986. The rate with which spontaneous mutation alters the electrophoretic mobility of polypeptides. PNAS 83:389-393.

"...gamete rates for point mutations... on the order of 30 per generation... ***The implications of mutations of this magnitude for population genetics and evolutionary theory are profound.*** *The first response of many population geneticists is to suggest that most of these occur in "silent" DNA and are of no real biological significance. Unfortunately for that line of reasoning... the amount of silent DNA is steadily shrinking.* ***The question of how our species accommodates such mutation rates is central to evolutionary thought."***

Kondrashov's Question

Kondrashov, A.S. 1995. Contamination of the genome by very slightly deleterious mutations: **Why have we not died 100 times over?** J. Theor. Biol. 175:583-594.

"Tachida (1990) concluded that VSDMs (very slight deleterious mutations) impairing only one function – its interaction with nucleosomes – may lead to too high a mutation load."

"Lande (1994) and Lynch et al. (1994)... concluded... VSDMs can rapidly drive the population to extinction..."

"Simultaneous selection against many mutations can lead to further decline of N_e and facilitate extinction (Li 1987; Lynch et al. 1984)."

***"I interpret the results in terms of the whole genome and show, in agreement with Tachida (1990), that VSDMs can cause too high a mutation load, even when $N_e = 10^6$-10^7...** conditions under which the load may be paradoxically high are quite realistic..."*

"...the load can become excessive even when U<1... as my analysis suggests – contamination by VSDMs implies an excessive load, leading to stochastic mutation load paradox."

"...selection processes at different sites interfere with each other."

"...because the stochastic mutation load paradox appears real – it requires a resolution."

"Chetverikov (1926) assumed the mutational contamination of a species increases with time, leading perhaps to its eventual extinction."

"accumulation of VSDMs in a lineage... acts like a time bomb... the existence of vertebrate lineages... should be limited to 10^6-10^7 generations."

If Dr. Kondrashov would accept his own data he would conclude that the Primary Axiom is wrong and that genomes must degenerate. Instead, he eventually appeals to "synergistic epistasis" to wave away the problems which he has so brilliantly characterized.

Lynch et al.'s Mutation Meltdown

Lynch, M., J. Conery, and R. Burger. 1995. Mutation accumulation and the extinction of small populations. The American Naturalist 146:489-518.

*"As deleterious mutations accumulate by fixation, there is a gradual decline in the mean viability of individuals... net reproductive rate is less... precipitates **a synergistic interaction between random genetic drift and mutation accumulation, which we refer to as mutational meltdown... the length of the meltdown phase is generally quite short."***

*"These results suggest **that for genetic reasons alone, sexual populations with effective population sizes smaller than 100 individuals are unlikely to persist for more than a few hundred generations**, especially if the fecundity is relatively low."*

"...our results provide no evidence for the existence of a threshold population size beyond which a population is completely invulnerable to a mutational meltdown...."

"...simultaneously segregating mutations interfere with each others' elimination by natural selection..."

Lynch *et al.* understand that genetic degeneration is a major factor for all currently endangered species. They openly acknowledge the problem of selection interference, yet they fail to go on to explain that the same would be true for most past extinctions, and that the basic process of extinction via genomic degeneration should logically apply to all higher genomes.

Howell's Challenge

Howell et al. 1996. Evolution of human mtDNA. How rapid does the human mitochondrial genome evolve? A. J. Hum. Genet. 59: 501-509.

"We should increase our attention to the broader question of how (or whether) organisms can tolerate, in the sense of evolution, a genetic system with such a high mutational burden."

Howell's challenge to us is based upon his own data, which suggested that the mutation rate just within the mitochondrial genome might be approaching one mutation per person per generation. He is right. Just 0.1-1.0 mitochondrial mutations per person creates insurmountable problems for evolutionary theory. Yet this is nothing compared to the hundred or more mutations simultaneously occurring within the other chromosomes.

Crow's Concerns

Crow, J.F. 1997. The high spontaneous mutation rate: is it a health risk?
PNAS 94:8380-8386.

"...The overall impact of the mutation process must be deleterious... **the typical mutation is very mild. It usually has no overt effect, but shows up as a small decrease in viability or fertility... each mutation leads ultimately to one 'genetic death'...** *would surely be an excessive load for the human population... so we have a problem."*

"...there is a way out... by judicious choosing, several mutations may be picked off in the same victim... all individuals with more than a certain number of mutations are eliminated... **of course... natural selection does not line up individuals and remove all those with more than a certain number of mutations... the unreality of this model kept me for many years from considering this as a way which the population deals with a high mutation rate...** *although truncation selection is totally unrealistic, quasi-truncation selection is reasonable."*

"It seems clear that for the past few centuries harmful mutations have been accumulating... The decrease in viability from mutation accumulation is some 1-2% per generation... *if war or famine force our descendants to a stone-age life they will have to be content with all the problems their stone-age ancestors had, plus mutations that have accumulated in the meantime... environmental improvements means that average survival and fertility are only slightly impaired by mutation...* **I do regard mutation accumulation as a problem. It is something like the population bomb, but with a much longer fuse."**

Dr. Crow acknowledges the fundamental evolutionary problems created by the discovery of high mutation rates, but tries to dismiss them using a very unrealistic theoretical model involving a very artificial selection system based on mutation count. Whether or not this artificial selection scheme employs truncation or "quasi-truncation" is just a matter of splitting hairs. He goes on to acknowledge that humanity must now be genetically inferior to our stone-age ancestors. This is an amazing (yet true) confession about the reality of genomic degeneration.

Dr. Crow also comments on the inherently deleterious nature of mutations:
J.F. Crow. 1958. Genetic effects of radiation. Bulletin of the Atomic Scientists 14:19-20.

"Even if we didn't have a great deal of data on this point, we could still be quite sure on theoretical grounds that mutations would usually be detrimental. For a mutation is a random change of a highly organized, reasonably smoothly functioning living body. A random change in the highly integrated system of chemical processes which constitute life is almost certain to impair it – just as a random interchange of connections in a television set is not likely to improve the picture."

Hoyle's Big Picture

Hoyle, F. 1999. *Mathematics of Evolution*. Acorn Enterprises, LLC, Memphis, TN. (note: unlike the others quoted here, Dr. Hoyle was not a geneticist, but a highly distinguished theoretical mathematician and physicist).

*"The aging process shows, indeed, that **statements one frequently hears, to the effect that the Darwinian theory is as obvious as the Earth going round the Sun, are either expressions of almost incredible naiveté or they are deceptions... with such widespread evidence of senescence in the world around us, it still seems amazing that so many people think it "obvious"** that the biological system as a whole should be headed in the opposite direction..."*

*"The best natural selection can do, subject to a specific environment, is hold the deleterious mutations in check. **When the environment is not fixed there is slow genetic erosion, however, which natural selection cannot prevent."***

*"...natural selection cannot turn back deleterious mutations if they are small, and over a long time a large number of small disadvantages escalate to a serious handicap. **This long term inability of natural selection to preserve the integrity of genetic material sets a limit to its useful life...***"

Eyre-Walker/Keightley's Degeneration

Eyre-Walker, A. and P. Keightley. 1999. High genomic deleterious mutation rates in Hominids. Nature 397:344-347.

"Under conservative assumptions, we estimate that an average of 4.2 amino-acid-altering mutations per diploid per generation have occurred in the human lineage..."

"...close to the upper limit tolerable by a species such as humans... a large number of slightly deleterious mutations may therefore have become fixed in hominid lineages... **it is difficult to explain how human populations could have survived... a high rate of deleterious mutation (U >>1) is paradoxical in a species with a low reproductive rate...** *If a significant fraction of new mutations is mildly deleterious, these may accumulate... leading to gradual decline in fitness."*

"...deleterious mutations rate appears to be so high in humans and our close relatives that it is doubtful that such species could survive..."

"...the level of constraint in hominid protein-coding sequences is very low, roughly half of all new non-synonymous mutations appear to have been accepted... if deleterious new mutations are accumulating at present, this could have damaging consequences for human health..."

These authors are still underestimating the extent of the mutation problem. They only consider the mutations within the protein-encoding portion of the genome. The functional genome is at least 10-30 fold larger than this. Even with these lower mutation rate estimates, they acknowledge a fundamental problem and conclude that many deleterious mutations have accumulated during human evolution, and are probably still accumulating. Doesn't this clearly demonstrate that we are in fact degenerating and *not* evolving?

Nachman and Crowell's Paradox

Nachman, M.W. and S.L. Crowell. 2000. Estimate of the mutation rate per nucleotide in humans. Genetics 156: 297-304.

"The human diploid genome... about 175 new mutations per generation. **The high deleterious mutation rate in humans presents a paradox.** *If mutations interact multiplicatively, the genetic load associated with such high U would be intolerable in species with a low rate of reproduction... for U=3, the average fitness is reduced to .05, or put differently,* **each female would need to produce 40 offspring for 2 to survive** *and maintain population size. This assumes that all mortality is due to selection... so* **the actual number of offspring required to maintain a constant population size is probably higher."**

According to Kondrashov (see p. 209), U (new deleterious mutations per person) is actually 10-30 fold higher than these authors claim (they are assuming 97% of the genome is silent junk). Furthermore, we know that, in reality, only a small fraction of total mortality can be attributed to selection. Despite their unrealistic assumptions, these authors still acknowledge a fundamental problem. However, they eventually wave it all away by evoking "synergistic epistasis."

Higgins and Lynch – More Meltdown

Higgins, K. and M. Lynch. 2001. Metapopulation extinction caused by mutation accumulation. PNAS 98: 2928-2933.

"Here we show that metapopulation structure, habitat loss or fragmentation, and environmental stochasticity **can be expected to greatly accelerate the accumulation of mildly deleterious mutations... to such a degree that even large metapopulations may be at risk of extinction."**

"...mildly deleterious mutations may create considerably larger mutational load... because individually they are nearly invisible to natural selection, although causing appreciable cumulative reduction in population viability."

"We find that the accumulation of new mildly deleterious mutations fundamentally alters the scaling of extinction time... causing the extinction of populations that would be deemed safe on the basis of demography alone."

"Under synchronous environmental fluctuations, the acceleration of extinction caused by mutation accumulation is striking... without mutation, extinction is 2,000 generations... **with mutation accumulation the extinction time is just slightly longer than 100 generations...***"*

"For a metapopulation in unfragmented habitat, mildly deleterious mutations are more damaging than highly deleterious mutations... just as in the case with large carrying capacity, **the mild mutational effects are the most damaging, causing minimal time to extinction.***"*

"Early work suggested... accumulation of deleterious mutations may threaten small isolated populations... here we show that accumulation of deleterious mutations may also be a significant threat to large metapopulations... **the decline is sudden, but extinction itself still takes a while to occur, the metapopulation may be completely inviable on intermediate or long time scales, although appearing healthy on short time scales.***"*

Higgins and Lynch make a strong case for genomic degeneration as a general problem for all mammals and all similar animal populations. They point out that currently existing genetic damage may ensure eventual extinction, even though it will take time to take effect. In the meantime, the species can still appear healthy and viable. Is that possible in the case of man? Human fertility and human sperm counts are both now dramatically declining (Carlsen et al., 1992). Many nations are now facing negative population growth (probably due to non-genetic causes). But is it not conceivable we could be in the early stages of mutational meltdown?

Kondrashov's Numbers

Kondrashov, S. 2002. Direct estimates of human per nucleotide mutation rates at 20 loci causing Mendelian diseases. Human Mutation 21:12-27.

"...the total number of new mutations per diploid human genome per generation is about 100... at least 10% of these are deleterious... analysis of human variability suggests that a normal person carries thousands of deleterious alleles..."

Since this paper, Dr. Kondrashov has indicated to me by way of personal communication that 100 was just a lower estimate and that 300 is his upper estimate. He also indicated that he believes up to 30% of the mutations may be deleterious. This means that, from his perspective, "U" (deleterious mutations per person per generation) would be 30-90. This is 100-fold higher than would have previously been considered possible. In the end, he dismisses the entire problem with "synergistic epistasis" and "truncation selection."

Loewe's Limit

Loewe, L. 2006. Quantifying the genomic decay paradox due to Muller's ratchet in human mitochondrial DNA. Genet. Res. 87:133-159.

"A surprisingly large range of biologically realistic parameter combinations should have led to extinction of the evolutionary line leading to humans within 20 million years..."

Loewe's limit for extinction is based upon the damage associated with the mitochondrial genome only, but the whole genome is degenerating roughly 200,000 times faster.

Lynch's Latest Analysis

Lynch, M. 2010. Rate, molecular spectrum, and consequences of human mutation. PNAS 107 (3): 961-968.

"From the present results, we infer that an average human gamete acquires approximately 38 de novo base-substitution mutations, approximately three small insertion/deletions in complex sequence, and approximately one splicing mutation... so it is likely that at the diploid level an average newborn acquires a total of 50 to 100 new mutations, a small subset of which must be deleterious."

Dr. Lynch's work confirms the analyses of others, that the human mutation rate is roughly 50-100 mutations per individual (i.e. 25-50 per gamete). If all types of mutation in all of the genome are considered, 50-100 is still too low. More importantly, it is no longer reasonable to assume that most mutations are perfectly neutral. Most mutations must be slightly deleterious – (i.e. nearly-neutral) see next quote.

"The vast majority of point mutations reside outside of coding regions (on the order of 40 per gamete), and it is likely that most of these will have very minor fitness effects, with averages almost certainly $<<10^{-2}$."

If there are 40 new mutations *per gamete* that do not affect protein coding, then there are 80 such new mutations per birth. Dr. Lynch is acknowledging that these are mostly NOT neutral, but are slightly deleterious.

"... although there is considerable uncertainty in the preceding numbers, it is difficult to escape the conclusion that the per-generation reduction in fitness due to recurrent mutation is at least 1% in humans and quite possibly as high as 5% ... over the course of a couple of centuries (approximately six generations), the consequences are likely to become serious, particularly if human activities cause an increase in the mutation rate itself (by increasing levels of environmental mutagens)."

Mutation rates may already be higher than Dr. Lynch estimates (even apart from a possible increase in mutagens), because: a) his analysis excludes the parts of the genome that are most subject to mutation; and b) because he assumes almost all mutations are within "junk DNA" and so are not deleterious.

"Without a reduction in the germline transmission of deleterious mutations, the mean phenotypes of the residents of industrialized nations are likely to be rather different in just two or three centuries, with significant incapacitation at the morphological, physiological, and neuro-biological levels."

As this book shows, the genetic degeneration that Dr. Lynch is documenting, cannot be halted by increasing selection intensity. This is because the mutation rate is way too high, because natural selection is way too inefficient, and most deleterious mutations are nearly-neutral and so are immune to selection.

In addition to recognizing the importance of mutations in our reproductive cells, Dr. Lynch points out that mutations in the rest of our body are rapidly building up – causing aging. By the time we are 60, we have tens of thousands of new mutations per cell. This is what limits our life expectancy, and no medical breakthrough can be expected to halt continuous mutation accumulation in virtually every cell of our body.

Big Science reveals human genome has incredibly high information-density.

The ENCODE Consortium, 2012. An integrated encyclopedia of DNA elements in the human genome. Nature 489: 57-74.

The ENCODE project took over 10 years and cost roughly 400 million dollars. It involved 442 scientists from all over the world, and resulted in a very large number of publications in various journals. The key summary publication came out in the journal Nature, and included the following statements:

"These data enabled us to assign biochemical functions for 80% of the genome, in particular outside the well-studied protein-coding regions."

"Many non-coding variants in individual genome sequences lie in ENCODE-annotated functional regions; this number is at least as large as those that lie in protein-coding genes."

"The newly identified elements also show a statistical correspondence

to sequence variants linked to human disease, and can thereby guide interpretation of this variation."

"Single nucleotide polymorphisms (SNPs) associated with disease by GWAS are enriched within non-coding functional elements, with a majority residing in or near ENCODE-defined regions that are outside of protein-coding genes. In many cases, the disease phenotypes can be associated with a specific cell type or transcription factor."

In a related Nature Video, the director of the ENCODE Project was interviewed by the Editor of Nature (Nature Video titled "Voices of Encode". Available at: http://nature.com/ENCODE).

Dr. Ewan Birney:
"It's likely that 80 percent will go to 100 percent... This metaphor of junk isn't that useful... It is very hard to get over the density of information. I think previously people thought the genome was quite a well-organized place with these genes that had kind of discrete places and a discrete quite sedate choreography, but that's just not what the data says. The data says it's like a jungle of stuff out there, things that we thought we understood and yet it's much, much more complex. And places of the genome that we thought were completely silent and they're teeming with life, teeming with things going on..."

The Editor of Nature:
"Human genetics has told us quite a bit about which areas of the genome are associated with human disease. The frustration has been most of those areas fall in non-coding parts of the genome. These are parts of the genome which we knew, until now, very little about and this is exactly where the ENCODE project comes in."

Appendix 2

How Many Nucleotides Can Effectively Be Selected at One Time?

How many traits or nucleotides can be simultaneously selected for in a given breeding population? This is a very important question, and one that has not really been addressed adequately before. It is relevant to artificial breeding, population biology, and evolutionary theory. The question can be dealt with on a mathematical basis.

Definition of C and c

Total selective cost (C) to a population is that fraction of the population that is *not* allowed to reproduce in order to achieve *all* selection. On the simplest level, we will assume that the fraction of the population which is selected against is C and that this fraction produces zero offspring. The remainder (1-C) is that part of the population which is selected for and is allowed to reproduce at the normal rate. Different species can afford different selective costs. For example, a plant species may produce one hundred seeds per plant. Such a species can afford to have a C value of 0.99. This means that 99% of the seedlings can be selected away and the population can still reproduce fully. In the case of man, the current human fertility rate is now roughly three children for every two adults. So in the human population only one child of the three can be selected away while still maintaining population size. In man, selective cost must be below 1/3 of the population and C must not exceed 0.33. In reality, even this cost is much too high. This is because there are many individuals who fail to reproduce for non-genetic reasons (accidental death, personal choice, etc.). We cannot know how often failure to reproduce is due to non-genetic effects, but it is surely very large. A realistic estimate of allowable selective cost in mankind must be less than 25%, probably near 10%. To be generous, we may assume C might be as high as 0.25. To determine upper theoretical limits for man, we may assume an unrealistically fertile human population wherein C = 0.50 (half of all children are eliminated from the breeding population for genetic reasons every generation).

Cost per trait (c) is that part of the population eliminated due to the presence of a specific trait (or nucleotide). If we are selecting against a given trait (or nucleotide), we need to decide how strongly we will select against it. In other words, how much of the total population are we willing to eliminate to improve that trait? The part of the population that is eliminated for that trait is the selective cost (c) for that trait, and represents the "selection pressure" for that trait. For example, if 10% of the population is eliminated to affect a given trait, then for that trait c = 0.10. If c = 0.01, then 1% of a population is prevented from reproducing in order to affect that trait.

Additive model

The simplest model to understand is the additive model. Here we assume that selection is additive and that selection for all traits is implemented simultaneously. For example, if we could afford to eliminate 25 individuals from a population of 100, we could simultaneously eliminate one individual to affect one trait and so we could affect 25 different traits (or 25 nucleotides). The general formulation would be as follows. Total population cost (C), would be the sum of all costs for each trait or nucleotide (c). So $C = c_1 + c_2 + c_3 \ldots c_n$, where "n" is the number of traits. Assuming that the selection pressure on each trait is the same, then $C = n \times c$. In the case where selection pressure per trait is 0.001 (1 individual is eliminated out of 1,000, to affect a given trait), and where total cost of selection is limited to 25% of the population, then $0.25 = n \times 0.001$. So in this instance, the maximal number of traits that can be selected for is 250. However, in such a case, even though 250 traits could be under selection, the selection pressure per trait would be vanishingly small, resulting in little or no selective progress over time. *Selective progress* approaches zero very rapidly, as more and more traits are put under selection (see Figure 6a, p. 90).

Multiplicative model

The multiplicative model is more realistic and slightly more complex than the additive model. In this model there is first selection for one trait (or nucleotide) and then what is left of the population is subjected to selection for the next trait (or nucleotide). Selection is sequential rather than simultaneous. After one round of selection, the remainder of the population is mathematically 1-c. If there are two traits one wishes to select for, then one multiplies the remainder of each, (1-c) x (1-c), and then subtract from 1 to see the total cost of selection. For example if we eliminate 10% of a population for one trait and 10% of the remainder for a second trait our total cost is 1 - [(1-0.1) x (1-0.1)] = 0.19. In other words, 81% of the population remains to reproduce after selection for these two traits. For many (n) traits under selection, assuming that each trait undergoes approximately the same selection intensity, the equation can be generalized to $C = 1- (1-c)^{n}$.

When I have plotted the number of traits under selection against the maximal allowable selection intensity per trait, assuming a multiplicative model and C = 0.25 (25% of a human population can be eliminated for all selective purposes). The shape of the curve is essentially identical to the additive model. As the number of traits under selection increases, the allowable selection pressure per trait falls off exponentially, rapidly approaching zero. This basic pattern does not change even where the population is extremely fertile. If we could assume an exceedingly fertile human population (C = 0.5), allowable selection per trait falls off extremely rapidly as "n" increases. Even when considering an extremely fertile species, such as a seed-producing plant wherein C might be as high as 0.99, maximal allowable selection pressures become very small when there are more than 1,000 traits (nucleotides) under selection. See Figure 6b, page 91.

What do these vanishingly small selection pressures mean? As the selection pressure for a trait approaches zero, selective progress also approaches zero, and the time to alter a trait via selection approaches infinity. As selective progress tends toward being infinitely small and infinitely slow, we realize we have a problem. This is because new mutations are constantly flooding into a population at high rates. We do not have "deep time" to remedy our degeneration problem. We need to eliminate mutations as fast as they arise or mutations become embedded in the population due to drift and fixation. Even more significantly, as the allowable selection pressures get very small, at some point effective selection truly *stops*. This is because of the phenomenon of "noise" and genetic drift. *A point will always be reached where selection halts altogether*, depending on population size and the total amount of biological "noise" associated with reproduction.

The exact threshold where selection breaks down depends on many variables that make it difficult to determine precisely. However, some common sense can help to approximate the point at which selection should stop or break down. A selection system for a given trait that cannot even remove one individual from a breeding population of 1,000 is certainly suspect. This corresponds to a selection cost for that trait of 0.001. Given the high level of noise within human populations, when the selection cost is less that 0.001, effective selection for that trait may cease entirely. Another way of saying this is as follows: in a population of 1,000 people, if we are not allowed to remove even one (whole) person to affect a given trait, selection for that trait has effectively stopped and random drift is probably operational. Using the cutoff point of 0.001 and the additive model, we can calculate the maximum number of traits we can select for simultaneously. In a realistic human population we can only select for about 500 traits. In an idealized (extremely fertile) human population we can only select for about 990 traits in a single generation* (see Table 2). Yet what we know about human mutation rates indicates that we need to select for millions of nucleotide positions every generation in order to stop genomic degeneration.

---

* *Kimura alludes to the same problem. Even though he does not show his calculations, he states that only 138 sites can be selected simultaneously when C=0.50, and s=0.01 (Kimura, 1983, p. 30).*

How many genic units can be selected simultaneously (assuming a minumum for c = .001)?

C	n^a	n^m
.25	250	300
.50	500	700
.99	990	4,600

n^a = The maximal number of genic traits that can be selected under an additive model.

n^m = The maximal number of genic traits that can be selected under a multiplicative model.

Table 2. How many mutations can be effectively selected simultaneously within a typical population?

The number of mutations (variant nucleotides) that can be effectively selected simultaneously depends on various factors, but a key factor is the fraction of the population that can be selectively eliminated every generation (the cost of selection), which we can designate as "C". Here we show three hypothetical populations. When "C" is .25, one quarter of the population can be selectively prevented from reproducing every generation – which only enables about 300 mutations to be under efficient selection (see details within text). This would represent intense selection, as might be possible for a mammal population with a very high rate of reproduction. When "C" is .50, half of the population can be selectively prevented from reproducing every generation, which only enables about 700 mutations to be under efficient selection. This would represent much more intense selection, perhaps possible for a fish population with a high rate of reproduction. When "C" is .99, then 99% of the population can be selectively prevented from reproducing every generation, which only enables about 4,600 mutations to be under efficient selection. This would represent extremely intense selection, as might be possible in a population of plants undergoing artificial breeding.

The Phenomenon of Unity and the Concept of Integrated Complexity

The puzzle of how to recognize Intelligent Design has been gradually coming together. There has always been an intuitive recognition of design in nature. This is the logical default perspective. To the extent that some people wish to reject the obvious, design was explicitly proclaimed through the Scriptures (Genesis through Revelation). Later, design was argued by essentially all of the "Founding Fathers" of science, including Copernicus, Bacon, Newton, Pasteur, Maxwell, Faraday, and Kelvin. Paley (1802) was the first to put forward the argument of *complexity* as evidence of design. This concept has more recently been refined by Behe (1996) into the argument of *irreducible complexity*. The complexity argument has been further elaborated into the two related arguments, that of *information theory* (Gitt, 1997; Gitt et al., 2013), and *specified complexity* (Demski, 1998). However, I believe there is still at least one more useful diagnostic of design, the phenomenon of Unity, which arises as a result of *integrated complexity*.

One diagnostic of design is the *comprehensive integration of a large number of components,* which is what I call **Integrated Complexity**. It underlies the easily recognizable natural phenomenon of **Unity**. Unity is an objective reality. Unity is readily recognized by any rational person, and is not merely subjective. Unity is therefore a legitimate subject of scientific analysis. Unity arises through the *comprehensive integration* of very many parts. A jigsaw puzzle has unity. A pile of sand does not.

A fighter jet is made up of thousands of component parts and countless atoms, but it has **Unity** of both function and form. This is what makes it readily recognizable as a product of design. It exists as a single integrated unit, above and beyond all its components. In its original, undegenerated state, every single component has a purpose and a place, and each part is perfectly integrated with all the rest. Despite its countless components, the jet exists in a non-plural state. This is the essence of the term "unity" (oneness). We do not say, "Oh, look at all those pieces of metal and plastic." We say, "Oh, look at that plane." It is not even remotely adequate to say that a plane is more than the sum of its parts. A jet is a new reality existing on a totally different level than any of its parts. It can fly. The parts cannot. In a similar manner, it is inadequate to say that a spaceship is more than lots of metal parts. It is inadequate to say that a book is more than its letters. It is also inadequate to say that life is more than the sum of its parts. These are all obscene understatements. We might as well state that there is more than one drop of water in the sea. These things are so grossly obvious, how can we justify even saying them out loud unless we are talking to someone in a trance?

A human being contains over 100 trillion cells, but we **are not** 100 trillion cells. I repeat – that is not what we are. We are each truly a **singular entity**, united in form and function and being. We are the nearly perfect integration of countless components, and as such we comprise a singular new level of reality. The separateness of our existence as people – apart from our molecules – is both wonderfully profound and childishly obvious. Only a deep spiritual sleep could blind us to this reality. We desperately need to wake up. When we awake to the reality of unity, we also awake to the reality of *beauty*. We begin to realize that what we call "beauty" is simply the recognition of the comprehensive unity of well-designed things. In this light, beauty is not merely subjective. In this new light, beauty, like unity, can be seen as a truly objective and concrete reality*.

In their more poetic moments, scientists sometimes refer to the beauty of unity as *elegance*. Elegance is design that is so excellent and wonderful that every detail, every aspect, comes together perfectly to define

---

*As a personal aside, the converse of beauty is ugliness. I would suggest that ugliness is also an objective reality. Ugliness is the corruption of design, the marring of unity. This is why a wart can objectively be considered ugly. It is why aging is an uglifying process. It is why rusting cars, biological deformity, wars, and lies are all truly ugly.

something new – **a comprehensively integrated whole**. Unity can be seen as the startling absence of loose ends or frayed edges. For example, in man, every cell has its place and function, in such a way as to specify **wholeness**. The human profile, like the profile of a sleek jet airplane, proclaims elegance of form and unity of purpose. I would like to submit to you that unity is the concrete and objective basis for what we call beauty. I believe it is also an unmistakable diagnostic for very high level design.

The amazing unity of a human body (our phenome) should be obvious to any thoughtful person who is even remotely acquainted with biology. When we see a human being, we do not think, "Look at all those cells and tissues." We see a single entity – a person.

What does this suggest about the human genome? The genome is the presumed basis underlying the phenome's unity. Yet amazingly, most modern geneticists see the genome as being essentially a disunited pile of nucleotides. All our collective genomes are said to merely comprise a "pool of genes". This is the very antithesis of unity. The genome is seen as a vast array of molecules, largely accidental and random. Each nucleotide supposedly arose and is "evolving" (or drifting) independently. This entire pattern of thought (i.e., man is just a bag of molecules) is termed *reductionism*. The typical modern geneticist sees the genome as primarily "junk DNA", within which are imbedded over a million parasitic "selfish genes" (they also acknowledge that there are some real bits of information – a few tens-of-thousands of functional genes). It is widely assumed that each selfish gene has its own selfish agenda, propagating itself at the expense of the whole.

How could this be true? In light of entropy and the second law of thermodynamics, does it seem possible that the phenome's amazing unity and order arises entirely from a fragmented and chaotic genome? Rationally, if the order and unity of the phenome derives from the genome, then shouldn't the genome be *more complex* and *more integrated* than the phenome?

Imagine entering the intergalactic starship *S.S. Phenome*. You go past doors labeled "Warp Speed Engine Room" and "Holodeck". Then you see a door marked "Office of the Senior Architect and the Chief Engineer". You open the door and you see an office that is a complete wreck. Papers are strewn everywhere, there is the smell of rotting food, and computer screens are broken. Standing on a desk are two chimpanzees fighting over a banana. Would you be so naive as to believe that you were actually looking at the Senior Architect and the Chief Engineer of the S.S. Phenome? Would you actually think the S.S. Phenome could have been *created* and *maintained* through this office in its degenerate and chaotic condition? Yet this is the modern view of the genome. This is the ruling paradigm regarding the genome's very nature, and describes the *idiotic master/genius slave* relationship of genome and phenome. In this light, shouldn't we be critically re-evaluating our view of the genome? Isn't it time for a paradigm shift?

If Integrated Complexity is actually a diagnostic of design, and if the genome really was originally designed, we would predict the genome should show extensive evidence of integration and unity. We should be able to discover many levels of unity of form and function within the genome. I believe this is now beginning to happen. I predict that this will be seen more and more in the coming years, as we unravel the many elaborate and multi-dimensional patterns within the genome. I predict that when we understand the genome better, we will see integration and unity at all levels. But I also predict that we will see more and more evidence of degeneration and corruption of the original design, since mutation is degenerative and selection cannot prevent mutational degeneration. The genome is clearly experiencing an enormous amount of change due to our high rates of mutation. But it seems to me what we are seeing is entirely "downhill" change. Random change cannot possibly be the origin of Integrated Complexity. Unity (comprehensively integrated complexity) simply cannot be built one mistake at a time (as the main body of this book clearly demonstrates).

The profound unity of life exposes reductionism for what it truly is: a type of spiritual blindness. Reductionism is simply a profound ignorance of the unity that is self-evident all around us. More specifically, the Primary Axiom, with its "gene pools" and independent evolution of individual nucleotides, is merely extreme reductionism applied to biology. It is thus inherently invalid. In a sense, this makes all the arguments of this book unnecessary. It is my personal conviction that even apart from the genetic arguments of this book the Primary Axiom is invalidated simply by the all-pervading reality of the phenomenon of Unity.

Can Gene Duplication and Polyploidy Increase Genetic Information?

In opposition to the main thesis of this book, some would like to argue that duplication is the key to understanding how genetic information can increase spontaneously. It is certainly true that duplications occur spontaneously within all genetic systems. Duplication is a form of mutation, and the size of a duplication can be very small (one or just a few nucleotides) or very large (one chromosome or all chromosomes together are duplicated). When one chromosome is doubled it is called *aneuploidy*, when all chromosomes are doubled, this is called *polyploidy*. As with word-processing errors, a single letter can be duplicated, a single word can be duplicated, a whole chapter can be duplicated, a whole book can be duplicated, or the whole library can be duplicated. The question is – "Do such duplications create new information?"

Iff I repeaaat a llettter, does it immmprove my sentenccce? If I repeat my sentence, do I tell you more? If I repeat my sentence, do I tell you more? If I repeat my sentence, do I tell you more? If this page occurred a second time elsewhere in this book, would the book be better? If every page of this book was in duplicate, would you learn twice as much from it? Obviously, all these types of duplications are deleterious regardless of the scale. They do not increase communication, they obviously disrupt it. How could anyone think this type of duplication is a realistic method for the spontaneous creation of useful new information? The answer is, of course, that such people imagine combining mutational duplication with almighty selection. But we have just dedicated most of this book to showing that while selection can slow mutational loss of information, it cannot stop it. Most emphatically selection cannot reverse this loss. It should be obvious by now, if you have read this book, that nearly all duplications will be both deleterious and nearly-neutral, like all other classes of mutation. This means selection will only be able to eliminate the very worst duplications. The rest will relentlessly accumulate and gradually destroy the genome.

Does biological observation support this common sense view of duplication? It most emphatically does! Let us consider the human population. Are there any polyploid humans? Of course not. Duplicating all the human genome is absolutely lethal. Are there any aneuploid humans? Yes there are – a significant number of people have one extra copy of one chromosome. Do these individuals have more information? Most emphatically they do not. While *aneuploidy* is entirely lethal for larger chromosomes, an extra copy of the smallest human chromosomes is not always lethal. Tragically, the individuals who have this type of "extra information" display severe genetic abnormalities. The most common example of this is Down's Syndrome, which results from an extra copy of chromosome 21. There are countless smaller duplications and insertions which also have been shown to cause genetic disease. It should be obvious by now that most duplications will be deleterious and nearly-neutral, like all other classes of mutation.

It is widely recognized that duplication, whether within a written text or within the living genome, destroys information. Rare exceptions may be found where a duplication is beneficial in some minor way (possibly resulting in some "fine tuning"), but this does not change the fact that random duplications overwhelmingly destroy information. In this respect, duplications are just like the other types of mutations.

After a given gene has been accumulating deleterious mutations for a long time, it is in a partially degenerated state. If that gene is then duplicated, the deleterious mutations are duplicated with it. Does such duplication in any way slow down the degeneration process? Obviously not! Upon careful consideration, we can see that once there is a duplicate copy of a gene, both copies will degenerate faster than before. Why is this? It is because each would then have a back-up copy and selection will become relaxed for both copies. It is often claimed that after a gene duplication one gene copy might then stay unchanged while the other might be free to evolve a new function. But neither of these events is actually feasible. Both copies will degenerate at approximately equal rates due to the accumulation of near-neutrals, as we have been learning. Neither can stay unchanged. Furthermore, gene conversion should theoretically be continuously cross-contaminating both the reputed "un-changing copy" and the reputed "evolving copy". Gene conversions should theoretically also allow mutations within each gene to jump into the other copy, which should effectively increase the mutation rate for both copies. This will clearly also accelerate degeneration. In summary, duplicate genes should clearly contribute to mutual accelerated degeneration due to relaxed selection and accelerated mutation accumulation, and due to mutation scrambling via gene conversion. As if this is not enough, Chapter 9 clearly shows how unreasonable the speculation is that one gene copy can evolve a new function while both copies are irrevocably degenerating.

What about polyploid plants? It has been claimed that since some plants are polyploid (having double the normal chromosome number), this proves that duplication must be beneficial and must increase information. Polyploidy was my special area of study for my PhD dissertation. Interestingly, it makes a great deal of difference how polyploidy arises. If somatic (body) cells are treated with the chemical called colchicine, cell division is disrupted, resulting in chromosome doubling but no new information. The plants that result are almost always stunted, morphologically distorted, and sterile. The reason for this should be obvious; the plants must waste twice as much energy to make twice as much DNA but with no new genetic information. The nucleus is roughly twice as large, disrupting proper cell shape and cell size. In fact, the plants actually have less information than before because a great deal of the information that controls gene regulation depends on gene copy number. Loss of regulatory control is loss of information. This is the same reason why an extra chromosome causes Down's Syndrome. Thousands of genes become improperly regulated because of the extra chromosome.

If somatic polyploidization is consistently deleterious, why are there any polyploid plants at all (e.g., potatoes)? The reason is that polyploidy can arise by a different process called "sexual polyploidization". This happens when an unreduced sperm unites with an unreduced egg. In this special case, all of the information within the two parents is combined into the offspring, and there can be a net gain in information within that single individual. But there is no more total information within the population. The information within the two parents was simply pooled. In such a case we are seeing pooling of information, but not any new information.

In a diploid organism, there can be two versions of the same gene. In such a heterozygous diploid, if one gene version is a dysfunctional mutant and the other is a functional non-mutant gene, the latter can act as a back-up copy of the former. Diploidy can thus be seen as a designed back-up system–designed in anticipation of the mutation problem. On the other hand, evolution cannot anticipate anything and so we can very reasonably conclude that it should never produce back-up systems. Sexual polyploidy essentially doubles potential heterozygosity, so there can be up to four versions of the same gene within the same individual. Such a system is thus doubly backed-up. Like the four redundant computers used on the space shuttle, there can be up to three mutant alleles at a given locus, but as long as the fourth is still functional, the plant is all right. So polyploidy does not provide a way to increase new information, but rather illustrates the importance of gene redundancy as a back-up system designed to effectively slow down degeneration. The cost of such back-up systems is that selection cannot remove mutations nearly as efficiently, so long-term degeneration is even more certain. In some special cases, the extra levels of genetic backup within a polyploid can outweigh the problems of disrupted gene regulation and reduced fertility, and so can result in a type of net gain. But such a "net gain" is more accurately described as a net reduction in the rate of degeneration.

What about duplicate genes and gene families? If having multiple gene versions can explain the utility of diploidy and polyploidy, it can likewise explain the utility of redundant copies of a given gene at different locations within the genome. Normally, when a redundant version of a gene is seen within another part of the genome, it is simply assumed by theorists that it must have arisen by an ancient gene duplication. They often add the general presumption of subsequent mutational divergence. But this is all based upon theoretical inferences, not observation. If a gene is redundant within the genome, such redundancy could just as logically be understood as having a designed function such as gene back-up or complex gene regulation.

The simple-minded notion that merely duplicating a gene might be beneficial is biologically naive. Yes, it is possible that a gene duplication might increase that gene's expression. In fact, this is sometimes seen. But simply increasing a gene's expression is usually deleterious (gene expression must be precisely regulated by elaborate and finely tuned molecular systems). Furthermore, duplication is a remarkably inefficient way to achieve such increased gene expression. How could evolution be so consistently inefficient?

Lastly, actual gene duplications not only mess up their own expression, they routinely mess up the expression of other genes. Much of my own career was spent in the production of genetically engineered plants. Industry and academia spent over a billion dollars in this endeavor. What was quickly discovered was that multiple gene insertions consistently gave lower levels of expression than single gene insertions. Furthermore, the multiple insertions were consistently less stable in their expression (Can you start to see that gene regulation is very complex?). Additionally, a large percentage of all transgenic plants displayed other genetic defects due to the disruptive effect of the extra DNA being randomly inserted into specific locations within the genome. Since the genome has a functional and highly specific architecture, any duplication or insertion should logically tend to disrupt that architecture. This is exactly what plant geneticists have been seeing.

The notion of gene duplication as a way to "evolve new information" has become very firmly entrenched within the evolutionary community. I believe this is partly because the "group think" has been saying "It must be true! How else could evolution have happened?" I also believe that when a mantra is mouthed often enough, it takes on the appearance of unassailable truth. But careful analysis of what information really is, and how it arises, combined with a healthy dose of common sense, should reveal to us that random duplications are consistently bad. It is my personal opinion that "evolution through random duplications" is for the most part a widely-held *philosophical assumption*, rather than a scientifically-defensible observation. I believe that while it sounds quite sophisticated and respectable, it does not withstand honest and critical assessment.

Author's note – *The most crucial aspect of the genome is that it carries a massive amount of **functional information**. It is very unfortunate that functional genetic information has been confused with "Shannon information". The simplest way to clarify this confusion is to explain that Shannon information deals with potential information, while genomic information deals with genuine functional information. If you buy a Scrabble game, it comes with a set of letters. These letters represent a certain amount of potential information. If you make a message to a friend with these letters, they then represent functional information. If you buy a second Scrabble game, you have doubled your potential information. But you have not yet created any additional functional information (that requires intelligent ordering of the new letters). It is useful to note that functional information is what is communicated through language. Shannon information applies only to potential information (what set of letters do I have?), and always assumes a linear, one-dimensional informational code. Shannon developed his statistical methods for electronic communication systems (how many electronic bits might I send through a wire?), and he explicitly stated his concepts should not be applied to functional biological information systems.*

Four Possible Objections

There are four possible objections to the thesis of this book which I would like to address in this appendix. These issues are not dealt with in the body of this book because they are for more advanced readers and would detract from the general readability of the main text.

Objection #1 – Persistence of various forms of life disproves Genetic Entropy.
Some claim that genetic entropy could not possibly be true because we are still here. Mice should degenerate must faster than mankind and mice are thriving. Bacteria and viruses should have gone extinct long ago.

Objection overruled:
These objections do not reflect a clear understanding of what I am saying about genetic entropy. My primary thesis is not that everything is going extinct (although I do hold that view), but is that many levels of evidence show that the neo-Darwinian theory is false. The mutation/selection process cannot create the genome, it cannot even stop the genome's continuous degeneration. Given only mutation/selection (given only neo-Darwinian theory) – all species must go extinct. I realize that conceivably there may be a counter-force to genetic entropy other than natural selection. That counterforce might be God, or aliens, or some unknown natural force. But if we are given only strict neo-Darwinian theory – yes, all life forms are doomed to extinction.

Why are we still here? Given the reality of genetic entropy, if there is no counterforce to genetic entropy beyond just natural selection, then our own existence suggests that there has not yet been enough time for genetic entropy to cause our extinction. This is consistent with a Biblical view of human history, but is blasphemy within evolutionary circles. For those who cannot abide with the idea of a Biblical timeframe, I suggest you consider either a type of God-assisted evolution or aliens – as a potential counter-force to genetic entropy.

Why are mice still here? It is not logical to assume mice should undergo genetic degeneration more quickly than mankind. It is true that mice have a much shorter generation cycle, hence many more generations per century – but this is offset by a lower mutation rate per generation. It is not clear to me that mice have more mutations per individual per year. While more mice generations are offset by fewer mutations per generation – mice have two key advantages; hyper-fertility and more selection cycles. Mice have many more cycles of selection per century. In man, opportunity for selection only arises every 20-30 years – only about 4 times per century. In mice, there are perhaps several hundred cycles of selection per century. This should greatly improve the selective removal of deleterious mutations – very significantly extending time to extinction. Mankind should go extinct before mice.

Why are bacteria and viruses still here? The same issues that apply to mice also apply to microbes. Microbes have vastly more generations per century, but this is offset by a much lower mutation rate per generation. While in man there are about 100 mutations per generation cycle, in bacteria there is only 1 mutation every 1,000 generations (i.e., cell divisions). In such microbes, selection should be able to keep up with the rate of deleterious mutations. Importantly, in microbial systems there is selection after every cell division. So there are about 1,000 cycles of selection for every mutation that occurs. In man it is reversed – there is only 1 cycle of selection for every 100 mutations. These advantages make most microbes especially resistant to genetic entropy. Yet microbes are still subject to genetic entropy because most deleterious mutations are nearly-neutral, and hence are invisible to selection.

RNA viruses, such as influenza and Ebola, are special cases – they have short generation times and very high mutation rates (due to absence of RNA repair enzymes). For this reason, it is widely understood that RNA viruses are prone to error catastrophe and spontaneous mutational meltdown, and this is well documented. In RNA viruses, entropic extinction of strains can be observed in less than a century (i.e., influenza) – and sometimes in a matter of just a few months (i.e., Ebola). So in these special cases we must again ask – why are RNA viruses still here? The answer is well known to microbiologists – viruses and bacteria can persist for very long periods of time in a dormant state and can re-emerge from "natural reservoirs". Microbiologists apply this knowledge within their own research labs all the time. They know that continuously-growing cultures are genetically unstable – so they back-up every strain they are studying in the freezer. If they go on vacation or put a project on hold for 10 years, they can let all the actively-growing strains go extinct, and start fresh by going to the freezer (their "natural reservoir") and revive the original less-mutated strains. Natural reservoirs of microbes can exist due to freezing, drying, semi-dormancy, or sporulation. Monitored over millennia, any specific microbial strain in nature probably spends much more time in a dormant or semi-dormant state than undergoing rapid growth. A strain may grow for a year and then be dormant or semi-dormant somewhere for a century. Therefore, microbes are not viable molecular clocks, and their persistence through thousands of years does not necessarily reflect vast numbers of cell divisions nor huge numbers of mutations.

Objection #2 – Mega-beneficial Mutations.

If there were occasional rare mutations with a profoundly beneficial effect, such mutations might outweigh all the harmful effects of the accumulating deleterious mutations. This might halt degeneration. For example, perhaps a single nucleotide substitution might increase the information content of the genome by 1%. This would effectively counteract the mutation (or even the deletion) of 1% of the functional genome. In this hypothetical situation, that single point mutation could create as much information as might be contained in 30 million nucleotide sites. In this manner, a few mega-beneficial mutations could theoretically counteract millions of deleterious point mutations.

Objection overruled:

The above scenario fails for four reasons:

a. The reductionist model of the genome is that the genome is basically a bag of genes and nucleotides, each gene or nucleotide acts largely in an additive manner. In such a model, essentially all information must be built up one tiny bit at a time, like building a pile of sand one grain at

a time. This is even true in the special case of large DNA
duplications. A duplicated region adds no new information
until beneficial point mutations are somehow incorporated
into it one nucleotide at a time. The reductionist theoretician
may give some lip-service to the importance of interactions
and synergy, but, in reality, he knows that the only way
to climb "Mount Improbable" is through a very long
series of infinitesimally tiny steps. We can ask ourselves,
rationally, "What type of improvements might we hope for
via misspellings within a jet assembly manual?" Obviously
any improvements, if they arose, would never involve large
increments of improvement. At best they would involve very
subtle refinements. At the heart of the Primary Axiom is
slow incremental improvement. Under the Primary Axiom,
we might safely say that a gene pool can only be filled up with
information one tiny drop at a time.

b. In a genome with 3 billion units of information, the average
beneficial mutation should only increase information by
about one part in 3 billion. Yes, some beneficials will have
more benefit than others, creating a natural distribution, but
it is entirely unreasonable to believe that *any* beneficial point
mutation could add as much information as, say, 30 million
functional nucleotides.

Some might object to this point as follows: *"There are
certainly lethal deleterious mutations. In these cases a single
point mutation can effectively negate 3 billion units worth
of information. In fairness, shouldn't the reciprocal be true
for beneficials? Shouldn't the maximal beneficial mutation
also be equal to 3 billion units of information?"* This line
of thinking takes us back to the naive, symmetrical-bell-
shaped-curve view of mutation. But we know that that view
is universally rejected. Why?

The extreme asymmetry of mutational effects has to do with
the fact that one is trying to climb "Mount Improbable". Yes,
it is conceivable that a mistake could cause you to stumble
up hill, but only by a few feet. You will never stumble uphill
by thousands of feet. However, a single error can easily cause

you to fall *downward* very substantial distances. Indeed, while climbing Mount Improbable, you could easily plunge a very great distance – to an instant death. In the same way, if you are building a house of cards, failures are very easy, and are often very catastrophic, but you can only go *upward* one card at a time. In a very similar way, mutational changes are profoundly asymmetrical.

c. The concept of using a few mega-beneficial mutations to replace the information being lost at millions of other nucleotide sites is not rational and leads to absurd conclusions. By this logic, just 100 mega-beneficial mutations, each of which might increase information by 1%, could replace the entire genome. One could delete all 3 billion bases within the genome and replace it with a genome consisting of just those 100 super-beneficial nucleotides. Indeed, if we could conceive of an information-doubling mutation (the mirror image of a lethal mutation), the entire rest of the genome could then be deleted. We would still have a fitness of 1.0, but based upon a genome of just one nucleotide. The mechanism of substituting a few mega-beneficials for millions of other information-bearing sites that are simultaneously being degraded by mutation would result in an effective genome size that was continuously and rapidly shrinking. This is obviously impossible. It would be like trying to improve a book by subtracting 1,000 letters for every new letter added.

d. Oft-cited examples of apparent "mega-beneficial mutations" are very misleading. For illustration, let us consider antibiotic resistance in bacteria, fur coat thickness in dogs, and homeobox mutations in fruit flies.

Chromosomal mutations within bacteria that confer antibiotic resistance appear to be mega-beneficial mutations. In the presence of an antibiotic, the mutant strain lives, while all the other bacteria die. So fitness has not merely been doubled relative to the other bacteria, it has increased infinitely, going from zero to one.

If you take a Samoyed (arctic) dog and put it in a very hot

desert it will die. A mutation to "hairless" will allow adaptation to the extreme heat, so the dog will live. Fitness has again increased from zero to one, an infinitely large increase.

Certainly the two examples above are both "mega-beneficial mutations" in terms of adaptation to a specific environment. But they are both loss-of-function mutations that reduce net information within the genome. In terms of information content, they are both still *deleterious* mutations. Almost all examples of what appear to be mega-beneficial mutations merely involve adaptation to a new environment. This is just a type of fine-tuning. It is not genome-building. The dramatic nature of these types of changes is not because the organism has "advanced" in any real way, but is only because everything else has died! It is only relative to the dead competitors that the mutant is seen as "improved". These types of mutations do not increase information, or create more specified complexity, or create in any way a higher form of life.

Regrettably, evolutionists have treated two very different phenomenon, *adaptation to environments* and *evolution of higher life forms,* as if they were the same thing. We do not need to be geniuses to see that these are different issues. Adaptation can routinely be accomplished by loss of information or even developmental degeneration (loss of organs). However, development of higher life forms (representing more specified complexity) always requires a large increase in information.

There is a special class of mutations that can profoundly affect the development of an organism: mutations arising within what are called "homeobox" genes. These mutations can cause gross re-arrangements of organs. For example, a single mutation can convert an insect's antennae into a leg, or can cause a fly to have four wings instead of two. These mutations certainly qualify as mega-mutations. Such dramatic changes in body form, arising from simple mutations, have greatly excited many evolutionists. This class of mutation has created a whole new field of speculation termed "EvoDevo" (evolutionary development). This type of mutation is widely assumed to provide the Primary Axiom with macro-beneficial mutations, and might allow for evolutionary saltations (big jumps forward).

It is indeed conceivable that macro-alterations caused by homeobox mutations might sometimes be beneficial. It is even conceivable that they might sometimes be beneficial in a substantial way. But how often would this realistically happen, and could such point mutations really counteract genome-wide degeneration?

In terms of a jet manual, a single misspelling might convert the command *"repeat loop 3 times"* to *"repeat loop 33 times"*. Or, a misspelling might convert the command *"attach assembly 21 into body part A"* into *"attach assembly 21 into body part Z"*. These typographical errors could result in very profound changes in the shape of the airplane, but would they ever be beneficial? If they were beneficial, could they effectively offset the loss of information arising from millions of other misspellings that are acting to degrade all the other components of the plane?

We can theoretically acknowledge that homeobox mutations might occasionally be useful in some ways. However, the actual examples given are in fact profoundly deleterious. The antennae-leg in the fly is actually just a monstrosity. It neither acts as an antennae nor a leg. The fly with the extra set of wings cannot use them (they are not attached to muscles or nerves). Those useless appendages only interfere with the functioning of the normal pair of wings, and the mutant flies can barely fly. It should be obvious that some random changes within any instruction manual will produce gross aberrations within the finished product. But would this in any way support the idea that mega-beneficial mutations are happening? Would this suggest that one such macro-mutation could increase total genomic information by as much as 1% (30 million nucleotides in man)? Would it suggest that one such a mutation could counteract the degenerative effects of millions of mutations happening throughout the rest of the genome? Obviously not!

In conclusion, as much as they might help prop up the Primary Axiom, mega-beneficial mutations cannot be honestly invoked.

Objection #3 – Noise can be averaged out.

If a population is essentially infinite in size, and is perfectly homogeneous, and if "noise" is both constant and uniform, and if there is unlimited time, then all noise effects might eventually be averaged out, and thus even near-neutrals might be subjected to selection. Under these conditions, it is conceivable that natural selection might eventually stop degeneration.

Objection overruled:

None of these basic requirements for eliminating noise, as listed above, are ever met in nature:

a.   Population size is never infinite, and in the case of man, population size has only become substantial in the last several thousands years. Evolutionists assume an effective evolutionary population size for mankind of only about 10,000. That small population would never have existed as a homogeneous gene pool, but would have only existed as isolated sub-populations – perhaps 100 tribes, each with about 100 individuals. Natural selection would have largely been limited to competition within each tribe. Under these conditions, there could be no significant noise averaging.

b.   Noise is never uniform. In particular, environmental noise is highly inconsistent both spatially and temporally. For a tribe within a given region, the most important source of non-genetic noise might result from climatic extremes, but for a tribe in another region it might be disease. For many generations, nutritional variation may be the main source of noise confounding selection, followed by cycles of disease or warfare. Under these conditions, there will be no significant noise averaging.

c. As fitness declines due to mutation accumulation, the genomic background itself will be changing. In reference to selection for a given nucleotide, there will be progressively more and more noise from all the other segregating mutations which are accumulating. While some aspects of environmental noise will scale with fitness (thus diminishing proportionately as fitness declines), some aspects of environmental noise will not scale with fitness, e.g., noise due to natural disasters. This latter type of noise, which does not diminish in concert with fitness decline, will grow progressively more disruptive to selection as fitness declines. Continuously increasing noise cannot be effectively neutralized by noise averaging.

d. When noise is high, selection becomes largely neutralized, resulting in rapid and catastrophic mutation accumulation. Given our low fertility and high mutation rate, there is little time for effective noise averaging to operate prior to our extinction. Noise averaging, to the extent it is happening at all, requires a huge number of selection events before there can be significant averaging. Since the hypothetical evolutionary human population would have been small, the only way to have huge numbers of selection events would be to average over many generations. However, long before noise averaging might help to effectively refine the selection process, the human population would go extinct (perhaps even before 1,000 generations). Fitness would reach zero long before mutational equilibrium could be reached. Noise averaging, even if it is actually happening, does not appear to be sufficient to halt the degeneration process soon enough to stop error catastrophe and extinction.

Objection #4 – The failure of the Primary Axiom is not a serious challenge to evolutionary thought.

What does it matter if the Primary Axiom is fatally flawed and essentially falsified? The Primary Axiom is just one of numerous mechanisms of evolution, and so is not crucial to evolutionary theory. Evolutionary researchers just need some more time and some more funding to work out the few "minor kinks" in their various theories.

Objection overruled:

This position is *damage control* and is clearly false:

a. **There is only *one* evolutionary mechanism.** That
    mechanism is mutation/selection (the Primary Axiom). There
    is no viable alternative mechanism for the spontaneous
    generation of information. It is false to say that mutation/
    selection is only one of various mechanisms of evolution. There
    are several types of mutations and there are several types
    of selection, but there is still only **one basic evolutionary
    mechanism** (mutation/selection). The demise of the Primary
    Axiom leaves evolutionary theory without any viable
    mechanism. Without any naturalistic mechanism, evolution
    is not significantly different from any faith-based religion.

b. Darwin's only truly innovative concept was the idea that the
    primary creative force in nature might be natural selection.
    Yet he had no concept of biological information, genetics
    or mutation - and therefore had no conception of what was
    actually being "selected" nor what was being "created". So he
    was entirely ignorant of all the problems addressed in this
    book. His general view, that natural selection could explain
    all aspects of biology, was simply his vigorously advanced
    philosophical position. Not until much later did the neo-
    Darwinists make a synthesis of genetics, mutation, and
    natural selection, creating the field of Population Genetics.
    Only then did Darwinism take on the appearance of real
    science. Ever since the mutation/selection mechanism was
    established, it has remained the singular lynch pin holding
    together all aspects of Darwinian thought.

c. Degeneration is the precise *antithesis* of evolutionary theory.
    Therefore the reality of Genetic Entropy is positively fatal
    to Darwinism. Many people are claiming that the concept of
    Intelligent Design cannot be approached scientifically and is
    only a matter of faith. However, it is obvious that in biology
    the "Null Hypothesis" of Intelligent Design is mutation/
    selection. We all know that to disprove a Null Hypothesis is
    to strongly support The Hypothesis. Therefore, any scientific
    evidence demonstrating that mutation/selection **cannot**
    create or preserve genomes is sound scientific evidence
    supporting Intelligent Design.

How has Academia Responded to These Findings?

The book - Genetic Entropy

When I first published this book nine years ago, I was moving into a new area of specialization (population genetics). I was an un-welcome new member in this relatively exclusive club. I asked several people in the field to critically examine my book before its publication – but they would not even respond, so I had to move ahead with publication with minimal critical feedback. Nine years have passed since the first edition of Genetic Entropy. How has the book faired?

Given its technical nature, this book has been relatively well read and well-acclaimed within conservative circles. I have to believe that many evolutionary biologists have also read it – as it is one of the principle works that openly challenges their paradigm in a meaningful way. Have I heard any serious refutation of this book's conclusions? From the scientists in the field who are qualified to respond – I have only heard deafening silence. This is true even though I have politely requested fair-minded feedback, after sending out complementary copies of this book and my related scientific papers. The relevant scientists, even the ones that were previously willing to dialogue with me to a limited extent, will not even respond to a friendly inquiry. This is very hard for me to understand, since science can only be advanced through open and honest dialogue. I am aware that some Darwinist blog sites have made some response – primarily resorting to personal insults and name-calling. However, to my knowledge there have been no serious rebuttals. I have certainly not heard any scientific response from respected people in the field. In a single case, a blogger from outside the field of biology made a long and biting attack, but his points were poorly informed, and his claims have been appropriately addressed within the blogosphere.

The academic community has received this book, along with my other scientific publications within the last 10 years, with silence. I asked a good friend who had carefully read this book, and who happens to be a geneticist and committed evolutionist, "why don't they engage my arguments?" His answer was startling and simple, "they do not have answers". I believe he is correct. Why should I be surprised that they do not have answers? Many of them have quietly acknowledged in their own papers all the problems I have outlined. Most of the top population geneticists who went before me have recognized the basic validity of the problems that I address in this book (see Appendix 1). I am certain that today's leaders in the field understand and privately acknowledge the problems that I am addressing. The only reason I can see, regarding why they would shun open dialogue, is that they would like to treat these very fundamental theoretical problems as if they were *trade secrets* – not for open dialogue and not for public consideration. If that is true, I hope they fail in protecting these "trade secrets". True science can only advance when there is open, honest, and civil dialogue. There can be no sacred cows – not even neo-Darwinian theory. I hope that the deep problems associated with neo-Darwinian theory will be brought into the light and that they will be examined in an honest and open way.

In summary, after its first 9 years, this book stands basically untarnished and requires no meaningful retraction or apology. In fact, the subsequent scientific developments during this time have greatly strengthened the thesis of this book. My biggest embarrassments, so far, have been some typos and misspellings. My biggest disappointment has been the silence, shunning and censorship which have been surprisingly effective in suppressing open and honest examination of the profound problems associated with the neo-Darwinian theory.

The program - Mendel's Accountant
Mendel's Accountant is the first comprehensive and biologically realistic numerical simulation available to the field for studying the mutation/ selection process. It is a powerful tool for both teaching and exploring otherwise inaccessible research questions in the field of population genetics. For more than 8 years, the field has refused to test, employ, or even acknowledge the existence of this important new tool. Yet Mendel is today's most potent tool for addressing the big questions of population genetics. Why would a field deliberately ignore a major new tool for its

own advancement? In the present case it seems obvious. Firstly, the developers of the new technology happen to be "politically incorrect" – they are mostly orthodox Christians. Believing Christians are the "lepers" within the western academic community. Western academia suspends its cherished standards of tolerance, academic freedom, unbiased peer-review, and simple standards of courtesy and fair play – when it comes to this especially despised minority. It is very clear that if certain "politically-incorrect" people are authors on a publication, that publication can be rejected or ignored without justification. Obviously, that is not how science is supposed to work. It does not happen if the author is Atheist, Muslim, Hindu, Wiccan, or believes in Gaia or Aliens. Even theologically-liberal Christians are often acceptable within western academia – as long as they are willing to salute the Darwinian mechanism. What we are seeing is a very specific type of bigotry, which is un-officially sanctioned on most campuses, and which is exclusively directed against scientists and students who happen to be orthodox Christians. It is very interesting to ponder why this is happening and why most of the people within academia refuse to take a stand against it.

I believe a second reason why the field is choosing to ignore this powerful new research tool is because the output from state-of-the-art numerical simulations is embarrassing for most players in the field. They would desperately like to ignore the new evidence, which is showing that their emperor is naked. They should have been able to see it all along, except they were blinded by the power of the "group think". They were also blinded by their idolization of certain "great men" who in reality were just like the rest of us – fallible.

Mendel's output empirically and scientifically shows that the neo-Darwinian theory does not work. It seems as if many in the field of population genetics have been deliberately hiding this simple fact from the broader scientific community. If so, science has been deliberately held back – presumably because so many people have committed their careers, their very identities, to defending a dying ideological paradigm from the 19th century. My hope is that somebody in the field will have the personal and professional integrity to break from the crowd, and initiate open, honest dialogue on all these issues. If my challenge to the Primary Axiom is misguided, let my colleagues show me my error, and I will retract my position. If they cannot show me where I am wrong on all of these many issues – then they need to openly and honestly acknowledge that there are serious problems with the now-ruling paradigm.

Glossary

Adaptation – Organisms interact with their external environment, and mutations can affect this interaction. Such mutations can affect adaptation to an environment, making the interaction better or worse. Adaptive mutations provide the best examples of beneficial mutations, and selection for such mutations is the basis for what is called "micro-evolution". However most of the information within a genome is not relevant to environmental adaptation, but controls the wonderfully complex inner-workings of a living system.

Adaptive degeneration – Adaption to a special environment is not normally accomplished by creation of any new gene or gene function, but generally results from the loss of useful functions or variants. Adaptive mutations generally involve a loss of information, typically due to a broken or defective gene or gene promoter.

Chromosome – Most genomes are divided into subunits called chromosomes. These are like volumes within an encyclopedia. Each human chromosome has tens of millions of nucleotides and thousands of genes.

Cost of selection – The cost of selection is the fraction of the population that must fail to reproduce to allow selection. In order to have selection operate, there must be surplus population every generation, such that the less fit individuals can be eliminated. This cost can be temporarily suspended as long as a population is continuously growing (everyone could reproduce, but some more than others), but in deep time, population growth must be merely episodic.

Entropy – In its most general or common usage, entropy means the universal tendency for things to degenerate apart from intelligent intervention. More specifically, entropy is a measure of disorder – which invariably increases. Entropy is sometimes defined as "the natural tendency for thing to go from order to disorder". It is also described as the "inability for machines to operate at 100% efficiency". It is also called "time's arrow", because entropy always increases in the big picture. Entropic degeneration is universal and we personally experience it every day of our lives.

Epistasis – Different mutations often interact, and when this happens, it is called epistasis. A deleterious mutation may be much more or less deleterious depending on the absence or presence of other mutations. Such epistasis creates non-heritable noise and strongly interferes with selection. Geneticists acknowledge that epistasis is important, but assume that positive and negative interactions largely cancel each other out.

Error catastrophe – The biological situation where deleterious mutations are accumulating faster than selection can remove them, leading to a continuous net decline in fitness every generation. Unless reversed, error catastrophe leads to the extinction of a population.

Functional information – When we use the word "information" in the normal sense of the word, we are speaking of functional information. Functional information communicates something – for a specific purpose. Data compression allows us to communicate more functional information using fewer numbers or characters.

Functional threshold – Any informative text string requires a minimal number of characters to convey its message. An isolated binary bit or nucleotide has no information. A typical sentence requires a dozen or more characters. A typical gene requires 1,000 or more characters. An emerging new gene function is not subject to positive selection until it has minimal functionality – i.e., enough nucleotides are in place to reach the functional threshold.

Gene – A biologically functional unit within a chromosome. Genes are made up of thousands or even millions of nucleotides. Genes are analogous to chapters in a book. A typical human gene is poly-functional, coding for many different RNAs and various protein forms. Genes are regulated by very complex machinery, including DNA sequences far beyond the gene's borders.

Gene pool – The abstract concept of a gene pool has no correspondence to reality. Genes (alleles, nucleotides), never exist in freely mixing pools, but only exist in living organisms, in the context of specific linkage blocks within chromosomes. The concept of a gene pool is sometimes useful when we need a mental picture of different alleles increasing or decreasing independently within a population.

Genetic drift – Because each new generation arises by a sampling of gametes produced from the previous generation, random sampling error will cause all alleles to randomly increase or decrease in frequency. Such genetic drift is the unavoidable result of Mendelian segregation and random gametic sampling. Drift is especially strong in small populations, and tends to negate almost all selection. Selection is essentially neutralized in very small populations (except selection against semi-lethal mutations), and alleles are quickly lost or fixed randomly regardless of their fitness effect.

Genetic entropy – The broad concept of entropy applies to biology and genetics. Apart from intelligent intervention, the functional genomic information within free-living organisms (possibly excluding some viruses) must consistently decrease. Like all other aspects of the real world we live in, the "natural vector" within the biological realm is degeneration, with disorder consistently increasing over time.

Genetic linkage – A chromosome is a linear molecule somewhat like a very long text message. Corresponding chromosome pairs can swap blocks of information, like two books might swap their final chapters. This type of informational swapping is limited to large blocks of DNA. Whole chapters are exchanged. Individual words or letters are not normally swapped. Within a linkage block (chapter), all letters and words are physically linked together and are never separated. The typical human linkage in block is about 30,000 nucleotides long. Linkage blocks are largely indivisible and are consistently inherited as a single unit.

Genetic load – The genetic load of a population consists of all deleterious mutations present within that population. When genetic load is increasing continuously, a population is in error catastrophe.

Genome – The entire genetic content of an organism. This includes all DNA, all genes, and all chromosomes. The functional genome is the entire physical genome, minus any portions that are biologically irrelevant (having no functional information and zero biological effect).

Genotype – A genotype is a personal version of the genome. It is a specific array of genetic alleles, present in a specific individual within a specific population.

Genotype value – The genotype value can be seen as the total information content of an individual's genome. It is that part of an individual's total biological functionality that is specified by the individual's genome. Genotype value is different from phenotype value because of environmental factors (phenotypic noise), which also affects an individual's biological functionality. The extent that a given mutation changes genotypic value is a function of its specific mutation fitness effect. Genotype value can be used as being synonymous with the term "genotype fitness".

Haldane's dilemma – The famous geneticist Haldane analyzed the cost of selection and found that, even given a steady supply of selectable beneficial mutations, the rate that such mutations can be selectively fixed is extremely slow (300 generations per fixed mutation). This means that forward evolution becomes impractical even within geological time frames. This problem has been confirmed by others.

Heritability – A traditional measure of the signal-to-noise ratio as it applies to selection. Specifically, it is the heritable variance divided by total variance. Total variance combines heritable variation (signal) and non-heritable variation (noise). Non-heritable noise includes all variance due to environmental effects, environment-by-genotype effects, epistatic effects, epigenetic effects, and dominance effects.

Information – The most useful definition of this word is its plain and ordinary sense – information is "that which is communicated through language". Biological information takes on many forms, due to the labyrinth of communication networks which enable life.

Integrated complexity – Perfectly integrated complexity results in Unity. Perfect integration arises when every piece of a puzzle is fitted to every other piece, with no missing parts and with no loose ends. Neither "co-option" nor "pre-adaptation" can explain this type of perfection (such mechanisms produce "jerry-built" contrivances). Natural selection lacks the almost infinite resolution needed to explain this type of perfection. A garbage pile is complex, but it is not integrated. However, assembled jigsaw puzzles and working jet planes manifest Integrated Complexity.

Kimura's box – Muller realized that mutations that had very small fitness effects would be unselectable. Kimura formalized this principle mathematically and described a threshold where mutational effects would become "effectively neutral" (i.e., unselectable). Kimura argued that most mutations would fall into this class and that the principle of "effectively neutral" applies equally well to both beneficial and deleterious mutations. In plotting mutational fitness effects, one can envision a zone (or "box") surrounding the neutral mark. The more non-heritable noise that exists within a genetic system, the larger the "no-selection" box. Kimura pointed out that population size helps define the size of this no-selection zone (small populations have more noise due to gametic sampling). However, the size of this no-selection zone is also affected by many other types of noise, including environmental and reproductive noise. In large genomes, the majority of mutations must fall within Kimura's no-selection box.

Mendel's Accountant (MENDEL) – The first comprehensive numerical simulation computer program that realistically models how genomes change over time in response to mutation/selection.

Muller's ratchet – There is a given ratio of good versus bad mutations that enter a genome – with bad mutations always being predominant. Therefore, the separation of rare good mutations from abundant bad mutations is essential to halting genetic degeneration. Where there is sexual recombination, this may be feasible. However, in whole genomes or in genomic regions where there is no sexual recombination, the good and bad mutations are inseparably linked and can not be teased apart. In such genomes (or in such chromosomal regions), the predominant bad mutations cannot be separated from the rare good mutations – resulting in a downward ratchet mechanism that guarantees net genetic degeneration.

Mutant allele – All new mutations arise as a single copy within a population. If over time that copy increases in frequency – there are more copies of that variant allele. A given mutant allele can increase or decrease in frequency within a population. If a mutant allele reaches a frequency of 1.0, it has reached "fixation" (all individuals in the population have two copies of the mutation – so the non-mutant form has disappeared from the population).

Mutant allele frequency – The fraction of all forms at a particular locus (for diploids this is the population size times two) that are the mutant form. If there are 2 copies of a mutation in a diploid population of 100, the mutant allele frequency is 1% and the non-mutant allele frequency is 99%.

Mutant locus – The location of a mutation, in terms of its position within a linkage block, within a chromosome.

Mutation – Any change in the genome that was not present previously. Mutational changes are directly analogous to word processing errors which arise in the copying of a text. There can be substitutions, deletions, insertions, duplications, inversions, etc.

Mutational meltdown – The final phase of error catastrophe. As a population's fitness continually declines, the population's fertility eventually begins to decline. When there are fewer offspring per female, then there is less surplus population available for the selective removal of accumulating deleterious mutations. This leads to accelerating fitness decline, which leads to accelerating fertility decline, and hence less and less selection. This final phase of degeneration leads to a rapid collapse of the population and relatively sudden extinction.

Mutation fitness effect – The biological effect of a mutation. Mutation fitness effects can be positive or negative, large or small. The mutation effect is expressed as the relative change in an individual's total biological functionality, due to a given mutation. A deleterious mutation with a fitness effect of -0.01 decreases an individual's genetic fitness by one percent. One percent of the genomic information is lost. Total biological functionality is reduced by 1%. These are all just alternative ways of describing the biological effect of such a mutation. Mutation effect is independent of environmental variation (phenotypic noise), and random aspects of reproduction (reproductive noise). Mutation effect is similar but not identical to the traditional concept of a selection coefficient (see Sanford et al., 2007a).

Mutation/selection chain – In the real biological world, this is the chain of events that links a mutational event to a selection event. A mutation affects a linkage block, which affects a chromosome, which affects a genotype, which affects a phenotype, which affects the reproductive fitness of an individual, which affects the actual transmission of the mutation into the next generation. There is biological noise at each link in this chain.

Natural selection – Natural selection is the natural tendency for those individuals who are less biologically functional within a population to reproduce less – compared to those who are more functional. When the more functional individuals reproduce, it is often called "survival of the fittest", but it would be better called "reproduction of the fittest". In nature there is also a great deal of randomness to reproduction. This important principle can be termed "survival (reproduction) of the luckiest". Because both principles are operational in nature, the most fit individuals simply have higher probability of reproduction than the unfit. They are often excluded from reproduction due to random events. This natural type of selection is also called "probability selection". It is a very ineffective form of selection (see truncation selection).

Nucleotides – Nucleotides are the four different molecules that constitute the "rungs" in the DNA ladder. They are typically represented as A, T, C, and G. Many specific nucleotides in a higher genome are poly-functional, affecting various biological processes simultaneously.

Phenome – An entire functional organism, combining all aspects of its genotype and phenotype. The outward expression of all the information of a genome within a specific environment.

Phenotype – The actual manifestation of the biologically functional individual. The phenotype is affected by both the genotype and the environmental factors surrounding the individual. Genotype and phenotype are correlated, but they are not identical.

Phenotype value – The actual biological functionality of an individual relative to other individuals in the population, as determined by the combination of genotypic effects and environmental effects, is called "phenotype value". It is what selection actually acts upon. It is what Mother Nature actually sees. Phenotype value is synonymous with the terms "phenotypic fitness" or "biological fitness", as reflected by the common use of these terms among biologists. However the concept of phenotype value (phenotypic fitness) is distinct from what population geneticists would formally define as "fitness". For clarity, we will use the term reproductive fitness to refer to the traditional population geneticist's definition of fitness (probability of reproduction), which is distinct from actual phenotypic fitness.

Poly-functional DNA – It is increasingly clear that there are multiple, overlapping, functional information systems within higher genomes. This means that many nucleotides do not have one function but actually have several functions (even as a letter in a crossword puzzle can be part of two words). Poly-functional DNA is interesting because it is poly-constrained and is severely limited in terms of having any potential beneficial mutations.

Population – An interbreeding group of individuals is a population. The population size is the number of individuals.

Primary Axiom – The foundational belief underlying all Darwinian thought is that *random mutation plus natural selection* can explain all aspects of life. Another term for this is neo-Darwinian theory.

Reproductive fitness – I define this term as the product of "phenotypic value" (phenotypic fitness) and "reproductive noise". Reproductive noise arises because actual success in reproduction is not just determined by biological functionality, but also by random reproductive factors. So phenotypic fitness and reproductive fitness are correlated, but not identical. The strength of the correlation between phenotype value and reproductive fitness depends upon the selection scheme employed. Artificial truncation will yield the highest possible correlation, while natural probability selection will yield the lowest correlation. What I am calling "reproductive fitness" is sometimes called "Darwinian fitness" or "Wrightian fitness", after Sewell Wright, the first to mathematically formulate "Darwinian fitness".

Selection – Selection can be viewed as differential reproduction, where some individuals reproduce more or less than others. Some individuals are differentially excluded from contributing to the next generation. Unless there is a surplus population (i.e., excess fertility), selection cannot happen without the population size shrinking due to the non-reproduction of certain individuals.

Selection Interference – The phenomenon where selection for one trait in a population confounds the selection for another trait in the same population.

Selection threshold – Any nucleotide, or set of nucleotides, is immune to natural selection unless the associated biological effect is sufficiently great so as to rise above the selection threshold. This threshold is dependent upon many factors, which act as "biological noise" interfering with selection. Mutations with fitness effects below the selection threshold are invisible to natural selection.

Shannon entropy – A statistical measure of complexity ("non-simplicity"). This statistic helps define the lower limits of potential information. An alphabetically ordered sequence of letters (a, b, c...) has low Shannon entropy, because the sequence is fixed and predictable. This limits the amount of information it carries. So low Shannon entropy means limited information potential. The same set of letters can be made "complex" by re-ordering them. Arranging them into a useful message that communicates something increases Shannon entropy, but so does just scrambling the letters. In the first case, true functional information is created (through intelligence). In the second case, there is still only potential information (a randomized set of letters). Therefore, increasing Shannon entropy should not be confused with increasing functional information. True information has high Shannon entropy, but so do randomized characters.

Shannon information – A statistical measure of potential information. More letters and more types of letters both increase potential information. However, unless letters are placed in a specified and meaningful sequence, there will always be zero functional information, and nothing can be communicated. By scrambling the letters of a coherent message, we maintain the same amount of Shannon information, but eliminate all functional (actual) information.

Synergistic epistasis – The term synergistic epistasis is normally only used in attempting to rationalize how genomes might be prevented from degenerating continuously. The basic concept is that epistasis (interaction) between deleterious mutations might be consistently negative. Therefore, as mutations accumulate, each new mutation has a greater and greater average deleterious effect. This is the exact opposite of the standard multiplicative population genetics model, wherein each mutation has less and less effect (one or both models must be wrong). The synergistic epistasis model is extremely artificial and biologically un-realistic. Even if the model is granted, it can be shown that this mechanism fails to stop degeneration when linkage and the interaction between mutations and non-mutations are also taken into account.

Truncation selection – When plant or animal breeders use artificial selection they typically use truncation selection. The best individuals are selected with certainty and the worst are excluded with certainty. This form of selection is not normally operational in nature. In special cases, where there is almost certain death for all but a few well-defined genotypes (i.e., antibiotic resistance in bacteria), episodes of truncation selection can happen in nature – but only for a specific trait. This is a very strong form of selection, but is not operational in natural populations except for rare episodes of very intense selection for a specific trait.

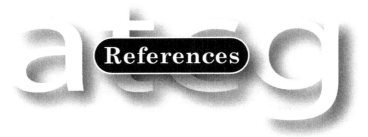

Anzai, T. et al. 2003. Comparative sequencing of human and chimpanzee MHC class I regions unveils insertions/deletions as the major path to genomic divergence. PNAS 100: 7708-7713.

Barrick, J.E. et al. 2009. Genome evolution and adaptation in a long-term experiment with Escherichia coli. Nature 461:1243-1247.

Bataillon, T. 2000. Estimation of spontaneous genome-wide mutation rate parameters: whither beneficial mutations? Heredity 84:497-501.

Bataillon, T. and S.F. Bailey. 2014. Effects of new mutations on fitness: insights from models and data. doi:10.1111/nyas.12460 Ann. N.Y. Acad. Sci. (2014) 1-17.

Baumgardner, J. et al. 2008. Mendel's Accountant: A New Population Genetics Simulation Tool for Studying Mutation and Natural Selection. In A. A. Snelling (Ed.) (2008). Proceedings of the Sixth International Conference on Creationism (pp. 87–98). Pittsburgh, PA: Creation Science Fellowship and Dallas, TX: Institute for Creation Research. https://www.icr.org/i/pdf/technical/Mendels-Accountant.pdf

Baumgardner J., W. Brewer and J. Sanford. 2013. Can Synergistic Epistasis Halt Mutation Accumulation? Results from Numerical Simulation, In: Marks II R.J. et al., (eds) *Biological Information – New Perspectives* (pp 312-337). http://www.worldscientific.com/doi/pdf/10.1142/9789814508728_0013

Behe, M. 1996. *Darwin's Black Box: Biochemical challenge to Evolution.* The Free Press. NY, NY.

Behe, M.J. 2007. *The Edge of Evolution.* Free Press. NY, NY.

Bejerano, G., et al. 2004. Ultraconserved elements in the human genome. Science 304:1321-1325.

Bergman, J. 2004. Research on the deterioration of the genome and Darwinism: why mutations result in degeneration of the genome. Intelligent design Conference, Biola University. April 22-23.

Bernardes, A.T. 1996. Mutation load and the extinction of large populations. Physica ACTA 230:156-173.

Brewer, W., J. Baumgardner and J. Sanford. 2013a. Using Numerical Simulation to Test the "Mutation-Count" Hypothesis. In: Marks II R.J., et al., (eds) *Biological Information – New Perspectives* (pp 298-311). http://www.worldscientific.com/doi/pdf/10.1142/9789814508728_0012

Brewer, W., F. Smith and J. Sanford. 2013b. Information loss: potential for accelerating natural genetic attenuation of RNA viruses. In: Marks II R.J., et al., (eds) *Biological Information – New Perspectives* (pp 369-384). http://www.worldscientific.com/doi/pdf/10.1142/9789814508728_0015

Britten, R.J. 2002. Divergence between samples of chimpanzee and human DNA sequences is 5% counting indels. PNAS 99:13633-13635.

Campbell, C.D. and E.E. Eichler. 2013. Properties and rates of germline mutations in humans. Trends in Genetics 29:575-584.

Carlsen, E., et al. 1992. Evidence for decreasing quality of semen during past 50 years. BMJ 305:609-613.

Carter, R.W. 2007. Mitochondrial diversity within modern human populations. Nucleic Acids Research 35(9): 3039-3045.

Carter, R.W. and J.C. Sanford. 2012. A new look at an old virus: patterns of mutation accumulation in the human H1N1 influenza virus since 1918. Theoretical Biology and Medical Modeling 9:42doi:10.1186/1742-4682-9-42. http://www.tbiomed.com/content/pdf/1742-4682-9-42.pdf

Charlesworth, B. 2013. Why we are not dead one hundred times over. Evolution 67:3354-3361.

Chen, J., et al. 2004. Over 20% of human transcripts might form sense-antisense pairs. Nucleic Acid Research 32:4812-4820.

Crow, J.F. 1997. The high spontaneous mutation rate: is it a health risk? PNAS 94:8380-8386.

Crow, J.F. and M. Kimura. 1970. *An Introduction to Population Genetics Theory*. Harper and Row. NY, NY p. 249.

Dawkins, R. 1986. *The Blind Watchmaker*. Norton & Company, New York.

Demski, W. 1998. *The Design Inference: Eliminating Chance Through Small Probabilities*. Cambridge University Press.

Dennis, C. 2002. The brave new world of RNA. Nature 418:122-124.

Elena, S.F., et al. 1998. Distribution of fitness effects caused by random insertion mutations in E. coli. Genetica 102/103:349-358.

Elena, S. F. and R.E. Lenski. 1997. Test of synergistic interactions among deleterious mutations in bacteria. Nature 390:395-398.

Ellegren, H. 2000. Microsatellite mutations in the germline: implications for evolutionary inference. TIG 16:551-558.

Eyre-Walker, A. and P. Keightley. 1999. High genomic deleterious mutation rates in Hominids. Nature 397:344-347.

Eyre-Walker A, and P.D. Keightley. 2007. The distribution of fitness effects of new mutations. Nat Rev Genet 8:610-618.

Felsenstein, J. 1974. The evolutionary advantage of recombination. Genetics 78: 737-756.

Flam, F. 1994. Hints of a language in junk DNA. Science 266: 1320.

Gabriel, S.B., et al. 2002. The structure of haplotype blocks in the human genome. Science 296:2225-2229.

Gardiner, K. 1995. Human genome organization. Current Opinion in Genetics and Development 5:315-322.

Gerrish, P.J. and R. Lenski. 1998. The fate of competing beneficial mutations in an asexual population. Genetica 102/103: 127-144.

Gibbs, W.W. 2003. The hidden genome. Scientific American. Dec.:108-113.

Gibson, P., J. Baumgardner, W. Brewer, and J. Sanford. 2013. Can Biological Information Be Sustained By Purifying Natural Selection? In: Marks II RJ et al., (eds) *Biological Information – New Perspectives* (pp 232-263). http://www.worldscientific.com/doi/pdf/10.1142/9789814508728_0010

Gitt, W. 1997. *In the Beginning was Information*. Literatur-Verbreitung Bielefeld, Germany.

Gitt, W., R. Crompton, and J. Fernandez. 2013. Biological Information – What is it? In: Marks II R.J. et al., (eds) *Biological Information – New Perspectives* (pp 11-25). http://www.worldscientific.com/doi/pdf/10.1142/9789814508728_0001

Hakimi, M.A. 2002. A chromatin remodeling complex that loads cohesion onto human chromosomes. Nature 418:994-998.

Haldane, J.B.S. 1957. The cost of natural selection. J. Genetics 55:511-524.

Higgins, K. and M. Lynch. 2001. Metapopulation extinction caused by mutation accumulation. PNAS 98: 2928-2933.

Hirotsune S., et al. 2003. An expressed pseudogene regulates the mRNA stability of its homologous coding gene. Nature 423:91-96.

Hochedlinger, K., et al., 2004. Reprogramming of a melanoma genome by nuclear transplantation. Genes and Development 18: 1875-1885.

Holladay, P.M. and J.M. Watt. 2001. De-generation: an exponential decay curve in old testament genealogies. Evangelical Theological Society Papers, 2001. 52nd Natl. Conf., Nashville, TN Nov. 15-17, 2000.

Howell, et al. 1996. Evolution of human mtDNA. How rapid does the human mitochondrial genome evolve? A. J. Hum. Genet. 59: 501-509.

Hoyle, F. 1999. *Mathematics of Evolution*. Acorn Enterprises, LLC, Memphis, TN.

Johnson, J.M., et al. 2005. Dark matter in the genome: evidence of widespread transcription detected by microarray tilling experiments. Trends in Genetics 21:93-102.

Kapranov, P., A.T. Willingham, and T.R. Gingeras. 2007. Genome-wide transcription and the implications for genome organization. Nature Reviews Genetics 8:413-423.

Karlin, S. 1998. Global dinucleotide signatures and analysis of genomic heterogeneity. Current Opinion in Microbiology. 1:598-610.

Kimura, M. 1968. Evolutionary rate at the molecular level. Nature 217: 624-626.

Kimura, M. and T. Ohta. 1971. *Theoretical Aspects of Population Genetics*. Princeton University Press, Princeton, NJ, pp 26-31, p 53.

Kimura, M. 1976. How genes evolve; a population geneticist's view. Ann. Genet.,19, no 3, 153-168.

Kimura, M. 1979. Model of effective neutral mutations in which selective constraint is incorporated. PNAS 76:3440-3444.

Kimura, M. 1983. *Neutral Theory of Molecular Evolution*. Cambridge Univ. Press, NY, NY. (p.26, pp 30-31).

Kondrashov, A.S. 1995. Contamination of the genome by very slightly deleterious mutations: why have we not died 100 times over? J. Theor. Biol. 175:583-594.

Kondrashov, A.S. 2002. Direct Estimate of human per nucleotide mutation rates at 20 loci causing Mendelian diseases. Human Mutation 21:12-27.

Koop, B.F. and L. Hood. 1994. Striking sequence similarity over almost 100 kilobases of human and mouse T-cell receptor DNA. Nature Genetics 7:48-53.

Kruuk, L.E.B. et al. 2000. Heritability of fitness in a wild mammal population. PNAS 97:698–703.

Lee, J. 2003. Molecular biology: complicity of gene and pseudogene. Nature 423:26-28.

Lenski, R.E. 2011. Evolution in Action: a 50,000-generation salute to Charles Darwin. Microbe 6(1):30-33.

Lesecque, Y., P.D. Keightley, and A. Eyre-Walker. 2012. A resolution of the mutation load paradox in humans. Genetics 191:1321-1330.

Loewe, L. 2006. Quantifying the genome decay paradox due to Muller's ratchet in human mitochondrial DNA. Genetic Research 87:133-159.

Lynch, M., et al. 1995. Mutational meltdown in sexual populations. Evolution 49 (6):1067-1080.

Lynch, M., J. Conery, and R. Burger. 1995. Mutation accumulation and the extinction of small populations. Am. Nat. 146:489-518.

Lynch, M. 2010. Rate, molecular spectrum, and consequences of human mutation. PNAS 107 (3):961-968.

Manuelidis, L. 1990. View of interphase chromosomes. Science 250:1533-1540.

Marks, II R.J., M.J. Behe, W.A. Dembski, B.L. Gordon, and J.C. Sanford. 2013. *Biological Information – New Perspectives*. World Scientific Publishing Co., Singapore (pp 1-559). http://www.worldscientific.com/worldscibooks/10.1142/8818

Mattick, J.S. 2001. Non-coding RNAs: the architects of eukaryotic complexity. EMBO reports 2:986-991.

Merila J. and B.C. Shelton. 2000. Lifetime reproductive success and heritability in nature. The American Naturalist 155:301-310.

Montañez, G., R. Marks, J. Fernandez, and J. Sanford. 2013. Multiple overlapping genetic codes profoundly reduce the probability of beneficial mutation, In: Marks II R.J. et al., (eds) *Biological Information – New Perspectives* (pp 139-167). http://www.worldscientific.com/doi/pdf/10.1142/9789814508728_0006

Morrish, T.A., et al. 2002. DNA repair mediated by endonuclease-independent LINE-1 retrotransposition. Nature Genetics:31:159-165.

Morton, N.E., J.F. Crow, and H.J. Muller. 1956. An estimate of the mutational damage in man from data on consanguineous marriages. PNAS 42:855-863.

Muller, H.J. 1950. Our load of mutations. Amer. J. Human Genetics 2:111-176.

Muller, H.J. 1964. The relation of recombination to mutational advance. Mutation Research 1:2-9.

Nachman, M.W. and S.L. Crowell. 2000. Estimate of the mutation rate per nucleotide in humans. Genetics 156:297-304.

Neel, J.V., et al. 1986. The rate with which spontaneous mutation alters the electrophoretic mobility of polypeptides. PNAS 83:389-393.

Nelson, C.W. and J.C. Sanford. 2011. The Effects of Low-Impact Mutations in Digital Organisms. Theoretical Biology and Medical Modeling, Vol. 8, (April 2011), p. 9. http://www.tbiomed.com/content/pdf/1742-4682-8-9.pdf

Nelson, C. and J. Sanford. 2013. Computational evolution experiments reveal a net loss of genetic information despite selection, In: Marks II R.J. et al., (eds) *Biological Information – New Perspectives* (pp 338-368). http://www.worldscientific.com/doi/pdf/10.1142/9789814508728_0014

Ohno, S., and T. Yomo. 1991. The grammatical rule for all DNA: junk and coding sequences. Electrophoresis 12:103-108.

Ohta, T. 1973. Slightly deleterious mutant substitutions in evolution. Nature 246:96-98.

Ohta, T. 1974. Mutational pressure as the main cause of molecular evolution and polymorphism. Nature 252:351-354.

Ohta, T. 1992. The nearly neutral theory of molecular evolution. Ann Rev Ecol Syst 23:263-286.

Ohta, T. 2002. Near-neutrality in evolution of genes and gene regulation. PNAS 99:16134-16137.

Paley, W. 1802. Natural theology: evidences of the existence and attributes of the Deity, collected from the appearances of nature.

Parsons, T.J. et al. 1997. A high observed substitution rate in the human mitochondrial DNA control region. Nature Genetics 15:363-368.

Patterson, C. 1999. *Evolution.* Comstock Publishing Associates, Ithaca, NY.

Provine, W.B. 1971. *The Origins of Theoretical Population Genetics.* University of Chicago Press, Chicago. pp 174-177.

Qui, S., A. McSweeny, S. Choulet, A. Saha-Mandal, L. Fedorova, and A. Fedorov. 2014. Genome evolution by matrix algorithms (GEMA): cellular automata approach by population genetics. Genome Biol. Evol. 6(4):988-999.

Rands, C.M, S. Meader, C.P. Pointing, G. Lunter, 2014. 8.2% of the Human Genome is Constrained: Variation in Rates of Turnover across Functional Element Classes in the Human Lineage. PLOS Genetics, 24 Jul 2014 DOI: 10.1371/journal.pgen.1004525.

ReMine, W. 1993. *The Biotic Message: Evolution versus Message Theory.* St. Paul Science, St. Paul, MN. 538 pages.

ReMine, W. 2005. Cost of Selection Theory. Technical Journal 19:113-125.

Rupe, C.L. and J.C. Sanford. 2013. Using numerical simulation to better understand fixation rates, and establishment of a new principle: Haldane's Ratchet. ICC. http://media.wix.com/ugd/a704d4_47bcf08eda0e 4926a44a8ac9cbfa9c20.pdf

Sandman, K., et al. 2000. Molecular components of the archaeal nucleosome. Biochimie 83: 277-281.

Sanford, J., J. Baumgardner, P. Gibson, W. Brewer, and W. ReMine. 2007a. Mendel's Accountant: a biologically realistic forward-time population genetics program. Scalable Computing: Practice and Experience 8(2):147-165. (http://www.scpe.org)

Sanford, J., J. Baumgardner, P. Gibson, W. Brewer, and W. ReMine. 2007b. Using computer simulation to understand mutation accumulation dynamics and genetic load. In: Shi et al. (Eds.), International Conference on Computational Science 2007, Part II, LNCS 4488 (pp.386-392), Springer-Verlag, Berlin, Heidelberg. http://bioinformatics.cau.edu.cn/ lecture/chinaproof.pdf

Sanford, J.C. 2008. *Genetic Entropy – Classroom Edition*. FMS Foundation, Inc. Waterloo, NY. 227 pages.

Sanford. J.C. et al. 2008. Using Numerical Simulation to Test the Validity of Neo-Darwinian Theory. In A. A. Snelling (Ed.) (2008). Proceedings of the Sixth International Conference on Creationism (pp. 165–175). Pittsburgh, PA: Creation Science Fellowship and Dallas, TX: Institute for Creation Research. http://www.icr.org/i/pdf/technical/Using-Numerical-Simulation-to-Test-the-Validity-of-Neo-Darwinian-Theory.pdf

Sanford, J. and C. Nelson. 2012. The Next Step in Understanding Population Dynamics: Comprehensive Numerical Simulation, Studies in Population Genetics, in: M. Carmen Fusté (Ed.), ISBN: 978-953-51-0588-6, InTech, Available from: http://www.intechopen.com/books/studies-in-population-genetics/the-next-step-in-understanding-population-dynamics-comprehensive-numerical-simulation.

Sanford, J. 2013. Session II Chair - Biological Information and Genetic Theory: Introductory Comments, In: Marks II R.J. et al., (eds) *Biological Information – New Perspectives* (pp 203-209). http://www.worldscientific.com/doi/pdf/10.1142/9789814508728_others02

Sanford, J., J. Baumgardner, and W. Brewer. 2013. Selection Threshold Severely Constrains Capture of Beneficial Mutations, In: Marks II R.J. et al., (eds) *Biological Information – New Perspectives* (pp 264-297). http://www.worldscientific.com/doi/pdf/10.1142/9789814508728_0011

Sanford J.C. 2014. *Biological Information – New Perspectives: A Synopsis and Limited Commentary* (46 pages). http://www.amazon.com/Biological-Information-Perspectives-Synopsis-Commentary-ebook/dp/B00IKTVD2C/ref=sr_1_1?s=digital-text&ie=UTF8&qid=1394477907&sr=1-1&keywords=biological+information+new+perspectives

Seaman, J. 2013. DNA.EXE: A Sequence Comparison between Human Genome and Computer Code. In: Marks II R.J. et al., (eds) *Biological Information – New Perspectives* (pp 385-401). http://www.worldscientific.com/doi/pdf/10.1142/9789814508728_0016

Segal E., et al. 2006. A genomic code for nucleosome positioning. Nature. 442(7104):772-778.

Shabalina, S.A., et al. 2001. Selective constraint in intergenic regions of human and mouse genomes. Trends in Genetics 17:373-376.

Shapiro, J.A., and R.V. Sternberg. 2005. Why repetitive DNA is essential to genome function. Biol. Rev. 80:1-24.

Simonsen L., et al. 1998. Pandemic versus epidemic mortality: a pattern of changing age distribution. Journal of Infectious Diseases 178:53-60.

Slack, F.J. 2006. Regulatory RNAs and the demise of 'junk' DNA. Genome Biology 7:328.

Storz, G. 2002. An expanding universe of non-coding RNAs. Science 296:1260-1263.

Sutherland, G.R. and R.I. Richards. 1995. Simple tandem repeats and human disease. PNAS 92: 3636-3641.

Tachida, H. 1990. A population genetic model of selection that maintains specific trinucleotides at a specific location. J. Mol. Evol. 31:10-17.

Taft, R.J. and J.S. Mattick. 2003. Increasing biological complexity is positively correlated with the relative genome-wide expansion of non-protein-coding DNA sequences. Genome Biology 5(1):P1.

The ENCODE Project Consortium. 2007. Identification and analysis of functional elements in 1% of the human genome by the ENCODE pilot project. Nature 447: 799-816.

The ENCODE Project Consortium. 2012. An integrated encyclopedia of DNA elements in the human genome. Nature 489:57-74.

Tishkoff, S.A. and B.C. Verrelli. 2003. Patterns of human genetic diversity: implications for human evolutionary history and disease. Annual Review of Genomics and Human Genetics 4:293-340.

Trifonov, E.N. 1989. Multiple codes of nucleotide sequences. Bull. of Mathematical Biology 51: 417-432.

Trifonov, E.N. 1997. Genetic sequences as product of compression by inclusive superposition of many codes. Molecular Biology 31(4): 647-654.

Vinogradov, A.E. 2003. DNA helix: the importance of being GC-rich. Nucleic Acid Research 31:1838-1844.

Weikart, R. 2004. *From Darwin to Hitler: Evolutionary Ethics, Eugenics, and Racism in Germany*. Palgrave MacMillan.

Wells, J. 2013. Not junk after all: non-protein-coding DNA carries extensive biological information, In: Marks II R.J. et al., (eds) *Biological Information – New Perspectives* (pp 210-231). http://www.worldscientific.com/doi/pdf/10.1142/9789814508728_0009.

Xue, Y., et al. 2009. Human Y chromosome base-substitution mutation rate measured by direct sequencing in a deep-rooting pedigree. Current Biology 19:1453-1457.

Yelin, R., et al. 2003. Widespread occurrence of antisense transcription in the human genome. Nature Biotechnology 21:379-386.

Index

H

I